ENVIRONMENTAL HEALTH LAW

This book is dedicated to Ann and Lucy

ENVIRONMENTAL HEALTH LAW

Francis McManus

MLitt, LLB(Hons), MREHIS
Lecturer in Law, Napier University

First published in Great Britain 1994 by Blackstone Press Limited, 9-15 Aldine Street, London W12 8AW. Telephone: 081-740 1173

© F. McManus, 1994

ISBN: 1 85431 317 7

British Library Cataloguing in Publication Data
A CIP catalogue record for this book is available from the British Library

Typeset by Montage Studios Limited, Tonbridge, Kent
Printed by Ashford Colour Press, Gosport, Hants

This book is printed on recycled paper

All rights reserved. No part of this book may be reproduced or transmitted in any form or by any means, electronic or mechanical, including photocopying, recording, or any information storage or retrieval system without prior permission from the publisher.

Contents

Preface	vii
Abbreviations	viii
Table of Cases	ix
Table of Statutes	xv
Table of Statutory Instruments	xxiv

1 Introduction — 1

The industrial revolution — Public health reform — Twentieth century — Enforcement of environmental health legislation

2 Nuisance — 8

Common law nuisance — Common law defences — Common law remedies — Statutory nuisances

3 Noise — 20

General background — Nuisance — Statutory control over noise — Other statutory controls — Aircraft noise — Road traffic noise — Other sources of noise — Insulation of buildings — Building regulations

4 Air Pollution — 33

Clean Air Act 1993 — Environmental Protection Act 1990 — Straw and stubble burning

5 Waste — 59

Definition of waste — Waste authorities — Control of waste dumping — Collection of controlled waste — Special waste and non-controlled waste — Inspectors — Default powers of the Secretary of State — Additional controls over the dumping of refuse, abandoned vehicles etc. — Litter — Transport of controlled waste — Radioactive waste

6 Water and Sewerage — 95

Water supply — Sewerage — Trade effluent

7 Public Health Control of Food — 114

Food Safety Act 1990 — Injurious food — Substandard food — Consumer protection — Subordinate legislation — Registration and licensing of food premises — Defences — Promotion of food safety — Food hygiene regulations — Milk and dairies

8 Health and Safety at Work — 143

Common law controls over the working environment — Statutory controls over work and workplaces — Factories Act 1961 — Offices, Shops and Railway Premises Act 1963 — Subordinate health and safety legislation

9 Housing — 179

House in disrepair and unfit houses — Renewal areas — Slum clearance — Overcrowding — Houses in multiple occupation — Common lodging-houses — Improvement grants — Caravan sites

10 Building Control and Buildings — 216

Building control — Buildings — Fire precautions

11 Control of Communicable Disease — 233

12 Pests — 244

Index — 248

Preface

Until recently environmental law as a subject in its own right received but scant attention from both academic establishments and practitioners. But winners have friends to be sure and the sharp upsurge in general interest in the subject has prompted many of the former to make frantic efforts to provide courses on the subject; environmental law sections and departments in a large number of law firms have sprung into existence overnight; and conferences on the subject of environmental law are being held in the most prestigious hotels where delegates are charged attendance fees that would have brought a blush to the cheeks of the medieval usurers. Life will never be quite the same again!

This book is intended for both student and practitioner. It should also be of assistance to environmental health officers as well as those studying environmental health law as part of a degree or professional course. The approach throughout is practical. The emphasis is therefore on what the law is as opposed to how it could be improved.

I relied on a number of people to make comment on earlier drafts of the book. I have to thank in this context Mr George Allen; Mr Ronald Ashton; Mr David Bayne; Ms Josephine Bisacre; Dr Douglas Brodie; Mr Thomas Burns; Mrs Val Finch; Ms Karen Fullerton; Mr James George; Mr Jeff Huggins; Ms Megan McGregor; Mr Donald Reid; Dr James Shepherd; and Mr Jeremy Strang. Needless to say however, all mistakes are my own.

I should also like to thank the staff of Blackstone Press for their help and encouragement throughout the entire project. I would also like to thank my wife Caroline for the way she has coped thus far with the trials and traumas brought about as a consequence of life with an eccentric author.

The law is considered correct as on the 1 May 1994.

Francis McManus
Balerno
1994

Abbreviations

CAA	Civil Aviation Authority
HASAWA	Health and Safety at Work etc. Act 1974
HMO	house in multiple occupation
NRA	National Rivers Authority
OSRPA	Offices, Shops and Railway Premises Act 1963
WCA	waste collection authority
WDA	waste disposal authority
WRA	waste regulation authority

Table of Cases

Adams v Flook and Flook [1987] BTLC 61	139
Aitchison v Howard Doris Ltd 1979 SLT (Notes) 22	153, 156
Aitchison v Reith and Anderson (Dingwall and Tain) Ltd 1974 JC 12	63
Allen v Gulf Oil Refining Ltd [1981] AC 1001	13, 20
Alphacell Ltd v Woodward [1972] AC 824	61
Anderson v Britcher (1913) 110 LT 335	128
Andreae v Selfridge and Co. Ltd [1938] Ch 1	20
Ashcroft v Cambro Waste Products Ltd [1981] 1 WLR 1349	62
Ashdown v Samuel Williams and Sons Ltd [1957] 1 QB 409	151
Associated Provincial Picture Houses v Wednesbury Corporation [1948] 1 KB 223	83
Austin Rover Group Ltd v HM Inspector of Factories [1990] 1 AC 619	149, 155
Babbage v North Norfolk District Council (1988) 57 P & CR 237	215
Baker v T. Clarke (Leeds) [1992] PIQR P262	146
Ball v Ray (1873) LR 8 Ch App 467	20
Ballard v Ministry of Defence [1977] ICR 513	165
Bamford v Turnley (1862) 31 LJ QB 286	10, 11
Barber v Co-operative Wholesale Society Ltd (1983) 81 LGR 762	128
Barnard Castle Urban District Council v Wilson [1902] 2 Ch 746	221
Barry v Cleveland Bridge and Engineering Co. Ltd [1963] 1 All ER 192	163
Bastin v Davies [1950] 2 KB 579	127
Belhaven Brewery Co. v McLean [1975] IRLR 370	150, 166
Bellew v Cement Ltd [1948] IR 61	9
Bennett v Rylands Whitecross Ltd [1978] ICR 1031	168
Bibby-Cheshire v Golden Wonder Ltd [1972] 1 WLR 1487	134
Blaker v Tilstone [1894] 1 QB 345	120
Bolton Metropolitan Borough Council v Malrod Insulations Ltd [1993] ICR 358	150
Bolton v Stone [1951] AC 850	11, 66
Breed v British Drug Houses Ltd [1947] 2 All ER 613	127
Bridlington Relay Ltd v Yorkshire Electricity Board [1965] Ch 436	11
British Railways Board v Liptrot [1969] 1 AC 136	165
Bromwich v National Ear, Nose and Throat Hospital [1980] ICR 450	163
Brown v Allied Ironfounders Ltd [1974] 1 WLR 527	169
Butler v Fife Coal Co. Ltd [1912] AC 149	147
Buxton v Minister of Housing and Local Government [1961] 1 QB 278	226

Table of Cases

Callow (F E) (Engineers) Ltd v Johnson [1971] AC 335	166
Cambridge Water Co. v Eastern Counties Leather plc [1994] 2 WLR 53	12
Campbell v Wallsend Slipway and Engineering Co. Ltd [1978] ICR 1015	159
Carmichael v Rosehall Engineering Works Ltd [1983] IRLR 480	154
Cartwright v GKN Sankey Ltd (1972) 12 KIR 453, (1973) 14 KIR 349	150, 164
Castle v St Augustine's Links (1922) 38 TLR 615	11
Cherry v International Alloys Ltd [1961] 1 QB 136	165
Chesterton Rural District Council v Ralph Thompson Ltd [1947] KB 300	220
Christie v Davey [1893] 1 Ch 316	9
City Fur Manufacturing Co. Ltd v Fureenbond (Brokers) London Ltd [1937] 1 All ER 799	118
Close v Steel Co. of Wales Ltd [1962] AC 367	165
Concentrated Foods Ltd v Champ [1944] KB 342	129
Cook v Square D Ltd [1992] ICR 262	145
Cooper v Wandsworth Board of Works (1863) 14 CB NS 180	53
Coventry City Council v Cartwright [1975] 1 WLR 845	16
Darby v GKN Screws and Fasteners Ltd [1986] ICR 1	151
David Greig Ltd v Goldfinch (1961) 59 LGR 304	119
Davidson v Handley Page Ltd [1945] 1 All ER 235	146
Davies v Massey Ferguson Perkins Ltd [1986] ICR 580	164
Davis (A C) & Sons v Environmental Health Department of Leeds City Council [1976] IRLR 282	172
Deary v Mansion Hide Upholstery Ltd [1983] ICR 610	161
Dew v Director of Public Prosecutions (1920) 89 LJ KB 1166	130
Dexter v Tenby Electrical Accessories Ltd [1991] Crim LR 839	168
Donoghue v Stevenson [1932] AC 562	156
Dunton v Dover District Council (1977) 76 LGR 87	20
Durham County Council v Peter Connors Industrial Services Ltd [1993] Env LR 197	63
Earl of Lonsdale v Nelson (1823) 2 B & C 302	230
Edwards v National Coal Board [1949] 1 KB 704	149
Evans v Sant [1975] QB 626	152
Findlay v Miller Construction (Northern) Ltd 1977 SLT (Sh Ct) 8	163
Finnie v John Laird and Son Ltd 1967 SLT 243	167
Fisher v Barrett and Pomeroy (Bakers) Ltd [1954] 1 WLR 351	133
Fisher v Bell [1961] 1 QB 394	117
Fisher v Port of London Authority [1962] 1 WLR 234	170
Foster v Flexile Metal Co. Ltd (1967) 4 KIR 49	166
Gagnon v Dominion Stamping Co. (1914) 7 OWN 530	10
Garner v John Thompson (Wolverhampton) Ltd (1968) 6 KIR 1	161
Gateway Foodmarkets Ltd v Simmonds (1978) 152 JP 11	118
George v Kumar (1981) 80 LGR 526	139
Gilling v Gray (1910) 27 TLR 39	20
Gillingham Borough Council v Medway (Chatham) Dock Co. Ltd [1993] QB 343	10
Goldman v Hargrave [1967] 1 AC 645	12
Goldup v John Manson Ltd [1982] QB 161	127, 128
Great Northern Railway v Lurgan Commissioners [1897] 2 IR 340	15
Greater Manchester Council v Lockwood Foods Ltd [1979] Crim LR 593	128
Griffith v Ferrier 1952 JC 56	163
Grimsby Borough Council v Louis C. Edwards and Sons (Manufacturing) Ltd [1976] Crim LR 512	136
Guild v Gateway Foodmarkets Ltd 1990 JC 277	119

Table of Cases xi

Hackney London Borough Council v Ezedinma [1981] 3 All ER 438	193
Haigh v Charles W. Ireland Ltd [1974] 1 WLR 43	150
Hall v Owen-Jones [1967] 1 WLR 1362	128
Halsey v Esso Petroleum Co. Ltd [1961] 1 WLR 683	20
Hammett (R C) Ltd v Crabb (1931) 145 LT 638	133
Harkins v McCluskey 1987 SLT 289	168
Harper v Mander and Germain Ltd (1992) *The Times*, 28 December 1992	167
Harrison v Southwark and Vauxhall Water Co. [1891] 2 Ch 409	9
Heath v Brighton Corporation (1908) 98 LT 718	11
Hicks v Sullam (High Court 4 February 1983 unreported	133
Hindle v Birtwistle [1897] 1 QB 192	165
Hollywood Silver Fox Farm Ltd v Emmett [1936] 2 KB 468	9, 21
Hooper v Petrou (1973) 71 LGR 347	118
Hudson v Ridge Manufacturing Co. Ltd [1957] 2 QB 348	147
Hunter v British Steel Corporation 1980 SLT 31	151
Huth v Clarke (1890) 25 QBD 391	225
Inglis v Shotts Iron Co. (1881) 8 R 1006	9
J and F Stone Lighting and Radio Ltd v Haygarth [1968] AC 157	162
J Miller Ltd v Battersea Borough Council [1956] 1 QB 43	128
Jenkins v Allied Ironfounders Ltd [1970] 1 WLR 304	168
James and Son Ltd v Smee [1955] 1 QB 78	235
Joy v News of the World (1972) 13 KIR 57	167
Kat v Diment [1951] 1 KB 34	129
Kennaway v Thompson [1981] QB 88	12, 20
Kilroe (T) and Sons Ltd v Gower [1983] Crim LR 548	155, 163
Kirk v Coates (1885) 16 QBD 49	128
Knight v Bowers (1885) 14 QBD 845	118
Knowles v Liverpool City Council [1993] 1 WLR 1428	144
Knox v Boyd 1941 JC 82	235
Kruse v Johnson [1898] 2 QB 91	28
Kyle v Laird 1951 JC 65	119
Lamb v Sunderland and District Creamery Ltd [1951] 1 All ER 923	133
Lambert (A) Flat Management Ltd v Lomas [1981] 1 WLR 898	8, 21
Lambton v Mellish [1894] 3 Ch 163	18
Lane v Gloucester Engineering Co. Ltd [1967] 1 WLR 767	164
Larner v British Steel plc [1993] ICR 551	168
Laws v Keane 1983 SLT 40	159
Leakey v National Trust [1980] QB 485	12
Leary v National Union of Vehicle Builders [1971] Ch 34	74
Leeman v Montagu [1936] 2 All ER 1677	20
London, Brighton and South Coast Railway Co. v Truman (1885) 11 App Cas 45	20
Lovell v Blundells and T. Albert Crompton and Co. Ltd [1944] KB 502	144
Macaulay v Mackirdy (1893) 20 R 58	136
MacFisheries (Wholesale and Retail) Ltd v Coventry Corporation [1957] 1 WLR 1066	138
MacKay v Drybrough and Co. Ltd 1986 SLT 624	174
Marshall v Ericsson Telephones Ltd [1964] 1 WLR 1367	168
Marshall v Gotham Co. Ltd [1954] AC 360	149
Matheson v Northcote College [1975] 2 NZLR 106	11
McCart v Queen of Scots Knitwear Ltd 1987 SLT (Sh Ct) 57	168
McColl v Strathclyde Regional Council 1983 SC 225, SLT 616	101, 221

McDonald's Hamburgers Ltd v Windle (1986) 151 JP 333	128
McFaulds v Reed Corrugated Cases 1993 SLT 670	168
McGuiness v Key Markets Ltd (1972) 13 KIR 249	165
McInnes v Onslow-Fane [1978] 1 WLR 1520	73
McLeod v Morton 1981 SLT (Sh Ct) 107	136
Meah v Roberts [1977] 1 WLR 1187	118, 127
Metropolitan Water Board v Avery [1914] AC 118	221
Metropolitan Water Board v Colley's Patents Ltd [1911] 2 KB 38	221
Millard v Serck Tubes Ltd [1969] 1 WLR 211	166
Miller v Jackson [1977] QB 966	9, 13
Mitchell v North British Rubber Co. Ltd 1945 JC 69	166
Mitchell v Westin (W S) Ltd [1965] 1 WLR 297	167
Mixnam's Properties Ltd v Chertsey Urban District Council [1964] 1 QB 214	215
Moore v Ray [1951] 1 KB 98	127
Morganite Special Carbons Ltd v Secretary of State for the Environment [1980] EGD 797	25
Morris v Breaveglen Ltd [1993] ICR 766	147
Motion v Mills (1897) 13 TLR 427	20
Naismith v London Film Productions Ltd [1939] 1 All ER 794	144
National Coal Board v Thorne [1976] 1 WLR 543	15
Naish v Gore [1971] 3 All ER 737	63
Nettleship v Weston [1971] 2 QB 691	65
Newton v John Stanning and Son Ltd [1962] 1 WLR 30	163
Newton v West Vale Creamery Co. Ltd (1956) 120 JP 318	128
NHBC Building Control Services Ltd v Sandwell Borough Council (1990) 50 BLR 101	226
Nolan v Dental Manufacturing Co. Ltd [1958] 1 WLR 936	146
Nor-Video Services Ltd v Ontario Hydro (1978) 84 DLR (3d) 221	11
Norse v Morganite Crucible Ltd [1989] 1 AC 692	163
Noss Farm Products Ltd v Lilico [1945] 2 All ER 609	133
Oliver v Goodger [1944] 2 All ER 481	118
Osborne v Bill Taylor of Huyton Ltd [1982] ICR 168	152
Overseas Tankship (UK) Ltd v Morts Dock and Engineering Co. Ltd [1961] AC 388	64
Pape v Cumbria County Council [1992] ICR 132	146
Paris v Stepney Borough Council [1951] AC 367	146
Paterson Zochonis and Co. Ltd v Merfarken Packaging Ltd [1983] 3 All ER 522	130
Paul Popper Ltd v Grimscy [1963] 1 QB 44	163
Pearce v Stanley-Bridges Ltd [1965] 1 WLR 931	166
Pengelley v Bell Punch Co. Ltd [1964] 1 WLR 1055	167
Pharmaceutical Society of Great Britain v Boots Cash Chemists (Southern) Ltd [1953] 1 QB 401	117
Pidgeon v Great Yarmouth Waterworks Co. [1902] 1 KB 310	221
Pollway Nominees Ltd v Havering London Borough Council (1989) 88 LGR 192	15
Powley v Bristol Siddeley Engines Ltd [1966] 1 WLR 729	163
Price v Cormack [1975] 1 WLR 988	61
Pyx Granite Co. Ltd v Ministry of Housing and Local Government [1958] 1 QB 554	215
Qualcast (Wolverhampton) Ltd v Haynes [1959] AC 743	146
Quiltotex Co. Ltd v Minister of Housing and Local Government [1966] 1 QB 704	181
R v AI Industrial Products plc [1987] ICR 418	163
R v Avon County Council, ex parte Terry Adams Ltd (1994) *The Times*, 20 January, 1994	83
R v Birmingham City Justice, ex parte Chris Foreign Foods (Wholesalers) Ltd [1970] 1 WLR 1428	122

Table of Cases   xiii

R v Board of Trustees of the Science Museum [1993] 1 WLR 1171	153
R v Fenny Stratford Justices, ex parte Watney Mann (Midlands) Ltd [1976] 1 WLR 1101	21
R v Gaming Board for Great Britain, ex parte Benaim and Khaida [1970] 2 QB 417	73
R v Hackney London Borough Council, ex parte Evenbray (1987) 86 LGR 210	193
R v Hackney London Borough Council, ex parte Thrasyvoulou (1986) 84 LGR 823	193
R v Lambeth London Borough Council, ex parte Clayhope Properties Ltd [1988] QB 563	181
R v Lord Kylsant [1932] 1 KB 442	129
R v Metropolitan Stipendary Magistrate, ex parte London Waste Regulation Authority [1993] 3 All ER 113	62
R v Secretary of State for Transport, ex parte Richmond-upon-Thames London Borough Council [1994] 1 WLR 74	30
R v Smith (1855) Dears CC 494	117
R v Swan Hunter Shipbuilders Ltd [1981] ICR 831	151
R v Thames Magistrates' Court, ex parte Polemis [1974] 1 WLR 1371	122
Re Findlay [1985] AC 318	73
Re Polemis and Furness, Withy & Co. Ltd [1921] 3 KB 560	64, 98
Re Ross and Leicester Corporation (1932) 96 JP 459	181
Renfrew Upper District Committee v Ranken (1928) 44 Sh Ct Rep 24	16
RHM Bakeries (Scotland) Ltd v Strathclyde Regional Council 1985 SC (HL) 17	12
Richard Thomas and Baldwins Ltd v Cummings [1955] AC 321	166
Rickards v Kerrier District Council (1987) 151 JP 625	223
Ridge v Baldwin [1964] AC 40	53
Riverstone Meat Co. Pty Ltd v Lancashire Shipping Co. Ltd [1960] 1 QB 536	133
RMC Roadstore Products Ltd v Jester, *The Times*, 8 February 1994	153
Roberts v Leeming (1905) 69 JP 417	129
Robertson v McKay 1924 JC 31	127
Robinson v Kilvert (1889) 41 ChD 88	11
Rodbourn v Hudson [1925] 1 KB 225	128
Roe v Minister of Health [1954] 2 QB 66	66
Rushmer v Polsue and Alfieri Ltd [1906] 1 Ch 234	9, 20
Rylands v Fletcher (1868) LR 3 HL 330	64
Salford City Council v McNally [1976] AC 379	15
Sandys v Small (1878) 3 QBD 449	129
Secretary of State for Education and Science v Tameside Metropolitan Borough Council [1977] AC 1014	69
Sedleigh-Denfield v O'Callaghan [1940] AC 880	12
Sheffield City Council v ADH Demolition Ltd (1983) 82 LGR 177	35
Sherratt v Gerald's the American Jewellers Ltd (1970) 68 LGR 256	133
Simpson v Hardie and Smith Ltd 1968 JC 23	165
Skinner v MacLean 1979 SLT (Notes) 35	129
Smedleys Ltd v Breed [1974] AC 839	127
Smith of Maddiston Ltd v Macnab 1975 JC 48	62
Smith v Scott [1973] Ch 314	20
South Suburban Gas Co. v Metropolitan Water Board [1909] 2 Ch 666	221
South Surbiton Co-operative Society v Wilcox [1975] IRLR 292	172
Southwark London Borough Council v Ince (1989) 21 HLR 504	28
Southwell v Ross [1945] 2 All ER 590	136
Sparrow v Fairey Aviation Co. Ltd [1964] AC 1019	166
Speed v Thomas Swift and Co. Ltd [1943] KB 557	145
St Helens Smelting Co. v Tipping (1865) 11 HL Cas 642 at p. 650	10
Stace v Smith (1880) 45 JP 141	136
Stagecoach Ltd v MacPhail 1988 SCCR 289	17
Sterling-Winthrop Group Ltd v Allan 1987 SLT 652	154
Strathclyde Regional Council v Tudhope 1983 SLT 22	23
Sturges v Bridgman (1879) 11 ChD 852	13

Swansea City Council v Jenkins (1994) *The Times*, 1 April 1994   227

Taylor v Coalite Oils and Chemicals Ltd (1967) 3 KIR 315   151
Taylor v Gestetner Ltd (1967) 2 KIR 133   168
Taylor v Lawrence Fraser (Bristol) Ltd [1978] Crim LR 43   133
TBA Industrial Products v Lainé [1987] ICR 75   165
Telfer v Glasgow Corporation 1974 SLT (Notes) 51   155
Tesco Stores Ltd v Edwards [1977] IRLR 120   173
Tesco Supermarkets Ltd v Nattrass [1972] AC 153   63, 133
Texas Homecare Ltd v Stockport Metropolitan Borough Council (1987) 152 JP 83   133
Thanet District Council v Kent County Council [1993] Env LR 391   59
Thorne v Heard and Marsh [1895] AC 495   130
Thornton v Fisher and Ludlow Ltd [1968] 1 WLR 655   164, 167
Thorpe v Brumfitt (1873) LR 8 Ch App 650   18
Torridge District Council v Turner (1991) 90 LGR 173   222
Towers and Co. Ltd v Gray [1961] 2 QB 351   118
Turner and Son Ltd v Owen [1956] 1 QB 48   119
Turtington v United Co-operatives Ltd [1993] Crim LR 376   134
Tyler v Woodspring District Council [1991] JPL 727   214

Uddin v Associated Portland Cement Manufacturers Ltd [1965] 2 QB 582   166

Walker v Baxter's Butchers Ltd (1977) 76 LGR 183   119
Wallhead v Ruston and Hornsby Ltd (1973) 14 KIR 285   164
Warner v Metropolitan Police Commissioner [1969] 2 AC 256   120
Wearing v Pirelli Ltd [1977] 1 WLR 48   165
Webb v Baker [1916] 2 KB 753   118
Webb v Knight (1877) 2 QBD 530   127
Webster v Lord Advocate 1985 SC 173   12, 13, 21
Wednesbury; see Associated Provincial Picture Houses v Wednesbury Corporation
West Bromwich Building Society Ltd v Townsend [1983] ICR 257   150
Westminster City Council v Select Management Ltd [1985] 1 WLR 576   156
Westwood v Post Office [1974] AC 1   170, 173
White v Bywater (1887) 19 QBD 582   128
Whitfield v H and R Johnson (Tiles) Ltd [1991] ICR 109   169
Williams v Friend [1912] 2 KB 471   129
Williams v Painter Brothers Ltd (1968) 4 KIR 487   168
Wilson v Tyneside Window Cleaning Co. [1958] 2 QB 110   144
Wivenhoe Port Ltd v Colchester Borough Council [1985] JPL 175   15
Woodhouse v Walsall Metropolitan Borough Council [1994] Env LR 30   133
Wychavon District Council v National Rivers Authority [1993] 1 WLR 125   61
Wyre Forest District Council v Secretary of State for Environment [1990] 2 AC 357   214

Table of Statutes

Adulteration of Food and Drugs Act 1872
   (35 & 36 Vict c.74)   5, 114
Alkali Act 1863   34
Alkali etc. Works Regulation Act 1906   34
   Part I   16
Animal Health Act 1991   243
Anthrax Prevention Act 1919   243

Building Act 1984   24, 216, 218, 223, 224, 226, 229, 230
   Part III   226
   s. 1   216
   s. 3   216
   ss. 6–8   217
   s. 11   217
   ss. 12–13   218
   s. 16   219, 223
   s. 16(1)–(2)   218
   s. 16(9)   219
   s. 17   219
   s. 17(1)   219
   s. 17(9)   219
   s. 18   219
   s. 21(1)   220
   s. 21(4)   220
   s. 22   220
   s. 23   218, 220
   ss. 24–25   220
   s. 32   222, 224
   s. 33   222
   s. 35   222, 224
   s. 36   223
   s. 36(1)   224
   s. 39   217
   ss. 40–41   223
   s. 42   217, 219
   s. 47   223, 224
   s. 47(2)   224

Building Act 1984 — *continued*
   s. 47(6)–(7)   224
   s. 48   224
   s. 48(1)   225
   s. 48(2)–(3)   224
   ss. 49–50   224
   s. 50(1)–(2)   225
   s. 50(5)–(6)   225
   s. 51   224, 225
   s. 52   225
   s. 52(5)   224
   s. 53   225
   s. 53(3)   225
   s. 54   225
   s. 55   226
   s. 57   226
   s. 59   227
   s. 59(1)(a)   227
   s. 59(1)(c)   227
   s. 64   227
   s. 64(2)   227
   s. 64(6)   227
   s. 65   227
   ss. 70–71   228
   s. 73   39
   s. 74   228
   s. 76   229
   s. 76(1)   229
   s. 77   229
   ss. 78–82   230
   s. 95   230
   s. 102   227

Caravan Sites and Control of Development Act 1960   213, 214
   s. 1(1)   213
   s. 1(4)   213
   ss. 2–4   214
   s. 5(1)   214

Caravan Sites and Control of Development
    Act 1960 — *continued*
  s. 5(2) 215
  ss. 7–9 215
  s. 29(1) 213
  Sch.1 214
Chancery Amendment Act 1858 13
Civil Aviation Act 1982
  s. 62 29
  s. 70(1) 29
  s. 77(1) 29
  s. 77(2) 30
  s. 78 30
  s. 78(1) 30
  s. 78(3) 30
  s. 78(6) 30
  s. 79 30
  s. 81 29
Clean Air Act 1956 6, 33, 40
Clean Air Act 1968 33
Clean Air Act 1993 8, 15, 33, 34, 36, 42,
    44, 45, 46
  Part I–III 44
  Part IV 42, 46
  Part V 46
  s. 1 44, 45
  s. 1(1)–(4) 34
  s. 2 35, 45
  s. 2(3) 35
  s. 2(4) 35
  s. 3(1) 34
  s. 4 36
  s. 4(1) 35
  s. 4(2) 35, 36
  s. 4(3) 36
  s. 4(5) 36
  ss. 5–14 38
  s. 5(3) 36
  s. 6 37, 45
  s. 6(1) 36
  s. 7 36, 45
  s. 7(2) 37
  s. 7(4) 37
  s. 8 37
  s. 10 37
  s. 10(2) 37
  s. 11 37
  s. 14(4) 38
  s. 15(2) 38
  s. 15(3) 38
  s. 16 39
  s. 18 40
  s. 18(2) 40
  s. 19 40
  s. 20 40, 41, 45
  s. 20(1)–(2) 40
  s. 20(4) 40

Clean Air Act 1993 — *continued*
  s. 21 40, 41
  s. 23 40
  s. 24 41
  s. 24(1) 46
  s. 25 41, 42
  s. 26 42
  s. 27(1) 41
  s. 27(2)–(3) 42
  s. 30–31 42
  s. 33 42
  s. 34 43
  s. 34(1)(a)–(b) 43
  ss. 35–38 43
  s. 36(6) 43
  ss. 41–44 44
  s. 42(4) 44
  ss. 45–47 45
  s. 51(1) 45
  ss. 52–53 45
  s. 56 46
  s. 58 46
  s. 60 46
  s. 64(1) 35
  Sch.1 40
Competition and Service (Utilities) Act 1992
    96, 97
Control of Pollution Act 1974 6, 21, 22
  Part III 17, 23, 25, 90
  s. 5 66, 76
  s. 17 86
  s. 30 59
  s. 50(8) 24
  s. 57(1) 27
  s. 58 21
  s. 60 23, 24
  s. 60(1)–(3) 23
  s. 60(4) 24
  s. 60(4)(a) 23
  s. 60(6)–(7) 23
  s. 61 23, 24
  s. 61(4)–(5) 24
  s. 63 25
  s. 64(3)–(4) 26
  s. 65(1)–(2) 26
  s. 65(4)–(5) 26
  s. 65(6) 26
  s. 66(1) 26
  s. 66(7)–(8) 26
  s. 67(3) 27
  s. 68 27
  s. 69(2) 26
  s. 71 27
  Sch.1 25
Control of Pollution Act 1976
  s. 61 24
  s. 61(9) 24

Table of Statutes

Control of Pollution Act 1976 — *continued*
  s. 62(1) 24
Control of Pollution (Amendment) Act 1989
  66, 92
  s. 1 92, 93
  s. 1(3)–(4) 93
  s. 2 66
  s. 3(5) 93
  s. 4 93
  s. 9 67
Countryside Act 1968
  s. 13(2) 31
Cross Act 1868 (31 & 32 Vict c.130)
  5, 179, 180
Crown Proceedings Act 1947
  s. 11 30

Drugs (Prevention of Misuse) Act 1964
  s. 1(1) 120

Employer's Liability (Defective Equipment) Act 1969 144
Environmental Protection Act 1990 6, 8, 14, 16, 21, 28, 34, 44, 46, 47, 50, 51, 53, 55, 58, 59, 62, 64, 65, 71, 73, 80, 83, 85, 87, 89, 91, 92, 217
  Part I 43, 46, 55, 56, 57
  Part II 60, 66, 67, 74, 86
  Part III 21, 44, 94
  Part IV 88, 92
  s. 1 46
  s. 1(5) 47
  s. 1(10) 50
  s. 2 47
  s. 2(6) 47
  s. 3 47
  s. 3(5) 49
  s. 4(2) 47
  s. 6 48, 54
  s. 6(1) 57
  s. 7 51
  s. 7(1)–(3) 48, 50
  s. 7(4) 49, 50, 57
  s. 7(5)–(8) 50
  s. 7(9) 51
  s. 7(10) 49
  ss. 8–9 51
  s. 10 51, 52
  s. 10(1) 51
  s. 10(4)–(5) 51
  s. 10(6) 52
  s. 11 52, 54
  s. 11(1)–(5) 52
  s. 11(6) 53
  s. 12 54
  s. 12(1)–(2) 53
  s. 13 53

Environmental Protection Act 1990
  — *continued*
  s. 14 53, 54
  s. 15 57
  s. 15(1) 54, 55
  s. 15(2)–(3) 54
  s. 15(5) 55
  s. 15(8)–(9) 55
  s. 16 55
  s. 16(6)–(7) 55
  s. 17 55, 57
  s. 18 55, 56
  s. 19(2) 57
  s. 20 56
  ss. 21–22 57
  ss. 23–27 57
  s. 28 51
  s. 30 59
  s. 32(2) 83
  s. 33 62, 63, 65
  s. 33(1) 61, 62, 63, 64
  s. 33(1)(a)–(b) 61, 62
  s. 33(1)(c) 62
  s. 33(2) 62
  s. 33(3) 62, 66
  s. 33(5) 62
  s. 33(7) 63
  s. 33(8) 61
  s. 34 65
  s. 34(1) 65, 67
  s. 34(1)(c) 66
  s. 34(2) 66, 67
  s. 34(3)–(4) 66
  s. 34(5)–(6) 67
  s. 35 66
  s. 35(2)–(3) 67
  s. 35(4) 68
  s. 35(6) 68, 69
  s. 35(7) 68
  s. 35(9) 68
  s. 35(10) 68
  s. 36 69
  s. 36(1)–(2) 68
  s. 36(3) 68, 73
  s. 36(4) 68, 69
  s. 36(5) 69
  s. 37 69, 74
  s. 37(1)–(2) 69
  s. 38 68, 71, 72, 73, 74
  s. 38(1)–(4) 70
  s. 38(5)–(6) 70, 72
  s. 38(8)–(10) 71, 72
  s. 38(12) 71, 72
  s. 39 68
  ss. 40–41 71
  s. 42 72, 73, 74
  s. 42(1)–(6) 71

Environmental Protection Act 1990
— *continued*
s. 43   74
s. 43(1)   73
s. 43(1)(c)   74
s. 43(1)(e)   74
s. 43(2)   74
s. 43(4)   74
s. 43(6)–(7)   74
s. 45   79, 84
s. 45(1)   76
s. 45(2)–(6)   77
s. 46(1)   77, 78
s. 46(3)   77
s. 46(3)(c)–(d)   78
s. 46(4)–(7)   78
s. 46(9)   78
s. 47(1)   78
s. 47(2)   78, 79
s. 47(4)–(8)   79
s. 48   79
s. 48(6)–(7)   80
s. 49   81
s. 49(1)   80
s. 49(1)(a)   81
s. 49(2)–(5)   80
s. 49(7)   81
s. 50   83
s. 50(1)–(5)   81
s. 50(7)–(10)   82
s. 50(11)   83
s. 51(1)–(2)   83
s. 51(4)–(6)   83
s. 52   84
s. 55   85
s. 57   85
s. 57(1)–(2)   85
s. 57(4)–(5)   85
s. 59(1)–(2)   64
s. 59(4)–(7)   64
s. 60   85
s. 61   75
s. 61(2)–(3)   76
s. 61(5)   76
s. 61(7)–(8)   76
s. 62   85, 86
s. 63   86
s. 63(2)   86
s. 64   74, 75
s. 65   74
s. 66   75
s. 66(2)   75
s. 68   60
s. 68(2)   86
s. 68(4)   86
ss. 69–70   86, 87
s. 71(2)   75

Environmental Protection Act 1990
— *continued*
s. 71(4)–(5)   75
s. 71(8)   75
s. 72   87
s. 73(6)   63, 64, 86
s. 74   68, 69
s. 75   59
s. 75(2)   59
s. 75(4)   59
s. 79   14
s. 79(1)   14, 16, 21, 28, 229
s. 79(1)(a)   14
s. 79(1)(b)   14, 15, 16, 18
s. 79(1)(c)–(e)   15, 18
s. 79(1)(f)   16
s. 79(1)(g)   16, 21
s. 79(1)(ga)   16, 21
s. 79(1)(h)   16, 18
s. 79(2)–(4)   15
s. 79(7)   17, 22
s. 79(7)(a)   18
s. 79(7)(d)–(g)   18
s. 79(9)   17
s. 79(10)   16
s. 80   18, 23, 24, 229
s. 80(1)–(4)   17
s. 80(5)   19
s. 80(7)   17
s. 80(9)(a)   24
s. 81(1)–(3)   18
s. 81(4)   18, 19
s. 81A   19
s. 82   22, 24
s. 82(1)   19
s. 86(2)   90
s. 87   88
s. 87(2)   88
ss. 88–89   89
s. 89(1)–(2)   90
s. 89(6)   90
s. 89(7)   91
s. 90   89
s. 90(3)   92
s. 91   90
s. 92   90, 91
s. 93   91
s. 93(1)   92
s. 93(2)   91
s. 94   91
s. 94(1)(a)   91
s. 94(4)   91
s. 95   92
s. 152   58
Sch.1, Part II   53
Sch.2, Part II   83

Table of Statutes   xix

European Communities Act 1972
   s. 2   48

Factories Act 1937   161
Factories Act 1961   15, 149, 157, 158, 161, 162, 168, 176
   Part I   163
   Part II   163
   s. 1   163
   ss. 2–3   164
   s. 4(1)   164
   s. 5(1)   164
   ss. 6–7   164
   s. 14   165, 166, 174
   s. 14(1)   164
   s. 15   165, 166
   s. 16   166, 167
   s. 28   167
   s. 28(1)   167, 168
   s. 29   168
   s. 29(1)   168
   s. 29(2)   169
   s. 72(1)   169
   s. 175   163
   s. 175(1)   162, 163
   s. 175(1)(a)–(e)   162
   s. 176   165
Factory Act 1833   147
Fire Precautions Act 1971   231, 232
   s. 1   231, 232
   s. 2   231
   s. 5   231
   s. 5A   231
   s. 6   231
   s. 7(1)   231
   s. 12   232
   s. 19   232
Fire Safety and Safety of Places of Sport Act 1987   231
Food Act 1984   114
   s. 2   127
Food and Drugs Act 1955
   s. 2   127
   s. 8   118
Food and Environment Protection Act 1985
   s. 1   137
   ss. 3–4   137
Food Safety Act 1990   6, 53, 114, 115, 116, 117, 119, 120, 121, 122, 124, 125, 129, 130, 131, 132, 134, 135, 136, 139, 141, 235
   s. 1(1)   114
   s. 1(2)   115
   s. 2(1)–(2)   115
   s. 3(2)–(4)   115
   s. 5   115
   s. 7   117

Food Safety Act 1990 — *continued*
   s. 7(1)   116, 117, 118
   s. 7(2)   117
   s. 8   120, 134
   s. 8(1)   117
   s. 8(1)(a)   120
   s. 8(2)   118
   s. 8(2)(c)   119
   s. 8(3)   120
   s. 8(4)   121
   s. 9   120, 121, 122
   s. 9(1)   121
   s. 9(3)–(9)   121
   s. 9(3)(a)–(b)   122
   s. 9(4)   122
   s. 9(6)   122
   s. 9(6)(b)   123
   s. 10   123
   s. 10(1)–(2)   123
   s. 11   123
   s. 11(1)   123, 124
   s. 11(2)   124
   s. 11(4)–(5)   124
   s. 11(6)   124, 125
   s. 12(1)   125
   s. 12(4)–(5)   125
   s. 12(6)   126
   s. 12(7)   125
   s. 12(8)–(10)   126
   s. 13   126
   s. 13(3)   126
   s. 13(5)   127
   s. 14   128, 134
   s. 14(1)   127
   s. 15   134
   s. 15(1)–(2)   129, 130
   s. 15(3)–(4)   130
   s. 16   130
   s. 16(1)   130, 131
   s. 16(2)   131
   s. 16(4)   131
   s. 17(1)–(2)   131
   s. 19(1)(a)–(b)   132
   s. 20   132, 133
   s. 21(1)   133, 134
   s. 21(2)   134
   s. 21(3)–(4)   134, 135
   s. 23   135
   s. 24   136
   s. 29   136
   s. 32   136
   s. 37(1)   123
   s. 53(1)   130

Health and Safety at Work etc. Act 1974
   15, 28, 53, 143, 148, 149, 153, 154, 156, 157, 158, 160, 161, 176, 217

Health and Safety at Work etc. Act 1974
— *continued*
　Part I   148, 149
　s. 2   149, 150, 155, 157, 158, 161
　s. 2(1)   149
　s. 2(2)   150
　s. 2(2)(a)   158
　s. 2(3)   152
　s. 3   28, 153, 155, 156, 157, 158, 161
　s. 3(1)   153, 154
　s. 3(2)   153
　s. 3(3)   153, 154
　s. 4   154, 155, 156, 157, 158, 161
　s. 4(2)   155
　s. 5   16, 157, 158, 161
　ss. 6–8   157, 158, 161
　s. 6(1)(a)   156
　s. 6(2)   156
　s. 6(4)   156
　s. 9   161
　s. 10–14   157
　s. 15(1)–(3)   149
　s. 16   157
　s. 16(2)   157
　s. 17   158
　s. 17(2)   158
　s. 18(1)   158
　ss. 19–20   159
　s. 20(2)   159
　s. 20(2)(a)   159
　s. 20(2)(f)   159
　s. 20(2)(g)   159, 160
　s. 20(2)(h)–(i)   159
　s. 20(6)   159, 160
　ss. 21–22   160
　s. 23   161
　s. 24(2)   161
　s. 33   149, 153, 155, 156, 157, 161
　s. 40   161
　s. 52(1)   148
　s. 53   154, 156
　Sch. 1   149
　Sch. 3   149
Housing Act 1903   180
Housing Act 1985   180, 182, 188, 189, 192, 193, 197, 205
　Part VI   180
　Part IX   186, 189
　Part X   189, 191
　Part XI   193, 199
　Part XII   198
　Part XVI   205, 206, 213
　s. 91   185
　s. 93   185
　s. 93(2)–(3)   185
　s. 93(4)–(5)   186
　s. 115   202

Housing Act 1985 — *continued*
　s. 183(3)   181
　s. 189   181, 184, 203, 205
　s. 189(1)   181
　s. 189(1A)–(1B)   181
　s. 189(4)   181
　s. 190   184, 206
　s. 190(1)   183
　s. 190(1A)   183
　s. 191   184
　s. 191A   184
　s. 193   184
　s. 207   181
　s. 207(2)   181
　s. 264   203
　s. 264(1)–(2)   186
　s. 265   187, 203
　s. 265(1)   187
　s. 265(2)   187
　s. 267   187
　s. 267(2)   186
　s. 268   188
　ss. 270–272   187
　s. 274   187
　ss. 277–278   186
　s. 279   187
　ss. 283–284   188
　ss. 286–287   188
　s. 289   189, 203
　s. 289(1)–(2)   189
　s. 289(2A)–(2B)   189
　s. 289(2F)   189
　s. 289(2F)(b)   189
　s. 289(3)–(4)   189
　s. 290   188, 189
　s. 304   187
　s. 324   189
　s. 325   189, 191
　s. 326   191
　s. 326(3)   191
　ss. 327–330   192
　s. 333   193
　s. 345(1)–(2)   193
　ss. 346–349   194
　s. 352   194, 195, 196, 197, 206
　s. 352(1A)   196, 208
　s. 352(2)–(3)   195
　s. 353   195
　s. 354   195, 197
　s. 355   196
　s. 358   196
　ss. 362–363   196
　s. 365   194, 195, 196
　s. 365(1)   195, 196
　s. 365(1A)(a)–(e)   195
　s. 365(2)   196
　s. 368   196

Table of Statutes

Housing Act 1985 — *continued*
  s. 369   197
  ss. 372–373   197
  ss. 375–376   195, 197
  s. 379(1)   197
  ss. 385–386   198
  ss. 392–393   198
  s. 401   198
  ss. 402–406   199
  ss. 408–409   199
  s. 411   199
  s. 604   182, 205
  s. 604(1)–(2)   182, 183
  s. 604(2)(a)–(e)   207
  s. 604(3)   183
  s. 604A   181, 186, 187, 189, 205
  Sch. 13
    Part I   198
Housing Act 1988
  Part I   209
Housing of the Working Classes Act 1890   5

Infectious Disease (Notification) Act 1889
  234

Land Compensation Act 1973   32
  s. 1(3)   32
  s. 20   32
Licensing Act 1964   28
  s. 4   28
Litter Act 1983   92
  ss. 3–5   92
  s. 10   92
Local Authority Social Services Act 1970
  243
  s. 29   243
Local Government Act 1972
  s. 235   28
Local Government and Housing Act 1989
  180, 182, 183, 186, 189, 193, 200, 203,
  206, 208, 209, 212
  Part VII   184
  Part VIII   199, 200
  s. 89(1)   184
  s. 89(3)   184
  s. 89(4)   185
  s. 90(1)   185
  ss. 101–102   200
  s. 104   200
  s. 105   201
  s. 105(1)   201
  s. 105(2)(a)–(c)   201
  s. 105(5)   202
  s. 106   201, 202
  s. 106(6)–(7)   202
  s. 107   202
  s. 107(5)   203

Local Government and Housing Act 1989
  — *continued*
  s. 108   203
  s. 109   203, 205
  s. 110   204, 205
  s. 110(1)   205
  s. 111   204
  s. 111(2)–(3)   204
  s. 111(3)(a)–(b)   204
  s. 111(4)   204
  s. 112   205
  s. 112(1)   205
  s. 113   205
  s. 114   206
  s. 114(1)   206
  s. 114(3)   206
  s. 115   205, 206
  s. 115(1)–(2)   207
  s. 115(2)(b)   208
  s. 115(3)   207, 208
  s. 115(3)(a)   207, 208
  s. 115(3)(c)–(g)   207
  s. 115(5)–(6)   208
  s. 115(9)   208
  s. 116   203, 208
  ss. 117–118   209
  s. 118(1)   208
  s. 118(5)   208
  s. 119(1)   209
  ss. 120–124   210
  s. 126   201, 211
  s. 127   211
  s. 127(5)   211
  s. 128   212
  s. 128(1)–(2)   211
  s. 128(3)   212
  s. 129   212
  s. 129(4)   212
  s. 131   212
  s. 136   201
  s. 138   200
Local Government Planning and Land
  Act 1980   25

Merchandise Marks Act 1887   118
Misuse of Drugs Act 1971   120

National Assistance Act 1948
  Part III   243
Noise Abatement Act 1960   20, 24
Noise and Statutory Nuisance Act 1993
  14, 17, 21, 22, 24
  s. 10(2)   19
  s. 62(1)   24, 25
  s. 62(2)   25
  s. 62(2)(d)   25
  s. 62(3)   25

Noise and Statutory Nuisance Act 1993
— *continued*
   Sch.2   25
Nuisance Removal Act 1848   233, 237
Nuisance Removal Act 1856   233

Offices, Shops and Railway Premises
   Act 1963   149, 157, 158, 169, 170,
   171, 172, 173, 174, 175, 176, 227
   s. 1(2)   169
   s. 1(2)(b)   170
   s. 1(3)(a)   170
   s. 1(4)   170
   ss. 2–4   170
   s. 5(1)   171
   s. 5(2)   171, 175
   s. 6   171, 175
   s. 6(2)   171
   ss. 7–8   171
   ss. 9–10   172, 175
   s. 10(2)   172
   ss. 12–13   172
   ss. 14–15   173
   s. 16   174
   s. 16(1)–(3)   173
   s. 16(4)   174
   ss. 17–19   174
   s. 42   174, 175
   s. 42(2)–(4)   174
   s. 42(6)–(7)   175
   s. 42(11)   175
   s. 42(13)   175
   s. 43   175
   s. 46(1)   175

Planning (Listed Buildings and Conservation
   Areas) Act 1990
   s. 1   188
Prevention of Damage by Pests Act 1949
   244, 247
   Part I   244, 246, 247
   Part II   245, 246
   s. 2   244
   ss. 3–6   245
   s. 8   246
   s. 13   246
   s. 13(1)–(2)   246
   ss. 14–16   247
   s. 22   247
Public Health Act 1848   4, 179, 237
Public Health Act 1872   5
Public Health Act 1875   5, 14
   s. 117   120
Public Health Act 1936   14, 216, 233
   s. 48   113
   s. 50   113

Public Health Act 1936 — *continued*
   ss. 85–86   242
   s. 90   113
   s. 92(1)(a)   28
   s. 93   229
   s. 140   104
   s. 259(1)   14
Public Health Act 1961   216, 233
   s. 17   113
   s. 34   88
Public Health (Control of Disease) Act 1984
   233, 236, 237, 240, 241
   ss. 10–11   234
   s. 13   242
   s. 16   234
   s. 17(1)–(2)   235
   s. 18   234
   s. 20   235
   ss. 21–23   236
   s. 23(6)   236
   ss. 24–26   237
   s. 28   237
   ss. 29–35   238
   ss. 36–38   239
   s. 39   240
   s. 39(2)   199
   ss. 40–45   240
   s. 46   240, 243
   s. 47-48   240
   s. 49(2)   199
   s. 56   240
   s. 61   240
   s. 71   241
   s. 73   241
   s. 74   240
   ss. 83–84   241
Public Health (Scotland) Act 1897   5, 16

Radioactive Substances Act 1960   93
Radioactive Substances Act 1993   93, 94
   s. 13   94
   s. 40   94
Refuse Disposal (Amenity) Act 1978
   s. 2   87
   s. 3   88
   s. 4   88
   s. 6   87
Rent (Agriculture) Act 1976   209
Road Traffic Act 1972
   s. 40   62
Road Traffic Act 1988
   s. 41(1)   31
   s. 41(2)(c)   31
   s. 42   31
Road Traffic Regulation Act 1984
   s. 99   88

Table of Statutes   xxiii

Sale of Food and Drugs Act 1875   5, 114
Sale of Goods Act 1893
  s. 24   118
Sanitary Act 1866   5
Sewage Utilisation Act 1865   5
Shaftesbury Act 1851 (14 & 15 Vict c.34)
  5, 179

Torrens Act 1875 (38 & 39 Vict c.36)   180
Torrens Act (31 & 32 Vict c.130)   5
Town and Country Planning Act 1947
  s. 29   229
Town and Country Planning Act 1971
  s. 54   188
Town and Country Planning Act 1990
  27, 68, 213, 214
  s. 70   27
  s. 192   68
Trade Descriptions Act 1968   63

Water Act 1989   96
Water (Fluoridation) Act 1985   104
Water Industry Act 1991   96, 97, 101, 105,
  106, 107, 108, 110
  Part VI   103
  ss. 37–38   96
  ss. 38A–38B   96
  s. 40   97
  s. 41   97
  s. 41(2)–(3)   97
  s. 42   97
  ss. 45–47   98
  s. 47(2)(g)   102
  s. 50   98
  s. 52   98, 99
  s. 53   99
  s. 54(1)–(2)   99
  s. 55   99
  s. 55(3)–(4)   99
  s. 56   99
  s. 60   99
  s. 61   100
  s. 62   100
  s. 64(1)–(3)   100

Water Industry Act 1991 — *continued*
  s. 65(1)   100
  s. 66(1)   101
  s. 67   101
  s. 68   101, 102
  ss. 69–70   102
  s. 72   102, 104
  s. 73   102
  s. 74   99, 102
  ss. 76–78   103
  s. 80(1)   103
  ss. 82–83   103
  s. 84   104
  s. 87   104
  s. 94(1)   104, 105
  s. 94(2)   105
  s. 95   105
  s. 97   105
  ss. 98–102   106
  ss. 104–105   107
  s. 106   107, 110
  s. 107   108
  s. 109   108
  s. 110A   108
  s. 111   110
  s. 111(1)–(2)   108
  ss. 112–114   109
  ss. 118–120   110
  s. 121(1)–(2)   111
  ss. 122–123   111
  ss. 124–127   112
  s. 129   112
  s. 131   113
  s. 138(1)   110
  s. 199   113
  s. 219   100
  s. 219(1)   105
  Sch.7   104
Water Resources Act 1991
  s. 85(3)   61
Water (Scotland) Act 1980   101
Wildlife and Countryside Act 1981
  s. 28(1)   69

Statutory Instruments

Air Navigation (Noise Certification) Order 1990 (SI 1990/1514)   29
  Art. 5   29
  Art. 5(1)–(2)   29
  Art. 6   29
Air Navigation Order 1989 (SI 1989/2004)   30
Air Quality Standards Regulations 1989 (SI 1989/317)   48
  Reg. 2   48
  Reg. 4   48
Anthrax Order 1991 (SI 1991/2814)   243
Anthrax Prevention Order 1971 (SI 1971/1234)   243
Asbestos Regulations 1969 (SI 1969/690)   163
Assistance for Minor Works to Dwellings Regulations 1990 (SI 1990/388)   212

Building (Approved Inspectors etc.) (Amendment) Regulations 1992 (SI 1992/740)   224
Building (Approved Inspectors etc.) Regulations 1985 (SI 1985/1066)   224
  Reg. 7   224
Building (Prescribed Fees etc.) Regulations 1985 (SI 1985/1576)   218
Building Regulations 1991 (SI 1991/2768)   32, 216
  Part E
    Sch. 1   32
  Reg. 10   217
  Reg. 16   222
  Reg. 17   222
  Sch. 1
    Part J   39

Canal Boats Regulations 1878 (SR & O Rev 1948, vol. 3, p.429)   240
Clean Air (Arrestment Plant) (Exemption) Regulations 1969 (SI 1969/1262)   37
Clean Air (Emission of Grit and Dust from Furnaces) Regulations 1971
    (SI 1971/162)   36
Clean Air (Height of Chimneys) (Exemption) Regulations 1969 (SI 1969/411)   38
Clean Air (Measurement of Grit and Dust from Furnaces) Regulations
    1971 (SI 1971/161)   37
Control of Asbestos at Work Regulations 1987 (SI 1987/2115)   177
Control of Noise (Code of Practice on Noise from Audible Intruder Alarms)
    Order 1981 (SI 1981/1829)   27
Control of Noise (Code of Practice on Noise from Model Aircraft) Order
    1981 (SI 1981/1830)   27
Control of Noise (Measurement and Registers) Regulations 1976 (SI 1976/37)   26

Statutory Instruments

Control of Pollution (Research and Publicity) Regulations 1977 (SI 1977/19) 43
Control of Pollution (Special Waste) Regulations 1980 (SI 1980/1709) 86
Control of Substances Hazardous to Health (Amendment) Regulations
   1990 (SI 1990/2026) 177
   Reg. 8-9 178
   Reg. 15 178
Control of Substances Hazardous to Health Regulations 1988 (SI 1988/1657) 177
   Reg. 6 177
   Reg. 7 177
Controlled Waste (Register of Carriers and Seizure of Vehicles) Regulations
   1991 (SI 1991/1624) 66
Controlled Waste (Registration of Carriers and Seizure of Vehicles)
   Regulations 1991 (SI 1991/1624) 93
   Reg. 10 93
   Reg. 11 93
Controlled Waste Regulations 1992 (SI 1992/588) 62
Crop Residues (Restriction on Burning) Regulations 1991 (SI 1991/1399) 58
Crop Residues (Restriction on Burning) Regulations 1991 (SI 1991/1590) 58

Dark Smoke (Permitted Periods) Regulations 1958 (SI 1958/498) 34
Department of Environment Circular 10/73 27
Department of Environment Circular 6/90 181

Employer's Health and Safety Policy Statements (Exception) Regulations
   1975 (SI 1975/1584)
   Reg. 2 152, 153
Environmental Protection (Applications, Appeals and Registers) Regulations 1991
   (SI 1991/507) 51, 55, 56
Environmental Protection (Duty of Care) Regulations 1991 (SI 1991/2839) 67
Environmental Protection (Prescribed Processes and Substances) Regulations 1991
   (SI 1991/472) 47
   Reg. 4 47
   Sch.1 47
      Part A 47
      Part B 47
   Sch.4-6 47
Environmental Protection (Waste Recycling Payments) Regulations 1992
   (SI 1992/462) 84

Factories (Cleanliness of Walls and Ceilings) (Amendment) Order 1974
   (SI 1974/427) 164
Factories (Cleanliness of Walls and Ceilings) Order 1960 (SI 1960/1794) 164
Fire Precautions (Factories, Offices, Shops and Railway Premises) Order 1989
   (SI 1989/76) 231
Fire Precautions (Hotel and Boarding Houses) Order 1972 (SI 1972/238) 231
Fire Precautions (Sub-surface Railway Stations) Regulations 1989 (SI 1989/1401) 232
Food Hygiene (General) Regulations 1970 (SI 1970/1172) 137, 141
   Reg. 6-7 137
   Reg. 8 138
   Reg. 9-13 138
   Reg. 17 139, 140
   Reg. 20 140
   Reg. 21-22 139
   Reg. 24-26 140
   Reg. 27 140
Food Hygiene (Markets, Stalls and Delivery Vehicles) Regulations 1970
   (SI 1970/1172) 140

Food Premises (Registration) Regulations 1991 (SI 1991/2825)   132
Food Safety (Sampling and Qualifications) Regulations 1990 (SI 1990/2463)   136

Gatwick Airport London Noise Insulation Grant Scheme 1980 (SI 1980/154)   30

Health and Safety (Display Screen Equipment) Regulations 1992 (SI 1992/2792)   176
   Reg. 2–4   176
Health and Safety (Enforcing Authority) Regulations 1989 (SI 1989/1903)
   Reg. 3   158
   Sch.1   158
Heathrow Airport London Noise Insulation Grant Scheme 1980 (SI 1980/153)   30
Homes Insulation Grants Order 1988 (SI 1988/1239)   213
Household Appliances (Noise Emission) Regulations 1990 (SI 1990/2179)
   Reg. 3–4   32
Houses in Multiple Occupation (Charges for Registration Schemes) Regulations 1991
   (SI 1991/982)   194
Housing Act (Overcrowding and Miscellaneous Forms) Regulations 1937
   (SR & O 1937/80)   192
Housing (Management of Houses in Multiple Occupation) Regulations 1962
   (SI 1962/668)   197
Housing (Management of Houses in Multiple Occupation) Regulations 1990
   (SI 1990/830)   197
Housing (Means of Escape from Fire in Houses in Multiple Occupation) Order 1981
   (SI 1981/1576)   196
Housing Renovation etc. Grants (Grant Limit) Order 1993 (SI 1993/553)   208
Housing Renovation Etc. Grants (Reduction of Grant) (Amendment) Regulations 1992
   (SI 1992/705)   204
Housing Renovation etc. Grants (Reduction of Grant) Regulations 1990 (SI 1990/1189)   204
Hydrogen Cyanide (Fumigation of Buildings) Regulations 1951 (SI 1951/1759)   247
Hydrogen Cyanide (Fumigation of Ships) Regulations 1951 (SI 1951/1760)   247

Litter Control Areas Order 1991 (SI 1991/1325)   89

Machinery (Safety) Regulations 1992 (SI 1992/3073)   156
Management of Health and Safety at Work Regulations 1992 (SI 1992/2051)   152, 176
   Reg. 3–4   152, 177
   Reg. 8   177
Manual Handling Operations Regulations 1992 (SI 1992/2793)   176
   Reg. 4   176
Milk and Dairies (General) Regulations 1959 (SI 1959/277)   141
   Part   6–9 142
   Part 5   141
   Reg. 6   141
   Reg. 8–9   141
Milk (Special Designation) Regulations 1989 (SI 1989/2383)   142
Ministry of Housing and Local Government Circular No 42/60   215
Motor Fuel (Lead Content of Petrol) (Amendment) Regulations 1985
   (SI 1985/1728)   42
Motor Fuel (Lead Content of Petrol) Regulations 1981 (SI 1981/1523)   42
Motor Fuel (Sulphur Content of Gas Oil) (Amendment) Regulations 1990
   (SI 1990/1097)   42
Motor Fuel (Sulphur Content of Gas Oil) Regulations 1976 (SI 1976/1989)   42
Motor Vehicles (Types Approval) (Great Britain) Regulations 1984 (SI 1984/981)   31

Noise at Work Regulations 1989 (SI 1989/1790)   178
   Reg. 6–7   178

Statutory Instruments

Noise Insulation Regulations 1975 (SI 1975/1763)
   Reg. 3   32

Oil Fuel (Sulphur Content of Gas Oil) Regulations 1990 (SI 1990/1096)   42

Prescribed Dangerous Machines Order 1964 (SI 1964/971)   174
Prevention of Damage by Pests (Infestation of Food) Regulations 1950
   (SI 1950/416)   246
Private Water Supplies Regulations 1991 (SI 1991/2790)   101
Provision and Use of Work Equipment Regulations 1992 (SI 1992/2932)   177
   Reg. 5–6   177
   Reg. 8   177
Public Health (Aircraft) Regulations 1979 (SI 1979/1434)   242
Public Health (Infectious Diseases) Regulations 1988 (SI 1988/1546)   234
   Reg. 5   239
Public Health (Prevention of Tuberculosis) Regulations 1925 (SR & O 1925/757)   242
Public Health (Ships) Regulations 1979 (SI 1979/1435)   242

Removal and Disposal of Vehicles Regulations 1986 (SI 1986/183)
   Reg. 5(1)   88
Road Vehicles (Construction and Use) Regulations 1986 (SI 1986/1078)   31
   Reg. 54   31
   Reg. 56–58   31
Road Vehicles (Construction and Use) Regulations 1986
   Reg. 97   31
Rules of the Air Regulations 1991 (SI 1991/2437)
   Reg. 5(1)   29

Sanitary Accommodation (Amendment) Regulations 1974 (SI 1974/426)   164
Sanitary Accommodation Regulations 1938 (SR & O 1938/611)   164
Sanitary Convenience Regulations 1964 (SI 1964/966)   172
Smoke Control Areas (Authorised Fuels) Regulations 1991 (SI 1991/1282)   40
Smoke Control Areas (Authorised Fuels) Regulations 1992 (SI 1992/72)   40
Smoke Control Areas (Exempted Fireplaces) Order 1991 (SI 1991/2892)   41
Street Litter Control Notices Order 1991 (SI 1991/1324)   91

Transfrontier Shipment of Hazardous Waste Regulations 1988 (SI 1988/1562)   93

Washing Facilities Regulations 1964 (SI 1964/965)   172
Waste Management Licensing Regulations 1994 (SI 1994/1056) 61, 69, 74
Water Supply and Sewerage Services (Customer Service Standards) Regulations 1989
   (SI 1989/1159)   105
Water Supply and Sewerage Services (Customer Service Standards) Regulations 1989
   (SI 1989/1383)   105
Water Supply (Water Quality) Regulations 1989 (SI 1989/1147)   101
Water Supply (Water Quality) Regulations 1989 (SI 1989/1837)   101
Workplace (Health, Safety and Welfare) Regulations 1992 (SI 1992/3004)   176

ONE
Introduction

Whereas environmental law covers a wide ambit ranging from the law relating to town and country planning through conservation to the pollution of the sea, environmental *health* law concerns itself with that aspect of the external environment which has close connection with human health. Of necessity, therefore, it deals with the law relating to a variety of situations as diverse as pollution of the land by waste, health and safety at work, food and housing, the only point of mutual contact being the influence the relevant activity has on human health. Environmental health law is therefore fragmented in nature. It is by no means a new subject. Indeed it has its roots in the early part of the 19th century. However, before alluding to the Victorian public health movement on which our modern environmental health law is founded, and in order to put the modern law in its historical context, it is useful to sketch a rough picture of the basic physical problems which confronted our forefathers.

THE INDUSTRIAL REVOLUTION

The industrial revolution forced many of those employed in the country to work in factories situated in towns. This caused a rapid expansion in the size of industrial towns. An unbearable strain was, as a consequence, placed on the housing stock. In order to accommodate the rapid influx of population, landlords, many of whom were also employers, either subdivided their houses or erected jerry-built property for the purpose. Living conditions were in the main grossly insanitary. It was not uncommon to find more than one family sharing a poorly lit and ventilated room in a house which also lacked a water supply and water closet. Cellars were also employed for the purposes of human habitation. Those who had to live there indeed occupied the lowest rung of the ladder of human degradation. The rapid expansion of industrial towns during the Victorian era resulted not only in high-density housing but also in the new factories being situated in such close proximity to houses that it was inevitable, in the absence of constraints imposed by planning law, that those living in the houses would be affected by the smoke and fumes belching from the factories.

The rapid growth of towns also placed great strain on public utilities such as water supply and drainage. The water companies or municipal authorities responsible for the public water supply were inclined simply to provide enough water to meet the immediate needs of the area served. No account was taken of the rapid expansion of the population. The result of this so-called 'droplet' method of water supply was a general shortage of water. This bore more heavily on the poor who often had to queue at public wells for their water. Another result of such a parsimonious and blinkered approach to water supply was the lack of a constant supply in the public water main. This often resulted in the water main being subject to negative pressure which facilitated the absorption of polluting matter such as excrement into the public water supply.

During the 19th century some tried to establish a link between alcohol and poverty. The poor were poor because of drink. Their lot could, it was believed, be improved simply by weaning them from drink. Furthermore, lack of a sufficient and wholesome water supply was often seen as a major cause of alcohol reliance by the working classes. Many temperance reformers therefore became involved in public health reform since they regarded a pure and copious water supply as an essential ingredient to the success of their cause.

As far as municipal drainage was concerned the outstanding problem was simply the lack of public sewers and drains. This prevented the installation of water closets in buildings. Another direct consequence of there being an insufficient number of sewers was the practice of using watercourses as sewers to convey both industrial and domestic effluent to the sea. Indeed in many of our great towns and cities such as London, Glasgow and Edinburgh the major watercourse running through the city was no less than an open sewer until well into the century.

Cholera was the most feared of the diseases which afflicted 19th century Britain. However, other diseases such as typhus, typhoid, smallpox, scarlet fever, dysentery and measles were endemic and occurred cyclically. Proliferation of disease during epidemics was normally, depending on the disease concerned, facilitated by overcrowding in dwellinghouses or by lack of ventilation. In the case of typhus, the lack of personal hygiene and lack of clothes-washing facilities in working-class homes, allowed the vector, namely lice, to breed. Tuberculosis or phthisis (the 'white plague') was also always present throughout the century. Contaminated milk supplies and overcrowding in houses facilitated its spread. One should also remember the prevalence of illnesses such as diarrhoea and influenza. The former had a pronounced effect upon the infant population especially during the summer months. Poor food hygiene practised in shops, especially those which sold dairy products, coupled with lack of refrigeration facilities in both shops and the home, ensured that diarrhoea was a constant torment especially to the young, and the disease enthusiastically carried them off in droves. Influenza pandemics occurred regularly throughout the 19th century. Indeed in 1847–8 some 50,000 deaths occurred from the illness, a figure which greatly exceeded that for cholera the following year. Of importance also was the fact that until well into the 20th century there was no effective cure for febrile diseases. Whether the patient fell foul of a febrile disease and survived an attack depended therefore on the personal defence system of the patient. Diet here was obviously important. The diet of the working classes was indeed poor unfortunately. Meat was seldom consumed. There was also a paucity of fresh fruit and vegetables which are valuable sources of vitamin C which plays an important part in immunity against disease.

PUBLIC HEALTH REFORM

While the woeful state of the environmental condition of urban Britain must have been pellucidly clear to anyone who had either eyes to observe the squalid living conditions or the filthy urban air, or a nose to smell the effluent covering the streets or the waste matter dumped immediately outside houses, it was that most feared disease, cholera, which dramatically and cruelly drew the attention of the public and, more importantly, the government, to the unsatisfactory state of the external environment and the deleterious effect it could have on human health. We all know now that cholera is water-borne, the causative micro-organism being the cholera vibrio. However, until the sterling work of Koch later in the 19th century established the true origins of the disease, it was widely held that diseases, especially febrile and enteric diseases, were generated by foul odour or 'miasms'. The miasmatists, as they were known, therefore believed that the essential prophylactic against cholera was to cleanse the external environment of refuse, excremental and organic matter. The theory which ran counter to the miasmatic theory was the contagion theory. This theory was based on the belief that disease was spread by personal contact with the host of the disease. However, until the work of Pasteur, Lister and Koch later in the century established the existence of pathogenic micro-organisms, it was impossible for the contagionists to base their theory on a sound theoretical terrain. The theory simply did not work. It is probable that the miasmatic theory found more staunch support south of the Border than north. One cannot, however, be certain. This interesting aspect of environmental history is indeed under-researched. More local studies of Victorian public health especially in Scotland, require to be done before a clearer picture can emerge.

There was also a political and economic aspect to the relative merits of each theory. If the contagion theory was to be given practical effect this meant imposing a *cordon sanitaire* around the relevant town or country as a whole. This meant the loss of trade and concomitant economic catastrophy. While the miasmatic theory possibly ranks as one of the greatest popular myths in British history, it did have the beneficial effect of linking the external environment with human health. In order to preserve human health therefore, it was necessary to ensure that the external environment was pure.

The first cholera outbreak in the United Kingdom occurred in 1831-2. It claimed roughly 32,000 lives. It marks the beginning, in the author's view, of the first environmental revolution in this country. Cholera made Britain look to its own sanitary condition and the laws which were believed to have a bearing on the external environment. While the cholera outbreak of the early 1830s may not have had a lasting effect on the sanitary administration of the various municipalities it affected (since the fervent municipal clean-up which preceded and continued during the outbreak of the epidemic was not sustained after the epidemic had abated) the disease prompted the Victorian public health reform movement which had perhaps its official origins in 1842 with the chilling report of that arch miasmatist and barrister-at-law turned sanitary reformer, Edwin Chadwick, on the *Sanitary Condition of the Labouring Population of Great Britain* which painted a truly lachrymose picture of the sanitary state of England's towns. Not only did the 1831-2 epidemic stimulate an awareness of the effect of the environment upon human health, it also acted as a catalyst in forging a closer relationship between central and local government inasmuch as the *ad hoc* Board of Health took upon itself to issue instructions to local boards of health on how to deal with the epidemic.

The late 1840s saw the miasmatic theory reach its zenith in terms of legislative expression with the passage of Nuisance Removal Acts. More important however, in terms of general public health was the Public Health Act 1848 which allowed local authorities to adopt its provisions and establish local boards of health which were given power to remove nuisances, construct sewers, and license slaughterhouses and lodging-houses. Power was also given to levy a rate to construct drains and sewers. Importantly, power was given to appoint a medical officer of health. Default powers were also given to the General Board of Health, a central government body, to force local authorities to establish local boards. However, regarded as autocratic and never popular, the General Board was finally abolished in 1858 and its powers transferred to the Privy Council.

The Sewage Utilisation Act 1865 and Sanitary Act 1866 increased the power of local authorities to provide drains and sewers. Of particular significance was the power conferred by the 1866 Act to create special drainage districts. The Public Health Act 1875, in the main a consolidating statute, represented the final phase in the development of a sound legislative foundation for the advancement of public health in England and Wales. English public health therefore had a head start over Scotland in this respect. Indeed, it was not until after the passage of the Public Health (Scotland) Act 1897 that public health took off in that country.

Mention should be made here of the Public Health Act 1872 which divided the country into sanitary areas and made the relevant local authority solely responsible for the enforcement of sanitary law in that area.

As far as housing was concerned, slow progress was made from the passage of the Shaftesbury Act 1851 (14 and 15 Vict c. 34) until the Cross Act and Torrens Act (31 & 32 Vict c. 130) between 1868 and 1882 which allowed local authorities to effect the demolition of unfit property on an area basis. However, it was the Housing of the Working Classes Act 1890 which constituted a landmark in the development of housing law inasmuch as it gave local authorities power to erect buildings for the working classes. This was of fundamental importance, since until 1890 it was left to speculative builders to build on the land left vacant. The dwellings thus built were too expensive for all but fairly well-heeled tradesmen.

Attempts were also made by private individuals to improve the housing of the working classes. One was the so-called 'five per cent philanthropy' movement which consisted of benevolently disposed persons combining to acquire property which could be rented at a low rent to the poor. The contributors then got a five per cent return on their investment. The movement failed to attract wide enough support and was nothing more than an interesting experiment. There also existed building societies. Individuals would contribute to a common fund which would be lent out for the purposes of buying or renting property. This failed to redound to the benefit of the poorer artisans or labourers since they simply could not afford to pay the appropriate rent or repay the loan for the purchase of property.

Finally, no discussion about public health reform would be complete without some mention of the common practice of the wilful adulteration of food which took place in the 19th century. To counter this problem several ineffective statutes were passed in the 1860s. The first breakthrough came in 1872 with the Adulteration of Food and Drugs Act 1872 (35 & 36 Vict c. 74). The Sale of Food and Drugs Act 1875 represented a determined attempt by Parliament to suppress the deliberate adulteration of food and drink by food manufacturers, wholesalers and retailers. The 1875 Act laid the foundation of the modern law governing the public health control of food.

TWENTIETH CENTURY

The first half of the 20th century saw environmental health law develop slowly and piecemeal. The momentum of the public health reform of the previous century was certainly lost. The First World War, the Depression, the Second World War and its aftermath all combined to ensure that priority was not given to matters environmental. However, there was some legislative action especially in the field of planning law and housing law. Things changed in 1952. It was in the winter of that year that the great volumes of smoke in London's air combined with its fog to produce a most horrendous smog which caused hundreds of deaths. The very young and the old were the worst affected. The disaster callously drew attention to the fact that the state of the atmosphere in Britain's towns had not substantially changed since the Victorian era. The main reason for this was that air pollution law was heavily nuisance-based. A smoke source had to be held to constitute a nuisance before any action could be taken. This was often difficult to do. The urban atmosphere became more polluted as time progressed. In the immediate aftermath of the smog disaster, the Beaver Committee was set up. Its findings formed the basis of the revolutionary Clean Air Act 1956 which relied not on the law of nuisance but on quantitative and qualitative standards for the control of pollution. The approach embodied in the 1956 Act represents a landmark in the postwar development of environmental law and, it is suggested, constitutes the beginning of the second environmental revolution in the United Kingdom.

Interest in the environment increased during the 1960s. In 1962 Rachel Carson's rather depressing but seminal *Silent Spring* drew attention to the harm pollution was having on the environment. Surprisingly, the environmental awareness of the 1960s did not result in immediate Parliamentary intervention. However, 1974 saw the passing of the Control of Pollution Act which represented the first statute in the United Kingdom to attempt to deal holistically with environmental pollution. In the 1980s attention again turned to the environment. Fear of the harm pollution could cause, especially to the ozone layer, plus awareness of so-called greenhouse gases as well as apprehension of the threat posed to our food by contamination from a variety of sources, combined to prompt renewed legislative activity in the form of the Environmental Protection Act 1990 and the Food Safety Act 1990 respectively.

ENFORCEMENT OF ENVIRONMENTAL HEALTH LEGISLATION

In England, metropolitan district councils are responsible, subject to certain limited exceptions, for environmental health. Non-metropolitan district councils are also responsible for this function. Non-metropolitan county councils are responsible for animal diseases, refuse disposal and consumer protection (e.g., certain aspects of food and drugs law). In Wales the allocation of local authority functions is roughly similar to that which obtains for England except that food and drugs and the disposal of abandoned vehicles are enforced by district councils.

TWO
Nuisance

It has already been mentioned in chapter 1 that nuisance removal played an important part in the development of public health reform in the United Kingdom. Whereas 19th-century environmental health law was largely nuisance-based, the centre of gravity, as far as the pollution of the environment is concerned, has now shifted to the law setting quantitative and qualitative standards, such control existing within a legal regime in which the enforcing authority also has appropriate licensing powers. However, nuisance law still has a role to play in environmental health law. Indeed such modern statutes as the Environmental Protection Act 1990 and the Clean Air Act 1993 both draw on the concept of nuisance to a limited extent.

This chapter is divided into a discussion of common law nuisance and statutory nuisance. A knowledge of the meaning of nuisance at common law is essential since the courts tend to give the expression 'nuisance' found in a statutory context, an identical meaning to that found in common law (see, for example, *A. Lambert Flat Management Ltd* v *Lomas* [1981] 1 WLR 898).

COMMON LAW NUISANCE

The courts recognise the general principle that one has a general right to enjoy one's property without interference from activities which take place outside that property. The law of nuisance can be enlisted by the plaintiff if such a right is prejudiced. The factors which the court takes into account when considering if a given state of affairs constitutes a nuisance are now discussed in turn. The list is not exhaustive, it is suggested. Furthermore no single factor is accorded a greater weighting than any other.

Social utility of the defendant's conduct

The court will take account of the public benefit which accrues from the defendant's conducting the activity which gives rise to the state of affairs complained of. The more socially useful such activity is the less likely it is to be condemned as a nuisance by the courts (*Harrison* v *Southwark and Vauxhall Water Co.* [1891] 2 Ch 409). However, the courts have carefully avoided constructing a hierarchy of activities weighted in terms of social worth for the purposes of nuisance law. Whereas the courts recognise the obvious social worth of factories (*Bellew* v *Cement Ltd* [1948] IR 61) there is no authority on how the courts would assess other activities such as forms of recreation (see, however, *Miller* v *Jackson* [1977] QB 966), transport, religious worship and education.

Motive of the defendant

The general rule is that the courts almost perfunctorily categorise a state of affairs as a nuisance if it has been motivated by spite. In *Christie* v *Davey* [1893] 1 Ch 316 the plaintiff's family were musically inclined and frequently played musical instruments to the annoyance of the defendant. The latter decided to retaliate by banging trays on the party-wall which separated his house from that of the plaintiff who successfully raised an action in nuisance. In *Hollywood Silver Fox Farm Ltd* v *Emmett* [1936] 2 KB 468 the plaintiff company bred foxes on its land. The defendant objected to this and decided to discharge guns along the boundary which separated his premises from that of the plaintiff. It was held that a nuisance existed.

Locality

The nature of the appropriate locality is taken into account by the court when it considers if a given state of affairs constitutes a nuisance. The leading case is *Bamford* v *Turnley* (1862) 31 LJ QB 286, where Pollock CB stated: 'That may be a nuisance in Grosvenor Square, which would be none in Smithfield Market'. In *Inglis* v *Shotts Iron Co.* (1881) 8 R 1006 the Lord Justice-Clerk stated (at p. 1021): 'Things which are forbidden in a crowded urban community may be permitted in the country. What is prohibited in enclosed land may be tolerated in the open.' This judicial approach can be explained on the grounds that people who live in localities where a certain state of affairs is commonly found will have become habituated to it and therefore less sensitive to it. However, the facts that a state of affairs is indigenous in the area does not give the defendant *carte blanche* to create a nuisance. This point was firmly made in *Rushmer* v *Polsue and Alfieri Ltd* [1906] 1 Ch 234 where the House of Lords upheld the grant of an injunction to restrain the defendant's use of printing presses during the night, notwithstanding that it was habitual practice for certain premises in that area to operate their presses during the night. The Canadian courts similarly have not been over-indulgent to industrialists in allowing them to operate with complete insensitivity to the rights of others. For example, in *Gagnon* v *Dominion Stamping Co.* (1914) 7 OWN 530 the constant use of steam hammers in an industrial neighbourhood was deemed to constitute a nuisance. The nature of the locality is only relevant, however, if the state of affairs solely affects personal comfort. If the state of affairs physically injures the plaintiff's property the locality principle is redundant (*St Helens Smelting Co.* v *Tipping* (1865) 11 HL Cas 642 at p. 650). It is suggested that the locality principle would also be redundant if the plaintiff suffered personal injury as a result of the state of affairs in question.

There is no authority on how the courts would apply the locality principle if the locality in which the state of affairs in question exists is physically separate and of a different type from that where the plaintiff's premises are situated. For example, such a problem could arise if the defendant's factory were situated in an industrial area but the plaintiff's dwellinghouse is located in a residential area. On the authority of *Gillingham Borough Council* v *Medway (Chatham) Dock Co. Ltd* [1993] QB 343, it is suggested that the relevant locality would be that of the defendant.

An interesting development in this area of law is the effect of planning permission on the character of the locality. In the *Gillingham* case it was held that the grant of planning permission by a local planning authority could have the effect of changing the character of a locality for the purposes of the law of public nuisance. Whether similar reasoning can be applied in relation to private law can only be clarified by subsequent decision. It is suggested that the grant of planning permission does not have this effect.

Duration and intensity

The length of time that a state of affairs exists as well as its intensity are taken into account when considering if it constitutes a nuisance. The leading case is *Bamford* v *Turnley* (1862) 31 LJ QB 286 in which Pollock CB stated (at p. 292):

> A clock striking the hour, or a bell ringing for some domestic purpose, may be a nuisance if unreasonably loud and discordant, of which the jury alone must judge; but although not unreasonably loud, if the owner from some whim or caprice made the clock strike the hour every 10 minutes, or the bell ring continually, I think that a jury would be justified in considering it to be a very great nuisance.

Time of day

The time of day at which the state of affairs exists is significant only in relation to an alleged noise nuisance. Thus the courts are more inclined to regard night noise a nuisance than noise which takes place during the day (*Bamford* v *Turnley* (1862) 31 LJ QB 286). The obvious rationale of the rule is that night noise is more likely to disturb than noise which exists only during the day.

Sensitivity of the plaintiff

As a general rule the courts are not indulgent to the oversensitive. This rule applies to the sensitivity of the plaintiff's person as well as that of his or her property. This robust judicial approach is well illustrated in the law of nuisance by *Heath* v *Brighton Corporation* (1908) 98 LT 718 where a priest failed in his action against the defendant municipality because it was proved that he was discomfited by the noise it made simply by virtue of his hypersensitive hearing. Similar reasoning is applied in relation to injury to property. Thus in *Robinson* v *Kilvert* (1889) 41 ChD 88 the plaintiff kept paper which was of a delicate nature. It was damaged by the heat generated from the defendant's premises. It was held that since an ordinary business would not have been affected by heat of such nature, the plaintiff failed. Similarly in *Bridlington Relay Ltd* v *Yorkshire Electricity Board* [1965] Ch 436 the court doubted whether the receipt of television signals could be protected by way of an injunction from external interference (but in *Nor-Video Services Ltd* v *Ontario Hydro* (1978) 84 DLR (3d) 221 damages were awarded for interference with transmission of a cable television service).

State of affairs

The alleged nuisance must emanate from a state of affairs. It must therefore not be transitory or evanescent in nature (see, for example, *Matheson* v *Northcote College* [1975] 2 NZLR 106). However, a single manifestation of a dangerous state of affairs is sufficient for liablity to lie (see, for example, *Bolton* v *Stone* [1951] AC 850 and *Castle* v *St Augustine's Links* (1922) 38 TLR 615).

Could the plaintiff have avoided the nuisance?

The courts have adopted an uncompromising stance to authors of nuisances by refusing to say that a person suffering from a nuisance should do everything reasonably possible to mitigate the suffering. This approach is implicit in the numerous decisions concerning noise nuisance where it has never been accepted, for example, that the plaintiff should go to the expense of having premises double or triple-glazed in order to reduce the effect of noise (see, for example, *Kennaway* v *Thompson* [1981] QB 88; *Webster* v *Lord Advocate* 1985 SC 173).

Is fault required?

Nuisance has traditionally been regarded as a tort of strict liability. In other words it is not necessary to prove that the defendant intended or, as is more common in practice, was negligent in allowing the adverse state of affairs to come into existence (see *Cambridge Water Co.* v *Eastern Counties Leather plc* [1994] 2 WLR 53). However, there are situations where liability lies only if the plaintiff has been negligent. For example, if the nuisance has been caused by a trespasser (*Sedleigh-Denfield* v *O'Callaghan* [1940] AC 880) or by nature (*Goldman* v *Hargrave* [1967] 1 AC 645; *Leakey* v *National Trust* [1980] QB 485), the defendant will be liable if reasonable steps are not taken to counter the effects of the adverse state of affairs. In assessing whether the necessary measures have been taken the courts employ a subjective approach taking into account the resources of the defendant.

As far as Scots Law is concerned, since the landmark decision of *RHM Bakeries (Scotland) Ltd* v *Strathclyde Regional Council* 1985 SC (HL) 17, *culpa* or fault is required before the defender is liable for nuisance.

Who is liable?

The author
The person who is responsible for the creation of a nuisance is liable at common law. The author of the nuisance need have no proprietary interest in the land on which the nuisance is situated.

The occupier
The occupier of land is normally liable for any nuisances which exist on it (*Sedleigh-Denfield* v *O'Callaghan* [1940] AC 880). However, an occupier is not liable for nuisances arising naturally or caused by trespassers unless insufficient steps were taken to combat the nuisance after the occupier became aware of its existence (see the discussion of fault above).

COMMON LAW DEFENCES

Coming to a nuisance

It is no defence that the plaintiff has come to the nuisance and thereby accepted its existence at the outset. In other words the general defence of *volenti* has no application in this aspect of nuisance law. Such an approach is well illustrated in the Scottish case of *Webster* v *Lord Advocate* 1985 SC 173, in which it was held that the pursuer, by moving into premises overlooking the Edinburgh Castle esplanade, did not thereby implicitly accept exposure to the noise from the military tattoo which was being performed on the esplanade (see also *Miller* v *Jackson* [1977] QB 966).

Prescription

The gist of this defence is that the law will not allow the plaintiff to succeed in a nuisance action if the plaintiff has acquiesced in the face of the nuisance for more than 20 years (*Sturges* v *Bridgman* (1879) 11 ChD 852). It must be shown that the state of affairs constituted an actionable nuisance for the entire 20-year period.

Statutory authority

Parliament can authorise the existence of a state of affairs which would normally rank as an actionable nuisance. Authorisation will usually be conferred by a private Act. The leading case is now *Allen* v *Gulf Oil Refining Ltd* [1981] AC 1001 in which an Act of Parliament authorised the construction and use of an oil refinery. Residents who lived in the vicinity of the refinery, were affected, *inter alia*, by noise, vibration and noxious odours and chemicals. It was held that since the nuisance was the necessary consequence of that which had been authorised, the defence of statutory authority succeeded.

COMMON LAW REMEDIES

Only very brief mention can be made here of the various common law remedies for nuisance. They are:

(a) Damages. The court can award the plaintiff damages to compensate for any personal discomfort or injury sustained to property.

(b) Injunction. The court can grant an injunction to prevent the creation, continuation or repetition of a nuisance. Since the passing of the Chancery Amendment Act 1858 the court has power to award damages in lieu of an injunction.

(c) Declaration. Sometimes the plaintiff may simply enlist the aid of the court to determine if a given state of affairs constitutes a nuisance. Such a determination is given in the form of a declaration which has no mandatory force. In other words the unsuccessful defendant is placed under no obligation to act on the decision. The declaration simply settles the respective rights of the parties to the dispute.

STATUTORY NUISANCES

Although a variety of statutes contain provisions relating to the abatement of nuisances, it has become customary to confine the term 'statutory nuisance' to the nuisances which could be dealt with under the various Public Health Acts, such as those of 1875 and 1936, and which are now dealt with under s. 79 of the Environmental Protection Act 1990 (as amended by the Noise and Statutory Nuisance Act 1993). Subsection (1) of s. 79 provides that the following matters constitute statutory nuisances:

(a) any premises in such a state as to be prejudicial to health or a nuisance;

(b) smoke emitted from premises so as to be prejudicial to health or a nuisance;

(c) fumes or gasses emitted from premises so as to be prejudicial to health or a nuisance;

(d) any dust, steam, smell or other effluvia arising on industrial, trade or business premises and being prejudicial to health or a nuisance;

(e) any accumulation or deposit which is prejudicial to health or a nuisance;

(f) any animal kept in such a place or manner as to be prejudicial to health or a nuisance;

(g) noise emitted from premises so as to be prejudicial to health or a nuisance;

(ga) noise that is prejudicial to health or a nuisance and is emitted from or caused by a vehicle, machinery or equipment in a street;

(h) any other matter declared by any enactment to be a statutory nuisance.

The Public Health Act 1936, s. 259(1) (as amended by the Environmental Protection Act 1990), makes the following statutory nuisances:

(a) any pond, pool, ditch, gutter or watercourse which is so foul or in such a state as to be prejudicial to health or a nuisance;

(b) any part of a watercourse, not being a part ordinarily navigated by vessels employed in the carriage of goods by water, which is so choked or silted up as to obstruct or impede the proper flow of water and thereby to cause a nuisance, or to give rise to conditions prejudicial to health.

It is suggested that the Environmental Health Act 1990, s. 79(1)(a), refers solely to the state of the premises as opposed to the use to which they are put. Premises may fall within the scope of the statute if they are in a state which (a) is prejudicial to the health of the occupants or others (b) is a nuisance.

As far as the phrase 'prejudicial to health' is concerned, it is not sufficient that the state of affairs interferes with personal comfort. Rather the premises must be likely to cause injury to health (*Salford City Council* v *McNally* [1976] AC 379). That which renders the premises prejudicial to health need not emanate from the premises in question. The cause of the danger to health may arise outside the premises (*Pollway Nominees Ltd* v *Havering London Borough Council* (1989) 88 LGR 192).

The courts accord the word 'nuisance' its ordinary meaning at common law (*National Coal Board* v *Thorne* [1976] 1 WLR 543). Therefore the non-occupiers of the premises must be affected (*National Coal Board* v *Thorne*).

Paragraphs (b) and (c) of s. 79(1) supplement the provisions of the Clean Air Act 1993. Section 79(2) of the 1990 Act provides that s. 79(1)(b) does not apply to various premises occupied by the Crown or visiting forces for the purposes of defence. Furthermore s. 79(3) provides that s. 79(1)(b) does not apply to the following:

(a) smoke emitted from a chimney of a private dwelling within a smoke control area,
(b) dark smoke emitted from a chimney or a building or a chimney serving the furnace of a boiler or industrial plant attached to a building or for the time being fixed to or installed on any land,
(c) smoke emitted from a railway locomotive steam engine, or
(d) dark smoke emitted otherwise than as mentioned above from industrial or trade premises.

Section 79(4) provides that s. 79(1)(c) does not apply to premises other than dwellinghouses.

Many of the situations which could fall within s. 79(1)(d) (which does not apply to steam emitted from a railway locomotive engine) could also be dealt with by provisions of the Factories Act 1961 and the Health and Safety at Work etc. Act 1974. In order to come within the scope of the nuisance limb of s. 79(1)(d) the state of affairs must materially affect the personal comfort of those residing outwith the premises. In *Wivenhoe Port Ltd* v *Colchester Borough Council* [1985] JPL 175 it was held that dust falling on the property of members of the public was insufficient to be categorised a statutory nuisance.

As far as s. 79(1)(e) is concerned it was held in *Great Northern Railway* v *Lurgan Commissioners* [1897] 2 IR 340 at p. 351 that the expression 'accumulation' implied some gradual accretion or heaping up of matter from day to day. It is suggested, in the absence of authority, that the accumulation could exist by reason of deliberate human conduct (for example, by dumping) as well as by the operation of nature, for example, by refuse matter being deposited by a stream on its banks. In the same case it was held that the expression 'deposit' meant something that was put down in some place and left there. Furthermore the words 'accumulation' and 'deposit' implied some degree of permanency. However, it is insufficient that the relevant danger manifests itself by the likelihood of people being injured by coming into contact with the deposit or accumulation while walking on the relevant land (*Coventry City Council* v *Cartwright* [1975] 1 WLR 845).

Under s. 79(1)(f) it has to be shown that the place or manner of keeping the animal causes the prejudice to health or nuisance. A kennel kept in close proximity to a neighbouring house, by reason of which the occupants are disturbed, would come within the scope of the paragraph, as would premises which became filthy and in turn presented a health risk by virtue of being too small to accommodate animals satisfactorily. It is suggested that s. 79(1)(f) would also be relevant to a situation in which zoonotic disease could be transmitted to humans by virtue of the place or manner in which animals are kept.

Paragraphs (g) and (ga) of s. 79(1), which deal with noise nuisances, are discussed in chapter 3.

By s. 79(1)(h), any matter declared to be a nuisance by any enactment is a statutory nuisance capable of being dealt with under the 1990 Act. Therefore any nuisance provision in any public general or private Act of Parliament would come within the scope of the paragraph, as would similar provisions in local authority by-laws. In most cases this would allow the courts to impose more severe penalties for failure to abate the nuisance in question.

As far as nuisance from watercourses, ditches etc. is concerned, it is sufficient that the state of the watercourse or ditch brings about an adverse state of affairs outside the ditch etc. which in turn causes a nuisance. In *Renfrew Upper District Committee* v *Ranken* (1928) 44 Sh Ct Rep 24, several ditches vested in the defender became a breeding ground for mosquitoes which invaded a residential district and attacked individuals residing there. It was held that this state of affairs constituted a nuisance in terms of the Public Health (Scotland) Act 1897.

The Environmental Protection Act 1990, s. 79(1), places a duty on every local authority to inspect its area to ascertain if statutory nuisances exist. Furthermore if a resident complains of a statutory nuisance, the authority must take reasonable steps to investigate the complaint. Section 79(10) provides that a local authority may not institute proceedings under paras. (b), (d) or (e) of s. 79(1) if proceedings might have been instituted under part I of the Alkali etc. Works Regulation Act 1906 or s. 5 of the Health and Safety at Work etc. Act 1974 (the provisions of which are enforced by HM Inspectorate of Pollution (HMIP).

Procedure for abatement of statutory nuisances

The Environmental Protection Act 1990, s. 80(1), gives a local authority power to serve a notice (called an abatement notice) if it is satisfied that a statutory nuisance exists, or is likely to occur or recur, in its area. The notice may require the abatement of the nuisance or prohibit its occurrence or recurrence. It may also require the execution of works and the taking of other necessary steps. The abatement notice must be served on the person responsible for the nuisance (s. 80(2)). The expression 'person responsible', other than in relation to vehicle noise nuisance, is defined by s. 79(7) as amended by the Noise and Statutory Nuisance Act 1993 as the person to whose act, default or sufferance the nuisance is attributable. If the nuisance arises from any defect of a structural character the notice must be served on the owner of the premises (Environmental Protection Act 1990, s. 80(2)). Where the owner of the premises cannot be found or the nuisance has not yet occurred, the notice must be served on the occupier of the premises. Where the person responsible for the nuisance cannot be found or the nuisance has not yet occurred, the notice must be served on the owner or occupier of the premises.

The person served with the notice may appeal against it within 21 days to the magistrates' court (s. 80(3)). An offence is committed if a person on whom a notice is served fails to comply with the notice (s. 80(4)). On the authority of *Stagecoach Ltd* v *MacPhail* 1988 SCCR 289, which concerned a prosecution under part III of the Control of Pollution Act 1974, the defendant cannot challenge the terms of a notice in the subsequent trial if the notice could have been challenged by way of appeal to the magistrate.

Defence of best practicable means

Under the Environmental Protection Act 1990, s. 80(7), the defence of best practicable means is available in proceedings relating to the abatement of statutory nuisances under the 1990 Act. Section 79(9) defines the expression 'best practicable means' as follows:

(a) 'practicable' means reasonably practicable having regard amongst other things to local conditions and circumstances, the current state of technical knowledge and the financial implications;

(b) the means to be employed include the design, installation, maintenance, and manner and periods of operation, of plant and machinery, and the design, construction and maintenance of buildings and structures;

(c) the test is to apply only insofar as compatible with any other duty imposed by law;

(d) the test is to apply only insofar as compatible with safety and safe working conditions, and with the exigencies of any emergency of unforeseeable circumstances.

The defence of best practicable means does not apply to nuisance falling within paras. (a), (d), (e), (f) and (g) of s. 79(7) unless the nuisance arises on industrial, trade or business premises. Furthermore the defence does not apply to a nuisance falling within s. 79(1)(b) unless the smoke is emitted from a chimney. The defence is not available in relation to a nuisance falling within s. 79(1)(c) or (h).

Supplementary provisions

Several authors
The Environmental Protection Act 1990, s. 81(1), gives statutory recognition to a rule which is well engrained in the common law, that is to say, that the author of a state of affairs is liable in nuisance notwithstanding that the state of affairs would not have constituted a nuisance without the presence of another state of affairs (*Thorpe* v *Brumfitt* (1873) LR 8 Ch App 650; *Lambton* v *Mellish* [1894] 3 Ch 163). Therefore, the occupier of a house would be liable if the smoke from its chimney created a nuisance only when combined with smoke from other premises. It would be irrelevant, in other words, that the smoke from the defendant's premises was insufficiently voluminous to annoy anyone.

Nuisance originating outside local authority's area
Nuisances often accord scant regard to administrative boundaries. For example, smoke or fumes emanating from premises in one administrative area can travel considerable distances and affect residents in another area. Section 81(2) of the Act therefore provides that a local authority which finds that a statutory nuisance exists or has occurred within its area, or has affected any part of that area, but appears to be wholly or partly caused by some act or default committed or taking place outside the area, can institute proceedings under s. 80 in the same way as it could had the nuisance emanated from within its own areas. Proceedings can be brought only in a magistrates' court having jurisdiction where the act or default is alleged to have taken place.

Default proceedings
If an abatement notice (see page 17) has not been complied with the local authority may abate the nuisance and do whatever is necessary in execution of the notice (s 81(3)). Any expenses reasonably incurred in abating the nuisance may be recovered from the person by whose act or default the nuisance was caused (s. 81(4)). If the nuisance was caused by the act of default of the owner of the premises then the expenses may be recovered from any person who is for the time being the owner of the premises. The court may apportion the expenses between the persons by whose acts the

relevant nuisance is caused in such manner as the court considers fair and reasonable (s. 81(4)). Therefore if a nuisance is caused by the combined effect of smoke emanating in different volumes from two chimneys, the person from whose premises the greater quantity of smoke is emitted can be required to bear the greater part of the expenditure.

A new s. 81A is inserted into the Environmental Protection Act 1990 by the Noise and Statutory Nuisance Act 1993, s. 10(2). One of its important provisions from a practical viewpoint is that where any expenses are recoverable under s. 81(4) from a person who is the owner of the premises and the local authority serves notice on that person under s. 81A, the expenses carry interest at such reasonable rate as the local authority may determine, from the date of service of the notice until the whole amount is paid. Furthermore, such expenses become a charge on the premises, that is to say that the charge ranks as a right *in rem* on the premises, and therefore enforceable against, for example, future owners of the premises concerned. A person served with such a notice can appeal to the county court.

It may happen that a nuisance is of such a magnitude that it would be prudent to institute proceedings in the High Court. Section 80(5) therefore allows the relevant local authority to institute such proceedings notwithstanding the local authority has suffered no damage from the nuisance in question. This provision overcomes any potential difficulties over whether the local authority had the requisite standing to institute proceedings.

Proceedings by private individuals
It is increasingly common for statutes dealing with environmental matters to allow private individuals as opposed to public authorities to invoke statutory law to abate an adverse state of affairs. Under s. 82(1) of the Environmental Protection Act 1990, a person aggrieved by a statutory nuisance can institute proceedings in a magistrates' court. In the absence of authority it is suggested that 'person aggrieved' simply means someone who is affected by the nuisance and could succeed in a nuisance action at common law.

THREE
Noise

GENERAL BACKGROUND

In comparison with its attempts to deal with other obvious environmental health problems such as unsound food and waste pollution, Parliament was relatively late in explicitly recognising noise as an environmental pollutant. It was only in 1960, when the Noise Abatement Act was passed, that the legislature turned its attention to noise. Before 1960 the main statutory control over noise took the form of local authority by-laws. The contribution of the common law to noise control has been significant also. The law of nuisance has been frequently invoked by private individuals to suppress unwanted noise. As far as the modern law is concerned, therefore, noise can be controlled both by statute and the common law. The various controls are now discussed in turn.

NUISANCE

Noise nuisances which have been the subject of litigation include a motley variety such as from print works (*Rushmer* v *Polsue and Alfieri Ltd* [1906] 1 Ch 234), building operations (*Andreae* v *Selfridge and Co. Ltd* [1938] Ch 1), a sawing mill (*Gilling* v *Gray* (1910) 27 TLR 39), singing (*Motion* v *Mills* (1897) 13 TLR 427), domestic birds (*Leeman* v *Montagu* [1936] 2 All ER 1677), cattle (*London, Brighton and South Coast Railway Co.* v *Truman* (1885) 11 App Cas 45), horses (*Ball* v *Ray* (1873) LR 8 Ch App 467), a power station (*Halsey* v *Esso Petroleum Co. Ltd* [1961] 1 WLR 683), petrochemical works (*Allen* v *Gulf Oil Refining Ltd* [1981] AC 1001), an unruly family (*Smith* v *Scott* [1973] Ch 314), powerboats (*Kennaway* v *Thompson* [1981] QB 88), a children's playground (*Dunton* v *Dover District*

Council (1977) 76 LGR 87), a military tattoo (*Webster* v *Lord Advocate* 1985 SC 173) and the firing of guns (*Hollywood Silver Fox Farm Ltd* v *Emmett* [1936] 2 KB 468). It must be emphasised, however that each of the above cases was decided on its own facts on the principles discussed in chapter 2.

Certain types of noise are capable of being measured by a noise level meter (see *R* v *Fenny Stratford Justices, ex parte Watney Mann (Midlands) Ltd* [1976] 1 WLR 1101). This in turn allows courts to refer to noise level standards. Standards in current use are included in the Wilson Report (Cmnd 2056, 1963) and British Standard No. 4142, both of which are largely concerned with setting standards governing levels of noise above which the average person would experience discomfort. Therefore noise has the advantage over, say, smell nuisance in that noise can be measured scientifically.

STATUTORY CONTROL OVER NOISE

Nowadays it is the norm for individuals adversely affected by noise not to seek redress by way of the common law but rather to use the public law. They can approach the appropriate local authority environmental health department which normally has officials who specialise in noise control. The present main legislative controls over noise are contained in the Control of Pollution Act 1974, the Environmental Protection Act 1990 the Noise and Statutory Nuisance Act 1993. These controls are now discussed.

Statutory noise nuisance

Action by local authorities

The majority of noise complaints local authorities receive from the public concern so-called neighbourhood noise which is now dealt with under the Environmental Protection Act 1990. The main effect of the Act is to make noise a statutory nuisance under part III of the Act. Under s. 79(1)(g), noise emitted from premises so as to be either prejudicial to health or a nuisance can be dealt with as a statutory nuisance (see chapter 2 for a general discussion of statutory nuisances). Noise is defined as including vibration. In *A. Lambert Flat Management Ltd* v *Lomas* [1981] 1 WLR 898 it was held that the expression 'nuisance' in s. 58 (now repealed) of the Control of Pollution Act 1974 bore its ordinary meaning at common law. It is suggested that the term 'nuisance' as now employed in s. 79(1)(g) of the Environmental Protection Act 1990 would be similarly construed.

Under the new para. (ga) of the Environmental Protection Act 1990, s. 79(1), as inserted by the 1993 Act, noise that is prejudicial to health or a nuisance and is emitted from or caused by a vehicle, machinery or equipment in a street now ranks as a statutory nuisance in terms of the Environmental Protection Act 1990. As far as vehicle noise is concerned, an abatement notice must be served on the person responsible for the nuisance which in relation to such noise includes the person in whose name the vehicle is for the time being registered and any other person who is for the time being the driver of the vehicle. In relation to noise nuisance from machinery or equipment, notice must be served on the person who for the time being is the operator of the machinery or equipment (s. 79(7)).

The Noise and Statutory Nuisance Act 1993 also gives local authorities increased powers in relation to noise from intruder alarms.

Action by private individuals

It is possible that a private individual may not, for a number of reasons, wish to complain to a local authority about noise which is found discomfiting. The Environmental Protection Act 1990, s. 82 (as amended by the Noise and Statutory Nuisance Act 1993), allows a magistrates' court, on the complaint of any person that he or she is aggrieved by a noise nuisance originating from premises or the street, to make an order requiring the abatement of the nuisance in question.

It could be argued that requiring a noise to be a nuisance before a local authority can intervene sets too high a standard. It could be said with some justification that the public should be protected from noise which, though falling short of constituting a nuisance in law, annoys the sufferer. Furthermore the locality factor which is engrained in nuisance law (see page 9) could have a regressive effect in that it could result in the courts denying relief in respect of areas most in need of protection. The concept of nuisance, however, does allow the courts to balance the defendant's right to generate noise with the complainant's right to a peaceable environment. Indeed the Batho Committee were sanguine about the role of nuisance in noise abatement and recommended that it should remain the ground for local authority intervention in relation to noise complaints (see p. viii of the Report of the Noise Review Working Party, 1990).

Construction sites

The carrying out of building operations presents a particular problem as far as noise is concerned since the machinery and plant commonly employed for the excavating, lifting, cutting and demolishing which takes place there have an inherent capacity to produce loud and often disagreeable noise. Site traffic may also pose a noise problem. The capacity of building sites to create such unwanted noise is enhanced by the fact that people tend to be more adversely affected by noise to which they are unaccustomed. Building site operations are generally of such short duration that residents in the vicinity of the site do not have the time to become habituated to site noise and are therefore more predisposed to being discomfited. The Control of Pollution

Act 1974 therefore accords special attention to noise from construction sites. Section 60 confers wide and detailed powers on local authorities in relation to noise from such sites. By s. 60(1) the section applies to:

(a) the erection, construction, alteration, repair or maintenance of buildings, structures or roads;
(b) breaking up, opening or boring under any road or adjacent land in connection with the construction, inspection, maintenance or removal of works;
(c) demolition or dredging work; and
(d) (whether or not also comprised in paragraph (a), (b) or (c) above) any work of engineering construction.

Under s. 60(2) a local authority is empowered to serve a notice imposing requirements as to the way in which building works are to be carried out. The terms which the local authority stipulates in the appropriate notice must be both practical and precise (*Strathclyde Regional Council* v *Tudhope* 1983 SLT 22). An important feature of the section is that it does not lay down any requirement that a nuisance must already exist before notice is served. The local authority may by notice specify the plant or machinery which is or is not to be used and the hours during which the works may or may not be carried out (s. 60(3)). Importantly, the notice may also specify the level of noise which may be emitted from the premises. The local authority must have regard to, *inter alia*, the provisions of any code of practice (see SI 1984/1992) issued under part III of the Act as well as the best practicable means to minimise the noise (s. 60(4)(a)). The notice must be served on the person who appears to the local authority to be carrying out or going to carry out the relevant works and on other persons appearing to the local authority to be responsible for or to have control over the works. Therefore notice could lawfully be served on the building contractor as well as the person commissioning the works (if they are different persons) such as the owner or occupier of the land concerned. Under s. 60(6) the notice may specify the time within which its terms are to be complied with and may require the person on whom notice is served to execute works as opposed to simply refraining from creating noise. The person served with a notice under s. 60 may appeal against it to a magistrates' court within 21 days from the service of the notice (s. 60(7)). It is a defence to proceedings under s. 80 of the Environmental Protection Act 1990 (which deals with statutory nuisances) to prove that the alleged offence is covered by a notice served under s. 60 of the Control of Pollution Act 1974.

Section 61 allows a person who intends to carry out building works to apply to the local authority for consent. If, as will most commonly be the case, the works require approval in terms of the building regulations made under the Building Act 1984, application under s. 61 of the Control of Pollution Act 1974 must be made at the same time as application for building regulations approval. The application must contain particulars of the works and the method by which they are to be carried out and, more importantly, the steps proposed to be taken to minimise the noise resulting from the works. There is no authority on how detailed the relevant particulars must be.

Under s. 61(4) if the local authority considers that it would not serve notice under s. 60 it must give consent to the application. A local authority, when considering whether to grant consent must (s. 61(5)) address its mind to the provisions of s. 60(4) which is discussed above. If consent is in fact granted the local authority can reduce the potential noise level from the site by attaching appropriate conditions to the consent, limiting, qualifying the consent to allow for any change of circumstances and limiting the duration of the consent. The applicant can appeal to the magistrates' court against either a refusal by the local authority to grant consent or any condition or qualification attached to a consent. In any proceedings for an offence under s. 50(8) (which makes it an offence to contravene the terms of a notice served by a local authority on a builder to reduce site noise) it is a defence to prove that the alleged contravention amounts to the carrying out of works in accordance with such a consent. A further advantage from the practical viewpoint of the builder is that such consent precludes a local authority from serving notice under s. 80 of the Environmental Protection Act 1990 (which deals with general nuisances) provided the relevant state of affairs is sanctioned by a consent notice (Environmental Protection Act 1990, s. 80(9)(a)). However, consent under the Control of Pollution Act 1976, s. 61 does not (by s. 61(9)) preclude an occupier who is aggrieved by an alleged nuisance taking action under the Environmental Protection Act 1990, s. 82.

Noise in streets

Noise in streets received express legislative attention in the United Kingdom for the first time when it came within the scope of the Noise Abatement Act 1960. Section 62(1) of the Control of Pollution Act 1974 (which in effect repeals and re-enacts the appropriate provisions of the 1960 Act) proscribes the use of a loudspeaker in a street between the hours of 9.00 in the evening and 8.00 in the following morning for any purpose. The Noise and Statutory Nuisance Act 1993 allows the Secretary of State by order to amend the times specified in s. 62(1). However, any order made may not amend the relevant times so as to permit the operation of a loudspeaker in a street at any time between the hours of 9.00 in the evening and 8.00 in the following morning. The section also makes it an offence to use a loudspeaker in a street at any other time for the purpose of advertising any trade or business. Schedule 2 to the 1993 Act allows a local authority on the application of any person to consent to the operation in its area of a loudspeaker which would otherwise contravene s. 62(1).

Section 62(2) exempts the operation of loudspeakers by certain classes of persons such as the police, fire brigade and the ambulance service. The section also exempts the use of a loudspeaker (for example, a loudspeaker integrated in a car radio system) to entertain or to communicate with the occupant of a vehicle provided the loudspeaker is not operated so as to give reasonable cause for annoyance to persons in the vicinity (s. 62(2)(d)). An important exemption in practice is that made in respect of the operation of a loudspeaker between noon and 7.00 in the evening of the same day provided that the loudspeaker is fixed to a vehicle used for the purposes of sale of a perishable commodity (for example, ice cream) for human consumption and is operated so as not to give reasonable cause for annoyance to persons in the vicinity (s. 62(3)).

Noise abatement zones

Perhaps the most revolutionary aspect of part III of the Control of Pollution Act 1974 is the concept of the noise abatement zone which is intended to prevent the levels of noise emanating from buildings in an area increasing over a period of time. Under s. 63 a local authority is empowered to designate by order, all or any part of its area, a noise abatement zone. The relevant order must specify the classes of premises to which it applies. A local authority could, for example, confine the scope of the order to commercial and industrial premises. Local authorities therefore have considerable discretion as to how comprehensive the relevant order is to be. Much will depend in practice on the nature of the localities concerned as well as the number of staff to enforce the provisions of the order. The procedure for constituting a noise abatement zone is set out in sch. 1 to the Act (as amended by the Local Government Planning and Land Act 1980). Prior to initiating such a scheme the local authority need not make a prior inspection of the area concerned (*Morganite Special Carbons Ltd* v *Secretary of State for the Environment* [1980] EGD 797). However, it would obviously be administratively desirable for the authority to inspect the relevant area. Provision is made in the schedule to the Act for proposals to be adequately publicised to allow individuals who have a proprietary interest in premises which will be covered by the order to make objections. In turn, the local authority must consider objections prior to making the order.

After a noise abatement zone has been established the local authority is required to measure the level of noise emanating from the premises concerned and record them in a register known as the noise level register which must be kept by the authority (Control of Noise (Measurement and Registers) Regulations 1976 (SI 1976/37)). After recording the appropriate noise level the local authority must serve a copy on the owner and occupier of the premises concerned (s. 64(3)). Any person served with such a notice can appeal to the Secretary of State against the record. The latter has complete powers of review and can also give directions to the local authority which the local authority must comply with (s. 64(4)). Under s. 65(1) the level of noise recorded in the noise level register in respects of any premises must not be exceeded except with the written consent of the local authority concerned. The local authority's consent may be given conditionally (s. 65(2)). An applicant for consent can appeal to the Secretary of State against the local authority's decision within three months of the date of being notified of it (s. 65(4)). Again the Secretary of State can review the local authority's decision. It is an offence under s. 65(5) to emit noise from any premises in contravention either of s. 65(1) or of a condition attached to a consent. The magistrates' court in convicting a person of such an offence, if satisfied that the offence is likely to recur, may make an order requiring the execution of any works necessary to prevent it continuing or recurring. It is an offence to contravene such an order without reasonable excuse (s. 65(6)). Default powers are given to the local authority to execute works if the person who was ordered to carry them out fails to do so (s. 69(2)).

It is possible that a local authority may wish to reduce the level of noise emanating from particular premises after the noise level for the premises has been recorded in the register. The local authority may be prompted to do so, for example, because of the encroachment of a housing development near the premises emitting the noise. Section 66(1) therefore gives a local authority the power to order the reduction of the level of noise emanating from any premises situated in a noise abatement zone if the noise is of such a level that it is not acceptable having regard to the purposes for which the order was made and that a reduction in that level would afford a public benefit.

There is no authority on the application of s. 66(1). However, it is suggested that whether or not a reduction was acceptable or would be of a public benefit would be assessed objectively by the court. The noise reduction notice may specify particular times, or days, during which the noise level is to be reduced. A person served with a noise reduction notice can appeal to a magistrates' court against the notice (s. 66(7)). It is an offence to contravene a noise reduction notice without reasonable excuse (s. 66(8)).

It may happen that either a new building will be constructed in an area where a noise abatement order is in operation or the use of an existing building will be changed to bring it within the scope of a noise abatement order. In such a case the local authority may on the application of the owner or occupier of the premises, or a person who is negotiating to acquire an interest in the premises, determine the level of noise which will be acceptable from those premises (s. 57(1)). Appeal against this predetermined level can be made to the Secretary of State within three months of the date the applicant owner or occupier is notified of the decision of the local authority concerned (s. 67(3)).

Miscellaneous provisions

It is important that industrial plant is designed in such a way that it emits the minimum amount of noise. Section 68 of the Control of Pollution Act 1974 allows the Secretary of State to make regulations for reducing noise from plant or machinery and limiting the level of noise which may be caused by any plant or machinery used in connection with building works. No such regulations have been made so far. Under s. 71 the Secretary of State can make codes of practice for minimising noise (see, e.g., the Control of Noise (Code of Practice on Noise from Model Aircraft) Order 1981 (SI 1981/1830), the Control of Noise (Code of Practice on Noise from Audible Intruder Alarms) Order 1981 (SI 1981/1829)).

OTHER STATUTORY CONTROLS

Town and Country Planning Act 1990

Planning law has an important role to play in the suppression of noise. The imposition of controls at the planning application stage of a development allows local authorities to take prophylactic measures against potential sources of noise nuisance. Local planning authorities can also take into account factors relating to noise when formulating both structure and local plans (see Department of the Environment Circular 10/73 and consultation draft PPG 20 1992 paras. 5–16). As far as individual planning applications are concerned, a planning authority can impose such conditions as it considers fit (Town and Country Planning Act 1990, s. 70). The planning authority has wide powers in this context. The authority could, for example, impose conditions governing the distance between the proposed building and existing buildings so as to prevent noise complaints. It could also impose conditions governing the level of noise which could lawfully be emitted from the buildings.

By-laws

Noise, a perennial pollutant without doubt, plagued our Victorian ancestors probably just as much as it does us. Since the 19th century, local authorities have used their various by-law-making powers to deal with the problem of noise. Indeed the oft-cited case of *Kruse* v *Johnson* [1898] 2 QB 91) centred on the legality of a by-law which purported to make certain types of street music illegal. Local authorities can now make by-laws under s. 235 of the Local Government Act 1972, *inter alia*, for the prevention and suppression of nuisances. By-laws could therefore be made to deal with noise problems which do not fall within the scope of Acts of Parliament and relevant subordinate legislation.

Health and Safety at Work etc. Act 1974

Section 3 of the Health and Safety at Work etc. Act 1974 places a duty on every employer to conduct his undertaking in such a way as to ensure that so far as reasonably practicable, persons not in his employment are not exposed to risks to their health or safety. Such a duty would cover, for example, risks posed to the health of occupiers of land by noise or vibration from industrial premises. However, it should be noted that the section is not restricted to noise from premises. Noise created by workers carrying out street repairs could fall within the scope of the section.

Environmental Protection Act 1990

Buildings are sometimes constructed in such a way as to be easily permeated by both impact and airborne noise. This would obviously discomfit any occupants. Section 79(1) of the 1900 Act provides that any premises in such a state as to be prejudicial to health or a nuisance are a statutory nuisance in terms of the Act. In *Southwark London Borough Council* v *Ince* (1989) 21 HLR 504 it was held that it was quite legitimate for the court to take external factors into account when considering if premises constituted a statutory nuisance under s. 92(1)(a) of the Public Health Act 1936 which the 1990 Act repeals and re-enacts. In *Southwark London Borough Council* v *Ince* the occupiers of dwellinghouses successfully brought an action against the owners of the house on the grounds that the noise and vibration from passing trains and traffic could permeate the walls of the premises so as to be prejudicial to their health.

Licensing Act 1964

It is common nowadays for proprietors of licensed premises to provide their patrons with entertainment in the form of music from live bands as well as from jukeboxes etc. Licensed premises therefore present an obvious potential problem as far as noise nuisance is concerned. Section 4 of the Licensing Act 1964 allows licensing justices to attach such conditions governing the tenure of the licence and any other matters as they think proper in the interests of the public. Clearly the power conferred by this section could be used to regulate the level of noise emanating from licensed premises.

AIRCRAFT NOISE

Aeroplanes are a common source of noise pollution. The controls over aircraft noise can roughly be divided into those which are directed to the control of noise from the flight of navigation of aircraft, and those which specifically relate to the control of noise from aerodromes. Each control is now discussed in turn.

Flight noise

One could reasonably anticipate that the law of nuisance would be of relevance here. However, under s. 70(1) of the Civil Aviation Act 1982 no action lies, *inter alia*, in respect of nuisance by reason only of the flight of an aircraft over any property so long as the provisions of any air navigation order, and any orders made under s. 62 (which relates to orders made during times of war and emergency) have been complied with and also that there is no breach of s. 81 (which proscribes dangerous flying).

The noise from low-flying aircraft presents an obvious problem. Regulation 5(1) of the Rules of the Air Regulations 1991 (SI 1991/2437) which in the main govern flight safety) prohibits low flying (an expression which is defined by the regulations) by aircraft. Helicopters are similarly prohibited. However, the CAA can give permission for helicopters to engage in low flying in specific cases.

Noise certification

The most important form of control over noise from aircraft is the Air Navigation (Noise Certification) Order 1990 (SI 1990/1514). Under art. 5(1), no aircraft to which the order applies may take off or land in the UK unless a noise certificate has been granted in relation to the aircraft. Article 5(2) makes certain exceptions to this requirement. Article 6 requires the CAA to issue a noise certificate if it is satisfied that the aircraft complies with the appropriate standards specified in the article. Furthermore, the CAA is empowered under art. 11 to direct the appropriate operator or commander not to make a particular flight if the provisions of art. 5 would be infringed.

Aerodrome noise

Section 77(1) of the Civil Aviation Act 1982 allows provision to be made by way of an Air Navigation Order for regulating the conditions under which noise and vibration may be caused by aircraft on aerodromes. Under s. 77(2) no action may lie in respect of nuisance by reason only of the noise and vibration caused by aircraft on an aerodrome as long as the provisions of the relevant order are complied with. The appropriate current order is the Air Navigation Order 1989 (SI 1989/2004). Under s. 78(1) of the Act the Secretary of State may designate aerodromes in relation to which certain requirements relating to noise and vibration apply. Only three airports in England have been so designated, namely, Heathrow, Gatwick and Stansted.

Under s. 78(3) the Secretary of State can prohibit aircraft taking off or landing at a designated aerodrome during certain periods of the day. In *R v Secretary of State for Transport, ex parte Richmond-upon-Thames London Borough Council* [1994] 1 WLR 74 it was held that it was not lawful for the Secretary of State to limit the number of night flights by means of a quota system based on the noise generated by the aircraft using the designated aerodrome, as opposed to the number of aircraft using the aerodrome.

Under s. 78(6) the Secretary of State may give directions to the person managing a designated aerodrome for the purpose of avoiding, limiting or mitigating the effect of noise and vibration connected with the taking-off or landing of aeroplanes at the aerodrome.

Under s. 79 of the Civil Aviation Act 1982 the Secretary of State may, by statutory instrument, make a scheme requiring a person managing a designated aerodrome to make a grant towards the cost of insulating buildings or parts of buildings against noise from aerodromes. This power has been exercised in relation to, for example, Heathrow and Gatwick (see, e.g., SI 1980/153 and 154).

Military aircraft

The problem of noise from low-flying military aircraft is exacerbated by the fact that their design is such that they have a greater capacity to create noise than civil aircraft. Furthermore, the legal controls which are discussed above are largely inapplicable to military aircraft. Indeed the Crown is generally immune from civil action in relation to noise from such aircraft (see the Crown Proceedings Act 1947, s. 11).

The Ministry of Defence keep noise from military aircraft under constant review. This is done by the Ministry's Noise Panel which has no statutory status. The Ministry provides noise compensation schemes for those living in the vicinity of military airfields. Such *ex gratia* compensation schemes are comparable to those in operation for aerodromes designated by the Secretary of State under s. 78 of the Civil Aviation Act 1982 (see above). Furthermore, the Ministry also financially compensates owners of dwellings which have depreciated in value as a result of noise and other physical factors resulting from the creation of new airfields or the extension of existing airfields.

ROAD TRAFFIC NOISE

Road traffic presents an obvious problem as far as environmental noise is concerned. The problem has become worse since the Second World War since more people are using cars. Furthermore, lorries and other commercial vehicles are now a more popular means of transport than the railway system. Section 41(1) of the Road Traffic Act 1988 allows the Secretary of State to make regulations governing inter alia, the use of motor vehicles on roads and the conditions under which they can be used. Power is also given to make regulations relating to the construction and equipment in vehicles under sub-section (2)(c) such regulations can make provision inter alia for noise. Section 42 makes it an offence for a person to fail to comply with such regulations. The main regulations presently governing the construction and use etc. of vehicles are the Road Vehicles (Construction and Use) Regulations 1986 (SI 1986/1078).

Regulation 54 of the Road Vehicles (Construction and Use) Regulations 1986 requires every vehicle propelled by an internal combustion engine to be fitted with an exhaust system including a silencer, which must be maintained in good and efficient working order. Regulations 56 to 58 make provision in respect of noise limits which vehicles must not exceed. Under reg. 97 no motor vehicle may be used in such a manner as to cause any excessive noise which could have been avoided by the exercise of reasonable care on the part of its driver. Contravention of these regulations is an offence under the Road Traffic Act 1988, s. 41(1).

The Motor Vehicles (Types Approval) (Great Britain) Regulations 1984 (SI 1984/981) as amended) make provision relating to noise and silencers in respect of vehicles.

OTHER SOURCES OF NOISE

Boats in national parks

The Countryside Act 1968, s. 13(2), allows a local authority to make by-laws for the prevention of nuisance from excessive noise in national parks. Such by-laws may require the use of effectual silencers on boats or vessels propelled by internal combustion engines, and prescribe rules with a view to imposing limits on the noise or vibration which may be caused by any boat or vessel.

Household appliances

Household appliances (for example, washing machines, spin driers) sometimes have the capacity to generate considerable noise. Regulation 3 of the

Household Appliances (Noise Emission) Regulations 1990 (SI 1990/2179) prohibits the manufacturer or importer of an appliance manufactured or imported by him or her on or after 28 February 1990 from marketing any such appliance unless the provisions of reg. 4 are complied with. Regulation 4 provides that where a manufacturer or importer of an appliance takes any steps to inform any person to whom the appliance is to be or may be marketed of the level of airborne noise emitted by the appliance, the level must be determined in accordance with art. 6(1) of the EC Directive set out in the schedule to the Regulations.

INSULATION OF BUILDINGS

Land Compensation Act 1973

The Land Compensation Act 1973, s. 20, allows the Secretary of State to make regulations imposing a duty or conferring a power on responsible authorities (e.g., local authorities and central government departments) to insulate buildings or to make grants in respect of the cost of such insulation against noise caused or expected to be caused by the construction or use of public works (which is defined by s. 1(3) as any highway, aerodrome or works on land provided or used in the exercise of statutory powers). Under reg. 3 of the Noise Insulation Regulations 1975 (SI 1975/1763), where the use of a highway first open to the public after 16 October 1972 (or in respect of which an additional carriageway has been or is to be constructed since that date) causes or is expected to cause noise at a level not less than the level specified in the regulations, then the appropriate highway authority is required to carry out, or make the appropriate grant in respect of carrying out, insulation work. Subject to certain exceptions grants may only be made in respect of dwellings and other buildings used for residential purposes.

Building regulations

It is important that houses are so constructed that their external walls are not easily permeated by external noise. The current regulations governing the construction of new buildings are the Building Regulations 1991 (SI 1991/2768). Under sch. 1 to part E of the regulations, walls and floors of houses must be able to resist both airborne and impact noise. The importance of the schedule is severely circumscribed by the fact that it only relates to flats or semi-detached houses. It does not apply to detached houses.

FOUR
Air pollution

One of the main consequences and indeed hallmarks of the Industrial Revolution was the pollution of the atmosphere by thick palls of smoke which belched out of factory chimneys. However, the legislation which local authorities could invoke to suppress such pollution was heavily nuisance-based. The local authority had to prove that a given source of smoke pollution constituted a nuisance in law. This necessitated proving a causal link between the smoke source in question and either physical injury to property or personal discomfort to individuals. Nuisance-based law palpably failed to ameliorate the problem. Such theoretical difficulty, coupled with a distinct lassitude on the part of local authorities to enforce smoke control legislation, ensured that the air of our cities and towns remained polluted during the entire Victorian period. Indeed it was not until the infamous London smog disaster terrorised that city in the winter of 1952, that the inadequacy of nuisance-based law as the mainstay of air pollution control, was cruelly exposed. The Beaver Committee was appointed in 1953 'to examine the nature, causes and effects of air pollution and the efficacy of present preventive measures; and to consider what further preventative measures are practicable'. The committee reported in 1954 (Report of the Committee on Air Pollution, Cmd 9322). It came to the general conclusion that the law, as it then stood, was defective. The recommendations which the committee made were almost entirely embodied in the Clean Air Act 1956 which was amended by the Clean Air Act 1968. These Acts have now been replaced by the Clean Air Act 1993, the main provisions of which are shortly discussed.

While smoke presented a major urban problem in Victorian Britain, it was not the sole pollutant. The chemical industry, with the production of alkali as its mainstay, was also an infamous source of noxious vapours and fumes. However patent the problem, what was equally clear, was the very substantial contribution made by the alkali industry to the national economy. Indeed, Parliament had to treat the industry with great caution. However, the Alkali Act was passed in 1863. This Act was consolidated in the Alkali etc. Works Regulation Act 1906 which has been replaced by the Environmental Protection Act 1990 which is discussed later in the chapter.

CLEAN AIR ACT 1993

Industrial provisions

Smoke etc.

Smoke was the most important pollutant which afflicted the United Kingdom in the postwar years. Indeed it was smog, a combination of smoke and fog, which caused the London smog disaster. Parliament recognised therefore that dark smoke had to be given special attention. Section 1(1) of the Clean Air Act 1993 provides that it is an offence to emit dark smoke from the chimney of any building. The occupier is liable for any such omission. Liability under the section is strict it is suggested. Section 1(2) prohibits the emission of dark smoke from a chimney (not being a chimney of a building) serving the furnace of any fixed boiler or industrial plant. The person having possession of the boiler or plant is liable in the event of the emission of dark smoke. Section 3(1) defines the expression 'dark smoke' as being as dark as or darker than shade 2 on the Ringlemann Chart. However environmentally beneficial it would be for all chimneys not to emit dark smoke, it would be neither practicable nor possible for furnaces to operate without emitting dark smoke. Section 1(3) therefore allows the Secretary of State to make regulations to permit the emission of prescribed forms of dark smoke for limited periods (see the Dark Smoke (Permitted Periods) Regulations 1958 (SI 1958/498)). In common with many statutes which make provision for offences of strict liability, the Act contains a statutory defence in relation to the emission of dark smoke from chimneys. It is a defence under s. 1(4) to prove:

(a) that the alleged emission was solely due to the lighting up of a furnace which was cold and that all practicable steps had been taken to prevent or minimise the emission of dark smoke;

(b) that the alleged emission was solely due to some failure of a furnace, or of apparatus used in connection with a furnace, and that —

(i) the failure could not reasonably have been foreseen, or, if foreseen, could not reasonably have been provided against; and

(ii) the alleged emission could not reasonably have been prevented by action taken after the failure occurred; or

(c) that the alleged emission was solely due to the use of unsuitable fuel and that —

(i) suitable fuel was unobtainable and the least unsuitable fuel which was available was used; and

(ii) all practicable steps had been taken to prevent or minimise the emission of dark smoke as the result of the use of that fuel;

or that the alleged emission was due to the combination of two or more of the causes specified in paragraphs (a) to (c) and that the other conditions specified in those paragraphs are satisfied in relation to those causes respectively.

The emission of dark smoke is not, of course, confined to chimneys. Section 2 of the 1993 Act therefore makes it an offence for an occupier of any industrial or trade premises to cause or permit the emission of dark smoke from such premises. A wide meaning was given to the expression 'industrial or trade premises' in *Sheffield City Council* v *ADH Demolition Ltd* (1983) 82 LGR 177 in which it was held that the expression covered a site where demolition work was being carried out (see page 61 for a discussion of 'causing' or 'permitting'). Liability under the section is strict it is suggested.

Section 2(3) provides that in proceedings for an offence under the section there shall be taken to have been an emission of dark smoke from industrial or trade premises in any case where material is burned on those premises and in circumstances in which the burning would be likely to give rise to the emission of dark smoke, unless the occupier or any person who caused or permitted the burning shows that no dark smoke was emitted.

Section 2(4) provides that it is a defence for the accused to prove that the alleged emission was inadvertent and that all practicable steps had been taken to prevent or minimise the emission of dark smoke. Section 64(1) defines the expression 'practicable' as reasonably practicable having regard, amongst other things, to local conditions and circumstances, to the financial implications and to the current state of technical knowledge.

Smoke from furnaces

It is important that there is statutory control over the design and operation of furnaces. Section 4(1) of the Clean Air Act 1993 provides that no furnace may be installed in a building or in any fixed boiler or industrial plant unless notice of the proposal to install it has been given to the local authority. Smoke is the result of incomplete combustion. A boiler functioning effectively should therefore create no smoke. This principle is recognised by the Act. Under s. 4(2) no furnace may be installed in a building or in any fixed boiler or industrial plant unless the furnace is so far as is reasonably practicable capable of being continuously operated without emitting smoke when burning fuel of a type for which the furnace was designed. It is made an offence to install a furnace in contravention of this provision. However any furnace installed in accordance with plans and specifications submitted to and approved for the purposes of s. 4 is, by virtue of s. 4(3) to be treated as complying with the provisions of s. 4(2).

Section 4 does not apply to the installation of domestic furnaces (s. 4(5)). However, the section does apply in relation to:

(a) the attachment to a building of a boiler or industrial plant which already contains a furnace; or

(b) the fixing to or installation on any land of any such boiler or plant.

Grit and dust

Another grave environmental problem posed by industrial boilers in urban post war Britain, was the emission of grit and dust. Section 5 of the Clean Air Act 1993 allows the Secretary of State to make regulations prescribing limits for the emission of grit and dust from the chimneys of furnaces, other than domestic furnaces. If emissions from a furnace chimney exceed those limits then the occupier of the building in which the furnace is situated is guilty of an offence. However, s. 5(3) provides that the defence of best practicable means applies in such circumstances. The current regulations are the Clean Air (Emission of Grit and Dust from Furnaces) Regulations 1971 (SI 1971/162). If no limit obtains in relation to a building containing a furnace then the occupier is placed under a duty to minimise the emission of grit and dust.

Grit arrestment plant can substantially reduce the amount of grit and dust being emitted from a furnace. By s. 6(1) of the Act, a furnace (other than a domestic furnace) must not be used in a building:

(a) to burn pulverised fuel; or

(b) to burn at a rate of 45.4 kg or more an hour, any other solid matter; or

(c) to burn, at a rate equivalent to 366.4 kW or more, any liquid or gaseous matter,

unless the furnace is provided with plant for arresting grit and dust which has been approved by the local authority or which has been installed in accordance with plans and specifications submitted to and approved by the local authority, and that plant is properly maintained and used. It is an offence to contravene the section.

The intention of the Act is to ensure that boilers most capable of generating grit and dust are provided with grit arrestment plant, but some types of furnace are quite capable of being operated without creating grit and dust to any significant extent, and s. 7 of the Act empowers the Secretary of

State to exempt furnaces from the requirements of s. 6. The current regulations are the Clean Air (Arrestment Plant) (Exemption) Regulations 1969 (SI 1969/1262). Section 7(2) of the Act also gives a local authority on the application of the occupier of a building, power to exempt a furnace from the requirement to have grit arrestment plant if it is satisfied that the furnace will not be prejudicial to health or a nuisance. The occupier may appeal to the Secretary of State against the refusal of a local authority to grant exemption under the section (s. 7(4)).

As far as domestic furnaces are concerned, s. 8 of the Act provides that such a furnace may not be used in a building:

(a) to burn pulverised fuel; or
(b) to burn, at a rate of 1.02 tonnes an hour or more, solid fuel in any other form or solid waste,

unless the furnace is provided with plant for arresting grit and dust which has been approved by the local authority or which has been installed in accordance with plans and specifications submitted to and approved by the local authority, and that plant is properly maintained and used. It is an offence to use a domestic furnace in a building in contravention of the provisions of the section.

In order that enforcing authorities can accurately ascertain the quantity of grit and dust being emitted from industrial plant, s. 10 of the Act provides that if a furnace in a building is used:

(a) to burn pulverised fuel;
(b) to burn, at a rate of 45.4 kg or more an hour, any other solid matter; or
(c) to burn, at rate equivalent to 366.4 kW or more, any liquid or gaseous matter,

the local authority may serve a notice on the occupier of the building directing that the provisions of s. 10(2) will apply to the furnace. This means that the occupier must comply with the requirements of the Clean Air (Measurement of Grit and Dust from Furnaces) Regulations 1971 (SI 1971/161) with regard to installing measuring and recording apparatus and making the results available to the local authority. It is an offence to fail to comply with those requirements. The occupier can, under s. 11 require the local authority to make the measurements if the furnace is used:

(a) to burn, at a rate less than 1.02 tonnes an hour, solid matter other than pulverised fuel; or
(b) to burn, at a rate of less than 8.21 MW any liquid or gaseous matter.

Section 12 gives the local authority power to require the occupier of any building to give the authority information about the furnaces in the building.

Section 13 provides that ss. 5 to 12 are to apply in relation to the furnace of any fixed boiler or industrial plant to as they apply in relation to a furnace in a building.

Chimneys
The height of a furnace chimney has an important influence on the dispersal of emissions. Section 14 of the Clean Air Act 1993 makes it an offence for the occupier of a building in which is situated a chimney served by a furnace to knowingly cause or permit the furnace to be used in the building:

(a) to burn pulverised fuel,
(b) to burn at a rate of 45.4 kilograms or more an hour, any other solid matter, or
(c) to burn, at a rate equivalent to 366.4 kilowats or more, any liquid or gaseous matter,

unless the height of the chimney serving the furnace has been approved by the local authority, and any condition subject to which the approval was granted, has been complied with. Fixed boilers and industrial plant are within the scope of the section (s. 14(4)).

By s. 15(2) a local authority may not approve the height of a chimney unless it is satisfied that it will be sufficient to prevent, so far as is reasonably practicable, the smoke, grit, dust, gases or fumes emitted from the chimney becoming prejudicial to health or a nuisance, having regard to:

(a) the purpose of the chimney,
(b) the position and descriptions of buildings near it,
(c) the levels of neighbouring ground, and
(d) any other matters requiring consideration in the circumstances.

Approval may be granted conditionally or unconditionally in relation to the rate or quality, or the rate and quality, of emissions from the chimney (s. 15(3)). If the local authority decides not to approve the chimney height, or decides to attach conditions to an approval, it must notify the applicant in writing of the reasons for its decision. In the case of a decision not to approve the height of a chimney, the local authority must specify the lowest height, if any, which it is prepared to approve, conditionally or unconditionally. An appeal lies to the appropriate minister against the decision of the local authority and the minister has complete powers of review in the matter.

The Clean Air (Height of Chimneys) (Exemption) Regulations 1969 (SI 1969/411) exempts chimneys serving certain types of boiler from the need to obtain approval.

The Clean Air Act 1993, s. 16, provides for local authority control of chimneys other than furnace chimneys. The section applies where plans are deposited for inspection under building regulations (see chapter 10) for the erection or extension of a building outside Greater London, or in an outer London borough, other than a building used or to be wholly used for one or more of the following purposes:

(a) as a residence or residences,
(b) as a shop or shops, or
(c) as an office or offices.

If the plans show a chimney carrying smoke, grit, dust or gases for the building then the local authority must reject the plans unless it is satisfied that the height of the chimney will be sufficient to prevent so far as is reasonably practicable, the smoke, grit, dust or gases from becoming prejudicial to health or a nuisance having regard to:

(a) the purpose of the chimney,
(b) the position and descriptions of buildings near it,
(c) the levels of the neighbouring ground, and
(d) any other matters requiring consideration in the circumstances.

If plans are rejected any person interested in the building may appeal to the Secretary of State.

Other legislation on chimneys
The Building Act 1984, s. 73, applies when a new building will, when erected, be higher than the chimney of an adjoining building. Where the chimney of the lower building is in the party-wall between it and the taller building or is 6 feet (about 1.8m) or less from the taller building, the local authority may by notice require the person who erects the taller building to raise the height of the chimney of the adjoining building, if it is reasonably practicable to do so, to make the chimney the same height as the taller building or its chimneys, whichever is the higher.

Part J of sch. 1 to the Building Regulations 1991 (SI 1991/2768) requires solid-fuel, oil and gas-burning appliances to be capable of normal operation without the products of combustion becoming a hazard to health.

Domestic provisions

Smoke control areas
Although industry was a major source of air pollution in postwar Britain, a significant quantity of smoke came from domestic premises. In its review of

atmospheric pollution the Beaver committee was of the opinion that half of all the smoke in the United Kingdom came from domestic chimneys, and therefore recommended the setting up of smoke control areas (Cmd 9322, 1954, p. 683), a proposal which Parliament adopted in the Clean Air Act 1956. It was really only after smoke control areas began to be established throughout the country that a substantial improvement in the quality of the air took place.

Section 18 of the Clean Air Act 1993 empowers a local authority to declare, by order, the whole or part of its area to be a smoke control area. The procedure for making the order is contained in sch. 1 to the Act. A local authority has wide discretionary power as to the nature and effect of a smoke control order in that it can make different provision for different parts of the area and also limit the operation of the order to specified classes of building in the area (s. 18(2)). It may also exempt specified buildings or classes of building or specified fireplaces or classes of fireplace in the smoke control area from the operation of the order, upon such conditions as may be specified in the order.

Since the Victorian era central government has enjoyed default powers over local authorities with regard to the carrying out of their public health functions. Section 19 of the Clean Air Act 1993 gives the Secretary of State, after consultation with a local authority, power to direct it to prepare and submit proposals for making and bringing into effect one or more smoke control orders within such period as the authority thinks fit. The Secretary of State has power to make an order declaring the authority to be in default if it fails to submit proposals timeously or if the proposals are rejected in whole or in part.

It is an offence under s. 20(1) for smoke to be emitted from the chimney of any building situated in a smoke control area. The occupier of the building is guilty of the offence. Furnaces of fixed boilers and industrial plant are within the scope of the section (s. 20(2)). Liability under the section is strict it is suggested. However, it is a defence to prove that the alleged emission was not caused by the use of any fuel other than an authorised fuel (s. 20(4)). Authorised fuels have low bituminous content and can therefore burn without creating smoke in any significant quantity. They are designated authorised fuels by statutory instrument (see, e.g., the Smoke Control Areas (Authorised Fuels) Regulations 1991 (SI 1991/1282) as amended by SI 1992/72).

The Secretary of State is given power by s. 21 to suspend or relax the operation of s. 20 if it appears necessary or expedient to do so in relation to the whole or any part of a smoke control area.

In order to secure that in practice the provisions of s. 20 are complied with, s. 23 makes it an offence to acquire or sell by retail any solid fuel for use in a building in a smoke control area.

Air pollution

The practical result of the making of a smoke control order is that, in order to avoid incurring legal liablity, many occupiers of premises need to adapt fireplaces in their premises to burn authorised smokeless fuels. But there are fireplaces in which non-smokeless fuel can be burnt without emitting smoke in appreciable quantities. The Secretary of State is therefore empowered under s. 21 to exempt such fireplaces from the need to comply with smoke control orders. A fairly large number of fireplaces have been designated 'exempted fireplaces' by statutory instrument (see, e.g., the Smoke Control Areas (Exempted Fireplaces) Order 1991 (SI 1991/2892)). The list of exempted fireplaces grows over time as new types come on to the market.

Normally the owner or occupier of premises will adapt fireplaces in the premises of his or her own volition before a smoke control order becomes effective. Sometimes, however, it may be necessary for a local authority to compel the carrying out of remedial works. Section 24 therefore provides that a local authority may, by notice in writing served on the occupier or owner of a private dwelling, which is, or will be, within a smoke control area, require the carrying out of adaptations in or in connection with the dwelling so as to avoid contravening s. 20. In order either to adapt an existing fireplace to burn authorised fuel, or, alternatively, to employ another mode of heating such as gas, oil, electricity or solar power heating, the relevant owner or occupier normally requires to incur expenditure. Adaptation in relation to existing fireplaces is normally required since for example, extra air is needed for fireplaces which burn smokeless fuel. It is also normally necessary to replace existing metal grates with grates which have thicker fire-bars which can tolerate the more intense heat generated by the burning of smokeless fuels. Section 25 of the Act, in essence, places a duty on a local authority to make a grant of a minimum of 70 per cent to the owner or occupier or any person interested in any 'old private dwelling' (that is to say a private dwelling which was erected or came into existence as such after 15 August 1964), if such a person incurs expenditure in carrying out adaptations in order to comply with s. 20 of the Act. The local authority can, if it thinks fit, pay a 100 per cent grant. The expression 'adaptation' is given a precise meaning by s. 27(1):

 (a) adapting or converting any fireplace;
 (b) replacing any fireplace by another fireplace or by some other means of heating or cooking;
 (c) altering any chimney which serves any fireplace;
 (d) providing gas ignition, electric ignition or any other special means of ignition; or
 (e) carrying out any operation incidental to any of the operations mentioned in paragraphs (a) to (d);

being works which are reasonably necessary in order to make what is in all the circumstances suitable provision for heating and cooking without contraventions of section 20.

The provision of any igniting apparatus or appliance operating by means of gas, electricity or other special means is to be treated, under s. 27(2), as the execution of works for the purpose of s. 25.

Any works of adaptation which are superfluous may not be taken into account for the purposes of grant (s. 27(3)). However, such works do not render that part of the work which is necessary, in order to avoid contravention, ineligible for grant.

It has already been explained that grants in respect of premises situated in smoke control areas are only available to owners and occupiers of private dwellings. However, the need to meet the requirements imposed by a smoke control order may prove burdensome to other categories of occupiers. Section 26 therefore gives local authorities the power to reimburse, to certain other owners or occupiers who have carried out adaptations, part of or the complete cost of the necessary works. The section applies mainly to churches, church halls, or other premises which are used in connection with the advancement of religion, education or social welfare, provided such activities are not conducted for profit.

Further controls over air pollution

Part IV of the Clean Air Act 1993 makes further provision concerning pollution of the atmosphere. Section 30 empowers the Secretary of State to make regulations governing the composition and contents of any kind of motor fuel for the purpose of limiting or reducing air pollution (see the Motor Fuel (Sulphur Content of Gas Oil) Regulations 1976 (SI 1976/1989) amended by SI 1990/1097 and the Motor Fuel (Lead Content of Petrol) Regulations 1981 (SI 1981/1523) amended by SI 1985/1728. Section 31 confers similar power to make regulations imposing limits on the sulphur content of oil fuel which is used in furnaces or engines (see the Oil Fuel (Sulphur Content of Gas Oil) Regulations 1990 (SI 1990/1096)).

Under s. 33 a person who burns insulation with a view to recovering metal from the cable, is guilty of an offence. Liability under the section is strict. It should be noted that there is no requirement that the relevant burning should cause a nuisance. Rather, the very act of burning the cable in question, grounds liability under the section.

Information about air pollution

One intention of the Clean Air Act 1993 is to allow local authorities to make a substantial contribution to air pollution control other than by way of

Air pollution

traditional law enforcement. Section 34 empowers a local authority to undertake or contribute towards the cost of investigation and research in air pollution and arrange for the publication of information on that problem.

Section 35 allows a local authority to obtain information about the emission of pollutants and other substances into the air by issuing notices under s. 36 (see below), by measuring and recording the emissions, and by entering into arrangements with occupiers of premises.

In order to facilitate effective enforcement of the provisions of the Act, s. 36 gives a local authority power to require the occupier of any premises in its area to furnish it, whether by way of periodic returns or by other means, estimates, or other information which may be specified in the notice, concerning the emission of pollutants and other substances into the air from the premises. If the notice relates to a process subject to part I of the Environmental Protection Act 1990, the person on whom the notice is served is not obliged to supply any information which, as certified by an inspector appointed under that Part, is not of a kind which is being supplied to the inspector for the purposes of that Part. The section applies to Crown premises (s. 36(6)). It is an offence for a person to contravene the provisions of the section.

A person served with a notice under s. 36, or any other person having an interest in the premises to which the notice relates, may appeal to the Secretary of State under s. 37:

(a) on the ground that the giving to the authority or the disclosure to the public of all or part of the information required by the notice would —

(i) prejudice to an unreasonable degree some private interest by disclosing information about a trade secret; or
(ii) be contrary to the public interest; or

(b) on the ground that the information required by the notice is not immediately available and cannot readily be collected or obtained by the recipient of the notice without incurring undue expenditure for the purpose.

Section 38 places a duty on the Secretary of State to make regulations prescribing the manner in which, and the methods by which local authorities are to perform their functions under s. 34(1)(a) and (b) (which relate to research and publication on the subject of pollution) and ss. 35 and 36 (obtaining information about the emission of pollutants etc. and obtaining information about air pollution). The Control of Pollution (Research and Publicity) Regulations 1977 (SI 1977/19) have effect as if made under s. 38.

Relationship with the Environmental Protection Act 1990

In order to avoid overlap with the relevant provisions of the Environmental Protection Act 1990, the Clean Air Act 1993, s. 41, provides that parts I to III of the latter Act (dark smoke, smoke, grit, dust and fumes; and smoke control areas) do not apply to any process which is designated a prescribed process under the Environmental Protection Act 1990 (see page 46).

Special cases

Colliery spoilbanks

One of the most visible and enduring signs of Britain's industrial past is the presence of mounds of colliery waste. Unfortunately, waste can ignite spontaneously and generate fumes which can cause a nuisance. Section 42 of the Clean Air Act 1993 places a duty on the owner of a mine or quarry, from which coal or shale has been or is being or is to be got, to employ all practicable means for preventing combustion of refuse deposited from the mine or quarry and for preventing or minimising the emission of smoke and fumes from the refuse. It is an offence for such a person to fail to do so. Section 42(4) provides that neither the provisions of part III of the Environmental Protection Act 1990 (which deals with statutory nuisances) nor any provision of parts I to III of the 1993 Act, apply in relation to smoke, grit or dust from the combustion of refuse deposited from any such mine or quarry.

Railway engines and vessels

Section 43 of the Clean Air Act 1993 Act makes s. 1 of the Act (which relates to the prohibition of emission of dark smoke from chimneys) applicable to railway locomotive engines, with the exception that the obligations to comply with the Act are placed on the owner of the engine. The owner of any railway locomotive engine is also placed under a duty to minimise the emission of smoke from the chimney on the engine. Failure to do so is an offence.

Section 44 makes the provisions of s. 1 applicable to vessels in waters to which the section applies. The duty to comply with the provisions of s. 44 rests on the owner, master or other person in charge of the vessel. References to a furnace in a building in s. 1 are to be interpreted as references to an engine of the vessel in question. The waters the Act applies to are waters not navigable by sea-going ships and all waters navigable by sea-going ships which are within the seaward limits of the territorial waters of the United Kingdom, and are contained in any port, harbour, river, estuary, haven, dock, canal or other place, so long as a person or body of persons is empowered by any Act to make charges in respect of vessels entering or using the relevant facilities.

Exemptions for purposes of research etc.

Section 45 empowers a local authority to exempt from various provisions of the Act premises the use of which is devoted to investigation or research into pollution of the air. Any person who has applied to the local authority for an exemption under the section can appeal to the Secretary of State against the decision of the authority not to exempt the appropriate premises.

Crown premises

Under general principles of constitutional law, the provisions of the Act do not apply to Crown premises which can be a source of air pollution. A local authority is given power under s. 46 to report to the responsible minister any circumstances which would normally ground liability under the Act if the relevant premises were not Crown premises. On receiving such a complaint the minister is placed under a statutory duty to carry out an investigation into the complaint and to take all practicable means to abate the relevant state of affairs if the complaint is found by the minister to be justified.

Miscellaneous provisions

Fumes and gases

Power is given to the Secretary of State by s. 47 to make regulations making the provisions of ss. 5, 6 and 7 of the Act applicable to fumes as the sections apply to grit and dust.

Offences

Section 51(1) provides that if, in the opinion of an authorised officer of a local authority, an offence is being or has been committed under ss. 1, 2 or 20 (prohibition of certain emissions of smoke) notification in writing must be given to the appropriate person within four days of the commission of the offence in question. The appropriate person is the occupier of the premises, the person having possession of the boiler or plant, the owner of the railway locomotive engine or the owner or master or other officer or person in charge of the vessel concerned. In proceedings for an offence under ss. 1, 2 or 20 it is a defence to prove that the provisions of s. 51(1) have not been complied with.

Section 52 provides that where an offence under the Act has been committed by a body corporate and the offence is proved to have been committed with the consent or connivance of, or to be attributable to any neglect on the part of any director, manager, secretary or other similar officer of the body corporate or any person who was purporting to act in any such capacity, that person as well as the body corporate commits an offence.

Section 53 provides that where the commission of an offence under the Act is due to the act or default of some other person that person commits an offence. Such person may be charged with and convicted of an offence whether or not proceedings are taken against any other person.

Powers of entry to premises etc.

Section 56 empowers any person authorised by the local authority to enter any land or vessel, *inter alia*, to determine whether any provision of the Act or delegated legislation made under the Act has been complied with and also to carry out inspections, measurements and tests. Such powers do not, however, extend to private dwellings except in relation to work under s. 24(1) (adaptations to dwellings in smoke control areas). The section goes on to make provision for entry to premises where admission has been refused.

A local authority is also given power by s.58 to serve notice on any person requiring such person to furnish the authority with any information the authority reasonably considers it needs in connection with parts IV or V of the Act.

Default powers

Section 60 contains a general default provision which allows the Secretary of State, if satisfied that any local authority has failed to carry out any function which it ought to have performed, to make an order declaring the authority to be in default and directing the authority to perform such functions as are specified in the order. If the defaulting authority fails to comply with any direction contained in an order the Secretary of State is empowered to make an order taking over such of the functions of the authority as the Secretary of State thinks fit.

ENVIRONMENTAL PROTECTION ACT 1990

Integrated pollution control and local authority air pollution control

Part I of the Environmental Protection Act 1990 introduces an entirely new legal regime as far as pollution of the environment in the United Kingdom is concerned. The expressions 'environment' and 'pollution of the environment' are, for the purposes of part I of the act, defined in s. 1. The 'environment' is defined as 'all, or any, of the following media, namely, the air, water and land; and the medium of air includes the air within buildings and the air within other natural or man-made structures above or below ground. 'Pollution of the environment' is 'pollution of the environment due to the release (into any environmental medium) from any process of substances which are capable of causing harm to man or any other living organisms supported by the envirionment'.

Prescribed processes

The main purport of part I is to require certain industrial processes which could have a detrimental effect on the environment to be authorised by the relevant enforcing authority. Section 2 gives the Secretary of State power to prescribe by regulations any description of process as a process for which authorisation is required. A wide meaning is given to the expression 'process' which is defined by s. 1(5) as 'any activities carried on in Great Britain, whether on premises or by means of mobile plant, which are capable of causing pollution of the environment'. Regulations under s. 2 may frame the description of a process by reference to any characteristics of the process or the area or other circumstances in which the process is carried on or the description of persons carrying it on. It is made an offence to carry on a prescribed process unless authorisation is obtained beforehand.

Section 2(6) allows regulations made by the Secretary of State to prescribe separately for each environmental medium the substances, the release of which into that medium, are to be subject to control. Furthermore, the regulations may provide that a substance is only prescribed for any environmental medium, so far as it is released into that medium in such amounts, over such periods, in such concentrations or in such other circumstances, as may be specified in the regulations. In relation to a substance of a description which is prescribed for release into the air, the regulations may designate the substance as one for central control or local control.

The Environmental Protection (Prescribed Processes and Substances) Regulations 1991 (SI 1991/472) designate a variety of processes which require to be authorised for the purposes of the Environmental Protection Act 1990. Schedule 1 to the regulations divides the various processes into two categories, namely 'part A' and 'part B' processes. Certain activities are exempted from being included in sch. 1, such as domestic activities connected with a dwellinghouse and the running of certain types of engines.

Part A processes are processes designated for central control and, therefore, by s. 4(2), subject to integrated pollution control (see *Integrated Pollution Control: A Practical Guide* (London: HMSO, 1993)). Part B processes are designated for local control. However, reg. 4 of the 1991 Regulations provides that a process is not to be deemed to be a part A process if it does not result in the release into the air of any prescribed substances listed in sch. 4 (including metals and phosphorus), or will release prescribed substances only in insignificant quantities and it cannot result in the release into water of any substance listed in sch. 5 (including mercury) and cannot result in the release into land of any substance listed in sch. 6 (including pesticides). Regulation 4 goes on to exempt a process from being categorised as a part B process unless it will, or there is a likelihood that it will, result in the release into the air of one or more of the prescribed substances in a quantity greater than that which is so trivial that it is incapable of causing harm, or its capacity to cause harm is insignificant.

Emission limits
Under s. 3 the Secretary of State is empowered to make regulations establishing standards, objectives or requirements in relation to particular

prescribed processes or particular substances. The regulations made under the section can, *inter alia*, in relation to releases of any substance from a prescribed process into any environmental medium, prescribe standard limits for the concentration, amount or amount in any period, of the substance, and also prescribe any other characteristic of the substance in any circumstances in which it may be released. In relation to any prescribed process the regulations may prescribe standards or requirements as to any part of the process. Regulations made under the section may establish for any environmental medium (in all areas or in specified areas) quality objectives or quality standards in relation to any substances which may be released in to that or any other medium from that process. No such regulations have been made thus far. However, the United Kingdom government has invoked powers conferred on it by s. 2 of the European Communities Act 1972 to make the Air Quality Standards Regulations 1989 (SI 1989/317). The Regulations implement Council Directives Nos. 80/779/EEC, 82/884/EEC and 85/203/EEC. Under reg. 2 a duty is imposed on the Secretary of State to take appropriate measures to ensure that the concentrations of sulphur dioxide and suspended particulates in the atmosphere measured in accordance with the Regulations, do not exceed the limits laid down in the Regulations. Under reg. 4 a duty is placed on the Secretary of State to take necessary measures to ensure that the mean annual value for the concentration of lead in the air, measured in accordance with the Regulations, does not exceed 2 micrograms of lead per cubic metre expressed as a mean annual concentration. Similarly a duty is placed on the Secretary of State to take any necessary measures to ensure that the concentration of nitrogen dioxide in the atmosphere measured in accordance with the regulations does not exceed the limit defined in Council Directive 85/203/EEC.

Authorisations
It is an offence for anyone to carry on a prescribed process unless the process has been authorised by the relevant enforcing authority and the process is conducted in accordance with the conditions which the enforcing authority has seen fit to impose (s. 6) (see the Secretary of State's Guidance Note, *Authorisations*, GG2(91)). Where an application has been made to the appropriate enforcing authority, the authority can grant the authorisation conditionally or unconditionally (see the Secretary of State's Guidance Note, *Applications and Registers*, GG3(91)). The Secretary of State is empowered to give, in relation to any application for an authorisation, directions as to whether or not the authority should grant the authorisation. This type of central government power is unusual in environmental law.
. The Secretary of State is empowered by s. 7(3) to give directions to the enforcing authorities as to the conditions which are, or are not to be included

Air pollution

in all authorisations, in authorisations of any specified description or in any particular authorisation.

Section 7(1) provides that there must be included in an authorisation such specific conditions as the enforcing authority considers appropriate, when taken with the general condition implied by s. 7(4), for achieving the objectives specified in s. 7(2). There must also be included any conditions which are specified in directions given by the Secretary of State in terms of the section. The objectives which s. 7(2) requires be achieved are:

(a) ensuring that, in carrying on a prescribed process, the best available techniques not entailing excessive cost will be used —

(i) for preventing the release of substances prescribed for any environmental medium into that medium or, where that is not practicable by such means, for reducing the release of such substances to a minimum and for rendering harmless any such substances which are so released; and

(ii) for rendering harmless any other substances which might cause harm if released into any environmental medium;

(b) compliance with any directions by the Secretary of State given for the implementation of any obligations of the United Kingdom under the Community Treaties or international law relating to environmental protection;

(c) compliance with any limits or requirements and achievement of any quality standards or quality objectives prescribed by the Secretary of State under any of the relevant enactments;

(d) compliance with any requirements applicable to the grant of authorisations specified by or under a plan made by the Secretary of State under section 3(5) above.

Section 7(4) implies in every authorisation a condition that, in carrying on the process to which the authorisation applies, the person carrying it on must use the best available techniques not entailing excessive cost:

(a) for preventing the release of substances prescribed for any environmental medium into that medium or, where that is not practicable by such means, for reducing the release of such substances to a minimum and for rendering harmless any such substances which are so released; and

(b) for rendering harmless any other substances which might cause harm if released into any environmental medium.

The expression 'best available techniques not entailing excessive cost' is a term of art which, in relation to a process, is defined in s. 7(10) as including:

'the number, qualifications, training and supervision of persons employed in the process and the design, construction, layout and maintenance of the buildings in which it is carried on'.

Section 1(10) provides that a substance is released into any environmental medium whenever it is released directly into that medium whether it is released into it within or outside Great Britain and 'release' includes:

    (a)   in relation to air, any emission of the substance into the air;
    (b)   in relation to water, any entry (including any discharge) of the substance into water.
    (c)   in relation to land, any deposit, keeping or disposal of the substance in or on land.

The narrow objectives contained in s. 7(2) are supplemented by a more general objective in relation to any process which is designated for central control and is likely to involve the release of substances into more than one environmental medium. For such a process the objective of the conditions must be to ensure that the best available techniques not entailing excessive cost will be used for minimising the pollution which may be caused to the environment as a whole, by the releases, having regard to the best practicable environmental option (BPEO) as respects the substances which may be released (s. 7(7)). The expression BPEO is not, rather surprisingly defined in the Act. However, in the influential 12th Report of the Royal Commission on Environmental Pollution (Cm 310, 1988) it is said that the BPEO procedure establishes, for a given set of objectives, the option that provides the greatest benefit or least damage to the environment as a whole at an acceptable cost in the long term as well as in the short term (para. 2.1).

Of prime significance in relation to air pollution is the requirement imposed by s. 7(5) to the effect that a local authority, when considering how its powers should be exercised in terms of s. 7(1) to (4) may consider only the effect of the relevant release on the air.

Section 7(6) provides that the obligation implied by virtue of s. 7(4) does not apply in relation to any aspect of a process which is regulated by a condition imposed by s. 7(1).

Section 7(8) provides that an authorisation for carrying on a prescribed process may, without prejudice to the generality of s. 7(1), include conditions:

    (a)   imposing limits on the amount or composition of any substance produced by or utilised in the process in any period; and
    (b)   requiring advance notification of any proposed change in the manner of carrying on the process.

Section 7 has effect subject to s. 28, which provides that no condition may be attached to an authorisation so as to regulate the final disposal by deposit in or on land of controlled waste. However, the enforcing authority is in such circumstances required to notify the appropriate waste regulation authority (s. 7(9)).

The Environmental Protection (Applications, Appeals and Registers) Regulations (SI 1991/507) make provision governing applications for authorisation.

Fees and charges etc.
An important principle enshrined in the Environmental Protection Act 1990 is that the polluter should pay. Section 8 therefore places a duty on the relevant enforcing authority to charge such fees as may be prescribed from time to time by the Secretary of State.

Transfer and variation of authorisations
Section 9 allows an authorisation for the carrying on of any prescribed process to be transferred by the holder to a person who proposes to carry on the process in the holder's place. An authorisation so transferred has the same effect as if authorisation had been directly granted to the person to whom the authorisation was transferred.

Wide power is also given to the relevant enforcing authority by s. 10(1) to vary an existing authorisation. The need for such a variation may be brought about by a change of circumstances. However, the enforcing authority is required to vary an authorisation if it appears to the authority that s. 7 requires conditions to be included which are different from the subsisting conditions. If the enforcing authority decides to vary an authorisation it is required to serve a variation notice on the person concerned. A variation notice must require the holder of the authorisation within a specified period to notify the local authority what action, if any, the holder of the authorisation proposes to take to ensure that the process is carried on in accordance with the authorisation as varied by the notice (s. 10(4)). The notice must also require the holder to pay the relevant fee.

If the enforcing authority is of the opinion that any action to be taken by the holder of an authorisation in consequence of a variation notice served under s. 10 will involve a substantial change in the manner in which the process is being carried on, the enforcing authority must notify the holder of its opinion (s. 10(5)). The expression 'substantial change' is defined in the section, in relation to any prescribed process, as a substantial change in the substances released from the process, or in the amount or other characteristic of any substance so released. The Secretary of State is empowered to give directions to enforcing authorities as to what does or does not constitute a substantial change in relation to processes generally, any description of process or any particular process.

The Secretary of State may, in relation to authorisations of any description or particular authorisations, direct the enforcing authorities to exercise their powers under s. 10, or to do so in such circumstances as may be specified in the direction (s. 10(6)). Alternatively, the Secretary of State may direct the enforcing authority not to exercise those powers, or not to do so in such circumstances or such manner as may be so specified.

It may happen that a person carrying on a prescribed process for which authorisation has been obtained wishes to make a change to the process. In such a case that person may, under s. 11, notify the enforcing authority at any time of that fact in the prescribed form. For the purposes of s. 11, 'change', in relation to a prescribed process, means a change in the manner of carrying on the process which is capable of altering the substances released from the process or of affecting the amount or any other chacracteristic of any substances so released. The person making the request for variation must furnish the enforcing authority with such information as may be prescribed or as the authority may by notice require. A s. 11(1) notice requires the enforcing authority, under s. 11(2), to determine:

(a) whether the proposed change would involve a breach of any condition of the authorisation;

(b) if it would not involve such a breach, whether the authority would be likely to vary the conditions of the authorisation as a result of the change;

(c) if it would involve such a breach, whether the authority would consider varying the conditions of the authorisation so that the change may be made; and

(d) whether the change would involve a substantial change in the manner in which the process is being carried on.

Under s. 11(3) and (4), if the enforcing authority concludes that the proposed change would not involve a substantial change, but at the same time would lead to or require variation of the conditions of the authorisation, then it must notify the holder of the authorisation of the variations which the authority is likely to consider making. The holder of the licence may then apply to the enforcing authority for the requisite variation of the conditions of the authorisation. If, however, the enforcing authority concludes that the proposal would involve a substantial variation of the conditions of authorisation, then the holder of the authorisation is placed under an obligation to apply for the relevant variation if it is decided to proceed with the change.

The holder of an authorisation who does not wish to make a relevant change in the process may, at any time, apply to the enforcing authority for a variation of the conditions of the authorisation under s. 11(5). Similarly

Air pollution

the holder of an authorisation may, if it is wished to make a change in the relevant process, and it appears that the change will require the variation of the conditions of the authorisation, apply to the enforcing authority for the relevant variation of the conditions of the authorisation under s. 11(6).

An enforcing authority can, in relation to an application for variation of the conditions of an authorisation, either refuse the application or vary the conditions. Prior to making its decision, the enforcing authority is required to comply with the requirements of part 2 of sch. 1 to the Act (which relates to notification of the application, publicity etc.). If it is decided to vary the conditions, the enforcing authority is required to serve a variation notice on the holder of the authorisation.

Revocation of authorisations

Section 12(1) empowers an enforcing authority to revoke an authorisation at any time by giving notice in writing to the relevant holder. Under general principles of administrative law it is suggested that the enforcing authority would have to give the holder of the authorisation a hearing before deciding to revoke the authorisation (see, e.g., *Cooper* v *Wandsworth Board of Works* (1863) 14 CB NS 180; *Ridge* v *Baldwin* [1964] AC 40). Furthermore, without prejudice to the generality of subsection (1), subsection (2) provides that the enforcing authority may revoke an authorisation where it has reason to believe that a prescribed process for which authorisation is in force has not been carried on for a period of 12 months. The Secretary of State is empowered to give directions to an enforcing authority as to whether the authority should revoke an authorisation.

Enforcement

The Environmental Protection Act 1990 establishes its own machinery for the enforcement of its provisions. The devices employed are analogous to those found in the relevant provisions of the Health and Safety at Work etc. Act 1974 and the Food Safety Act 1990.

Section 13 of the Act allows an enforcing authority to serve an enforcement notice if it is of the opinion that the person carrying on a prescribed process under an authorisation is contravening any condition of the authorisation or is likely to contravene any such condition. The relevant enforcement notice must state that the authority is of the opinion that the authorisation is being contravened, and it must also specify the matters constituting the contravention or the matters making it likely that the contravention will arise. The Secretary of State is empowered to give directions to the enforcement authority as to whether the authority should exercise its powers under the section and as to the steps which must be taken under the section.

Section 14 empowers the enforcing authority, if it is of the opinion that carrying on a prescribed process under an authorisation involves an imminent risk of serious pollution of the environment, to serve a prohibition notice on the person carrying on the process. In contrast to the grounds governing the service of an enforcement notice, a prohibition notice may be served whether or not the process in question contravenes a condition of the authorisation, and may relate to any aspect of the process. The prohibition notice must state that the authority is of the opinion that an imminent risk of pollution is involved, specify the risk involved in the process and the steps that must be taken to remove the risk as well as the period within which the relevant steps must be taken. The notice must also direct that the authorisation shall, until the notice is withdrawn, wholly or to the extent specified in the notice, cease to have effect to authorise the carrying on of the process. Where the direction applies only to part of the relevant process it may impose conditions to be observed in carrying on the part which is authorised to be carried on. The Secretary of State can, in relation to the carrying on of a prescribed process, give directions to the enforcing authority as to whether the authority should perform its duties under s. 14 and the matters to be specified in any prohibition notice which the enforcing authority is directed to issue. The enforcing authority which has served a prohibition notice on any person is required to withdraw the notice when it is satisfied that the steps required by the notice have been taken.

Appeals

Section 15(1) of the Act allows the following persons to appeal against the decision of an enforcing authority to the Secretary of State:

(a) a person who has been refused the grant of an authorisation under s. 6 of the Act,
(b) a person who is aggrieved by the conditions attached to an authorisation,
(c) a person who has been refused a variation of an authorisation under s. 11,
(d) a person whose authorisation has been revoked under s. 12.

No appeal may be made, however, against a decision of an enforcing authority that implements a direction of the Secretary of State.

A person on whom a variation notice, an enforcement notice or a prohibition notice is served may appeal against it to the Secretary of State (s. 15(2)).

The large majority of appeals made under the section will centre on technical matters (see the Secretary of State's Guidance Note, *Appeals*, GG5 (91)). Section 15(3) therefore allows the Secretary of State to refer any matter involved in an appeal made under the section to a person appointed by the Secretary of State for that purpose. Furthermore the Secretary of

State, instead of determining any appeal personally, may direct that the appeal, or any matter involved in it, be determined by a person appointed for that purpose. Such delegation of quasi-judicial power by the Secretary of State is indeed unusual in administrative law.

If either party to the appeal so requests or the Secretary of State decides, an appeal may take the form of a hearing (s. 15(5)).

Wide power is given to the Secretary of State on appeals made under the section against a decision of an enforcing authority. The decision may be affirmed. Where the decision was a refusal to grant an authorisation, the Secretary of State may direct the enforcing authority to grant the authorisation or to vary it as the case may be. Where the decision related to the conditions attached to an authorisation, the Secretary of State can quash all or any of the conditions. A decision to revoke an authorisation may be quashed by the Secretary of State. The Secretary of State is also empowered to direct on appeal that certain conditions attach to the authorisation.

The bringing of an appeal under s. 15(1) against revocation of an authorisation has the effect of suspending the revocation until the determination or withdrawal of the appeal (s. 15(8)).

On an appeal relating to an enforcement notice or prohibition notice, the Secretary of State may either quash or affirm the notice. The bringing of such an appeal however, does not have the effect of suspending operation of the notice (s. 15(9)). The obvious intention of this provision is to prevent the holders of authorisations using the appeal machinery as a delaying tactic.

The Environmental Protection (Applications, Appeals and Registers) Regulations 1991 (SI 1991/507) govern appeals.

Appointment and powers of inspectors etc.

Wide power is given to the Secretary of State under s. 16 to appoint a sufficient number of suitably qualified inspectors for enforcing the provisions of the Act relating to prescribed processes designated for central control. One of such inspectors is required to be designated as the chief inspector for England and Wales. The functions capable of being exercised by the chief inspector under the Act may be delegated to any other inspector appointed under the section. Section 16(6) empowers local authorities to appoint a suitable number of inspectors as the authority considers necessary for enforcing the provisions of part I of the Act. Section 16(7) provides that an inspector may not be liable in any civil or criminal proceedings for anything done or purported to be done in the performance of the functions conferred on the inspector under ss. 17 or 18 of the Act (which are discussed below) provided the court is satisfied that the act was done in good faith and that there were reasonable grounds for doing it.

Section 17 confers both wide and detailed powers on inspectors. The powers are exercisable in relation to:

(a) premises on which a prescribed process is, or is believed on reasonable grounds to be, carried on, and

(b) in relation to premises on which a prescribed process has been carried on (whether or not the process was a prescribed process when it was carried on) the condition of which is believed (on reasonable grounds) to be such as to give rise to a risk of serious pollution of the environment.

The powers conferred on the inspectors include:

(a) power to enter premises at any reasonable time when entry is deemed necessary, or at any time, if the inspector is of the opinion that there is a risk of serious pollution of the environment,

(b) power to make necessary examinations and investigation,

(c) power to require that, in relation to any premises which the inspector has power to enter, those premises or any part of the premises be left undisturbed for so long as is necessary for the purpose of any examination or investigation,

(d) power to take measurements, photographs and recordings,

(e) power to take samples of any articles or substances found in or on any premises which the inspector has power to enter, and of the air, water or land in, on or in the vicinity of, the premises,

(f) power to dismantle or test or subject to any process any article or substance found in or on any premises which the inspector can enter,

(g) power to take possession of and detain any article or substance in order that it can be examined or used in criminal proceedings,

(h) power to require persons to give relevant information.

If an inspector discovers an article or substance which the inspector has reasonable cause to believe presents an imminent danger of serious harm, s. 18 gives the inspector power to seize the article and cause it to be rendered harmless whether by destruction or otherwise.

Publicity
The general public should have access to information which relates to the environment. Section 20 imposes a duty on each enforcing authority, in relation to the various prescribed processes for which it is the enforcing authority, to maintain a register in accordance with regulations made by the Secretary of State (see the Environmental Protection (Applications, Appeals and Registers) Regulations 1991 (SI 1991/507)) containing particulars of the following:

(a) applications for authorisation made to that authority,
(b) authorisations which have been granted by the authority,
(c) notices issued by the enforcing authority under part I of the Act,

Air pollution

   (d)   appeals made under s. 15,
   (e)   information obtained or furnished in pursuance of the conditions of authorisations or under any provision of part I,
   (f)   directions given to the authority by the Secretary of State,
   (g)   such other matters relating to the carrying on of prescribed processes or any pollution of the environment caused thereby as may be prescribed.

The duty to provide such a register is subject to the provisions of ss. 21 and 22 which relate to exclusion from the registers of matter relating to national security or information which is confidential.

Offences under the Act

Sections 23 to 27 relate to offences under the Act. Section 23 makes the following offences:

   (a)   contravention of s. 6(1) (which requires prescribed processes to be authorised),
   (b)   failure to comply with or contravention of any requirement or prohibition imposed by an enforcement notice or a prohibition notice,
   (c)   failure to comply with any requirement imposed under s. 17 (which relates to powers of inspectors),
   (d)   intentionally to obstruct an inspector in the exercise of his or her duties,
   (e)   failure, without reasonable excuse, to provide the relevant authority (in terms of s. 19(2)) with information which it considers it reasonably needs,
   (f)   making false statements to an enforcing authority.

It is also an offence falsely to pretend to be an inspector. The section also makes provision for penalties in respect of offences.

Section 24 gives an enforcing authority power to institute proceedings in the High Court if it is of the opinion that proceedings in respect of an offence for failure to comply with an improvement notice or prohibition notice would not afford an adequate remedy. This would allow the enforcing authority to apply for an injunction to prevent the continuance of a dangerous state of affairs.

Section 25 provides that in any proceedings for an offence relating to a failure to comply with the general condition implied under s. 7(4) in every authorisation for a prescribed process to the effect that the best available techniques not entailing excessive cost is employed, it is for the accused to prove that there was no better available technique than that in fact used.

Section 26 provides that where a person is convicted of an offence relating to either the carrying on of a prescribed process without authorisation or contrary to the relevant conditions, or the failure to comply with any requirement of an enforcement notice or prohibition notice, the convicting court may, in addition to or instead of imposing any punishment, order the convicted person to remedy the relevant state of affairs if it is within the person's power to do so.

STRAW AND STUBBLE BURNING

Smoke caused by the burning of straw and stubble can cause considerable discomfort, firstly to those living near the fields where the practice takes place and secondly, to motorists using roads situated alongside the fields in question. Section 152 of the Environmental Protection Act 1990 gives the appropriate minister power to make regulations prohibiting or restricting the burning of crop residues on agricultural land by persons engaged in agriculture. The regulations may also provide for exemptions from any prohibition or restriction imposed. The Crop Residues (Restriction on Burning) Regulations 1991 (SI 1991/1399 and SI 1991/1590) have been made under the Act.

FIVE
Waste

DEFINITION OF WASTE

The Environmental Protection Act 1990 controls arrangements for dealing with waste, which is defined in s. 75(2) as including any substance which constitutes a scrap material or any effluent or other unwanted surplus substance arising from the application of any process, and any substance or article which requires to be disposed of as being broken, worn out, contaminated or otherwise spoiled. The expression 'controlled waste' is defined in s. 75(4) as meaning 'household, industrial and commercial waste or any such waste'. The expressions 'household', 'industrial' and 'commercial' waste are also defined by s. 75. As far as these three types of waste are concerned, the factor which determines whether waste falls into the appropriate category is the nature of the premises the relevant waste derives from in contradistinction to the nature of the waste itself. In *Thanet District Council* v *Kent County Council* [1993] Env LR 391 it was held that seaweed did not constitute controlled waste in terms of the Control of Pollution Act 1974, s. 30.

WASTE AUTHORITIES

The Environmental Protection Act 1990, s. 30, provides that waste regulation authorities (WRAs) for England are as follows:

    (a)   for any non-metropolitan county, the county council;
    (b)   for Greater London, the authority constituted as the London Waste Regulation Authority;
    (c)   for the metropolitan county of Greater Manchester, the authority constituted as the Greater Manchester Waste Disposal Authority;

(d) for the metropolitan county of Merseyside, the authority constituted as the Merseyside Waste Disposal Authority;

(e) for any district in any other metropolitan county in England, the council of the district.

In Wales, each district council is the WRA for its district.

The following are constituted waste disposal authorities (WDAs):

(a) for any non-metropolitan county in England, the county council;
(b) in Greater London, the following:

(i) for the area of a London Waste disposal authority, the authority constituted as the waste disposal authority for that area;
(ii) for the City of London, the Common Council;
(iii) for any other London borough, the council of the borough;

(c) in the metropolitan county of Greater Manchester, the following:

(i) for the metropolitan district of Wigan, the district council;
(ii) for all other areas in the county, the authority constituted as the Greater Manchester Waste Disposal Authority;

(d) for the metropolitan county of Merseyside, the authority constituted as the Merseyside Waste Disposal Authority;
(e) for any district in any other metropolitan county in England, the council of the district;
(f) for any district in Wales, the council of the district.

The following are waste collection authorities (WCAs):

(a) for any district in England and Wales not within Greater London, the council of the district;
(b) in Greater London, the following:

(i) for any London borough, the council of the borough;
(ii) for the City of London, the Common Council;
(iii) for the Temples, the Sub-Treasurer of the Inner Temple and the Under Treasurer of the Middle Temple respectively.

Section 68 places a general duty on the Secretary of State to keep under review the discharge by WRAs of their functions under part II of the Act. Such a power is quite innovatory in relation to waste as far as the United

Kingdom is concerned, and provides a new and important dimension in relations between central and local government. Not perhaps since the era of Chadwick has central government enjoyed such a degree of control as far as waste removal is concerned.

CONTROL OF WASTE DUMPING

A recurring theme in waste control law to date has been the prevention of the unauthorised dumping of waste on land. Section 33(1) of the Environmental Protection Act 1990 makes it an offence for any person to:

(a) deposit controlled waste, or knowingly cause or knowingly permit controlled waste to be deposited in or on any land unless a waste management licence authorising the deposit is in force and the deposit is in accordance with the licence;

(b) treat, keep or dispose of controlled waste, or knowingly cause or knowingly permit controlled waste to be treated, kept or disposed of —

   (i) in or on any land, or
   (ii) by means of any mobile plant,

except under and in accordance with a waste management licence;

(c) treat, keep or dispose of controlled waste in a manner likely to cause pollution of the environment or harm to human health.

Penalties for contravening s. 33(1) are prescribed in s. 33(8).

The Waste Management Licensing Regulations 1994 (SI 1994/1056) exempt certain activities listed in the regulations from the requirements of s. 33(1)(a) and (b).

Paragraph (a) of s. 33(1) is concerned with 'knowingly causing' and 'knowingly permitting' unlicensed waste depositing. In *Wychavon District Council* v *National Rivers Authority* [1993] 1 WLR 125, which concerned an offence under what is now the Water Resources Act 1991, s. 85(3), it was held, following *Alphacell Ltd* v *Woodward* [1972] AC 824, that 'causing' implied some positive act on the part of the defendant, whereas the act of 'permitting' did not necessarily involve positive physical action. Therefore, one cannot 'cause' a given state of affairs simply by acquiescing in its face. However, mere passive inaction on the part of the defendant can, it is suggested, constitute 'knowingly permitting' (*Price* v *Cormack* [1975] 1 WLR 988). Whereas, for liablity to lie in respect of someone 'knowingly permitting' controlled waste to be deposited, it is necessary that the defendant has actual knowledge of the facts concerning the relevant deposit, it is not necessary that the defendant in addition knows that the deposit is unlawful, for example, by virtue of its flouting the conditions of the relevant waste management licence (*Ashcroft* v *Cambro Waste Products Ltd* [1981] 1 WLR 1349). In the Scots case of *Smith of Maddiston Ltd* v *Macnab* 1975 JC 48 it was held that it was sufficient for liability to lie in repect of 'permitting' a vehicle to be used in contravention of the Road Traffic Act 1972, s. 40, that the defender had simply shut his eyes to the obvious and allowed another to do something where a contravention was likely, not caring whether a contravention took place or not. It is suggested that this decision is authoritative as far as the interpretation of the Environmental Protection Act 1990, s. 33, is concerned. For example, a transferor of waste would be liable under s. 33(1) if he or she wilfully ignored the fact that the person to whom the waste was transferred for disposal did not possess a waste management licence.

As far as the meaning of 'deposit' is concerned, it is not necessary that the waste in question is in its final resting place. The waste can be in a temporary location and still constitute a deposit within the meaning of the Act (*R* v *Metropolitan Stipendary Magistrate, ex parte London Waste Regulation Authority* [1993] 3 All ER 113).

Section 33(1) does not apply to household waste from a domestic property which is treated, kept or disposed of within the curtilage of the dwelling by or with the permission of the occupier of the dwelling (s. 33(2)). Therefore, the dumping of putrescible material on one's garden for the purposes of fertilisation would not come within the ambit of s. 33(1). Similarly, the storage of refuse in receptacles situated in one's garden for collection by the relevant waste collection authority or private collector would not come within the scope of s. 33(1). Section 33(3) allows the Secretary of State to make regulations excluding s. 33(1)(a), (b) or (c) from having effect in prescribed cases (see the Controlled Waste Regulations 1992 (SI 1992/588)).

While some controlled waste is conveyed by rail, ship, and even by barge, the majority of controlled waste in Britain is conveyed by motor vehicle. It is imperative, therefore, that stringent legal controls obtain in relation to waste carried by vehicles. The Environmental Protection Act 1990, s. 33(5), provides that where controlled waste is carried in, and deposited from, a motor vehicle, the person who controls or is in a position to control the use of the vehicle is to be treated as knowingly causing the waste to be deposited for the purposes of s. 33(1)(a) whether or not that person gave any instructions for that to be done. Thus, as far as the deposit from such vehicles is concerned, the driver as well as the driver's employer, would be liable under s. 33(1), irrespective of whether the deposit of the waste was carried out at the behest of the vehicle driver or the employer. An example of the practical application of s. 33(5) would be where controlled waste is deposited from a vehicle on to land without a licence to authorise the deposit.

Section 33(7) provides that it is a defence for any person charged with an offence under s. 33 to prove:

(a) that he took all reasonable precautions and exercised all due diligence to avoid the commission of the offence; or

(b) that he acted under instructions from his employer and neither knew nor had reason to suppose that the acts done by him constituted a contravention of subsection (1) above; or

(c) that the acts alleged to constitute the contravention were done in an emergency in order to avoid danger to the public and that, as soon as reasonably practicable after they were done, particulars of them were furnished to the waste regulation authority in whose area the treatment or disposal of the waste took place.

While it seems probable that 'reasonable precautions' and 'due diligence' are separate concepts, there is a tendency for the courts to regard them as integrated. In *Tesco Supermarkets Ltd v Nattrass* [1972] AC 153, which concerned a prosecution under the Trade Descriptions Act 1968, it was held that the question whether the defendant, a large retailer, had taken reasonable precautions and exercised all due diligence was a question of fact which depended on all the circumstances of the business carried on by the defendant. If an offence under the 1968 Act occurred by virtue of the act of an employee, the employer had to be able to prove that the employee was suitably instructed and supervised in relation to the state of affairs which was the subject-matter of the offence. In relation to large businesses, however, such supervisory duties could be delegated to 'superior servants', for example, managers, and still attract the statutory defence, provided it was reasonable to delegate the supervisory duties in question.

In certain circumstances one can avail oneself of the defence of due diligence by having appropriate tests carried out by one's employees and also an independent expert (*Naish v Gore* [1971] 3 All ER 737). Failure to ensure that one's instructions are carried out will, however, negate the defence (*Aitchison v Reith and Anderson (Dingwall and Tain) Ltd* 1974 JC 12). Moreover, the defence of due diligence is unlikely to succeed if the defendant has not taken reasonable measures to be satisfied that the dumping will not contravene the section (*Durham County Council v Peter Connors Industrial Services Ltd* [1993] Env LR 197).

Civil liability

Section 73(6) provides that where any damage is caused by waste which has been deposited in or on land, any person who deposited it, or knowingly caused or knowingly permitted it to be deposited under s. 33(1) is liable for the damage except where the damage was due wholly to the fault of the person who suffered it or was suffered by a person who voluntarily accepted the risk of the damage being caused. The liabililty imposed by the Act does not prejudice the rights a plaintiff would enjoy under common law. For example, an occupier of land could still invoke the rule in *Rylands v Fletcher* (1868) LR 3 HL 330 as well as the law of nuisance and negligence in respect of damage caused by illegally deposited refuse.

One interesting point is whether the rules of remoteness of damage would be governed by the so called 'directness' rule in *Re Polemis and Furness, Withy & Co. Ltd* [1921] 3 KB 560 or the foreseeability rule enunciated in *Overseas Tankship (UK) Ltd v Morts Dock and Engineering Co. Ltd* [1961] AC 388. Since liability under s. 73(6) is strict it is suggested in the absence of authority that the appropriate test would be the directness test.

Removal of unlawful deposits of waste

Section 59(1) empowers both a WCA and a WRA by notice to require the occupier of land on which controlled waste has been dumped in contravention of s. 33(1) to do one or both of the following:

(a) remove the waste from the land within a specified period, not less than 21 days,
(b) take steps to eliminate or reduce the consequences of the deposit of the waste.

The person upon whom notice is served may appeal against any requirement to the magistrates' court (s. 59(2)). The court must quash the notice if it is satisfied that the appellant neither deposited nor knowingly caused nor knowingly permitted the deposit of the waste, or that there is a material defect in the notice. In any other case the court may modify the requirement or dismiss the appeal (s. 59(4)). Where an appeal is made against any requirement imposed under s. 59(1), the making of the appeal has the effect of suspending the effect of the requirement until the appeal is determined. The court is empowered to extend the period within which the relevant remedial work must be carried out (s. 59(4)). Section 59(5) makes it an offence to fail to comply with a notice served under s. 59(1). If the occupier fails to carry out the required remedial work then the authority can do it and can recover the cost from the occupier (s. 59(6)). In certain circumstances, a WRA or WCA may remove waste which has been unlawfully deposited on land without the need to serve notice on the occupier of the land. Section 59(7) provides that where the illegally dumped waste poses a threat of pollution to the land, water or air or a threat to human health, or there is no occupier of the land or the occupier neither made nor knowingly permitted the deposit of the waste, the authority may remove the waste from the land and/or take other steps to eliminate or reduce the consequences of the deposit. Costs may be recovered from the occupier of the land from the person who deposited or knowingly permitted the deposit of any of the waste.

Duty of care

The Environmental Protection Act 1990 adopts a holistic approach to waste. Central to this notion is the concept of the duty of care which s. 34(1) imposes on a variety of persons who deal with waste in any way. This important subsection provides:

> ... it shall be the duty of any person who imports, produces, carries, keeps, treats or disposes of controlled waste or, as a broker, has control of such waste, to take all such measures applicable to him in that capacity as are reasonable in the circumstances —
> (a) to prevent any contravention by any other person of section 33 above;
> (b) to prevent the escape of the waste from his control or that of any other person; and
> (c) on the transfer of the waste, to secure —
>
> (i) that the transfer is only to an authorised person or to a person for authorised transport purposes; and
> (ii) that there is transferred such a written description of the waste as will enable other persons to avoid a contravention of that section and to comply with the duty under this subsection as respects the escape of waste.

The obvious intention of the Act is to place a statutory responsibility on all those who deal with controlled waste from its very creation to its ultimate disposal to prevent environmental harm accruing from the waste. At the time of writing there is no authority on the interpretation of the section. It will be interesting to observe the extent, if any, to which the rules governing the breach of a duty of care at common law will pervade the judicial interpretation of s. 34. It is suggested that such concepts would be applicable. Therefore, in determining if the relevant duty has been breached, one would adopt an objective approach (*Nettleship* v *Weston* [1971] 2 QB 691). That is to say, in determining whether an importer, carrier etc. has breached its duty under the section, one would consider how a reasonably competent person in a given situation would have acted. One would also require to take into account the magnitude of the risk in relation to the measures necessary to avoid the breach in question (*Bolton v Stone* [1951] AC 850). Furthermore, one would also need to ascertain, where applicable, whether the person acted in conformity with the current state of knowledge (*Roe v Minister of Health* [1954] 2 QB 66).

In order to avoid bringing millions of householders within the ambit of the duty of care provisions, s. 34(2) excludes occupiers of domestic property in relation to household waste produced on their own property. Liability would lie however, in respect of waste produced elsewhere, for example, on a neighbour's property.

Authorised persons etc.

Section 34(3) defines who are 'authorised persons' for the purposes of s. 34(1)(c). As far as England and Wales is concerned, the following are authorised persons:

(a) any authority which is a waste collection authority for the purposes of part II of the Act,

(b) any person who is the holder of a waste management licence under s. 35 of the Act or a waste disposal licence under s. 5 of the Control of Pollution Act 1974,

(c) any person who does not require a waste management licence by virtue of being exempted by regulations made under s. 33(3) of the Environmental Protection Act 1990,

(d) any person registered as a carrier of controlled waste under the Control of Pollution (Amendment) Act 1989, s. 2 (see the Controlled Waste (Register of Carriers and Seizure of Vehicles) Regulations 1991 (SI 1991/1624)),

(e) any person who is exempted from the requirement to be registered under the 1989 Act by virtue of regulations made under that Act.

Section 34(4) provides that the following are authorised transport purposes for the purposes of s. 34(1)(c):

(a) the transport of controlled waste within the same premises between different places in those premises;

(b) the transport to a place in Great Britain of controlled waste which has been brought from a country or territory outside Great Britain not having been landed in Great Britain until it arrives at that place; and

(c) the transport by air or sea of controlled waste from a place in Great Britain to a place outside Great Britain.

The word 'transport' is given the same meaning as in the Control of Pollution (Amendment) Act 1989 where it is defined as including the transport of that waste by road or by air, sea or inland waterway but does not include moving that waste from one place to another by means of any pipe or other apparatus that joins those two places (s. 9).

Regulations, codes of practice, offences etc.

The Secretary of State is empowered under s. 34(5) to make regulations imposing requirements on any person who is under a duty of care imposed by s. 34(2) as respects the making and retention of documents and the furnishing of documents or copies of documents. The Environmental Protection (Duty of Care) Regulations 1991 (SI 1991/2839) have been made under this provision. The regulations make detailed provision concerning the transfer of controlled waste.

It is made an offence under s. 34(6) to fail to comply with the duty of care imposed by s. 34(1) or any requirement imposed under s. 34(5).

An important provision in practical terms is the power given to the Secretary of State to make codes of practice for the purpose of providing practical guidance on how the duty of care should be discharged. A code of practice entitled, *Waste Management. The Duty of Care. A Code of Practice* (1991) has been issued under this provision. While a breach of a provision of the code is not an offence, the relevant provision of the code is admissible in proceedings brought under s. 34(6). Furthermore the code must be taken into account where it appears to the court relevant to any question which has to be determined in such proceedings.

Waste management licences

The centrepiece of part II of the Environmental Protection Act 1990 is the provisions establishing a licensing regime for controlled waste. Section 35(2) provides that a licence shall be granted by a WRA:

> (a) in the case of a licence relating to the treatment, keeping or disposal of waste in or on land, to the person who is in occupation of the land; and
> (b) in the case of a licence relating to the treatment or disposal of waste by means of mobile plant, to the person who operates the plant.

A licence may be granted on such terms and conditions as appear to the WRA to be appropriate. The conditions imposed may relate to the activities which the licence authorises and to the precautions to be taken and works to be carried out in connection with or in consequence of those activities. Conditions may be imposed in a licence which are to be complied with before the activities which the licence authorises have begun or after the activities which the licence authorises have ceased (s. 35(3)). This gives wide power to the WRA in relation to the making of appropriate conditions. An important provision is that relating to conditions which are to be complied with after the activities which the licence has authorised have ceased. A condition could be attached to a landfill site relating to the nature of the site cover, screening the site etc.

An interesting and important provision of s. 35 is subsection (4) which allows a WRA to require the holder of a licence to carry out works or do other things, notwithstanding that the holder is not entitled to carry out the works or do the thing in question. Any person whose consent would be required is required to grant, or join in granting, the holder of the licence such rights in relation to the land as would enable the holder of the licence to comply with any requirement imposed by the licence. For example, the owner of adjoining land could, under this section, be compelled to confer a legal right, in the form of an easement, on the holder of a site licence, allowing the site holder the right to construct a drain through the former's property in order to adequately drain the site.

Power is given to the Secretary of State to make regulations relating to the conditions which may be included in a licence (s. 35(6)). Furthermore, the Secretary of State is empowered to give the WRA directions as to the terms and conditions which are or are not to be included in a licence (s. 35(7)). WRAs are generally required to have regard to any guidance issued to them by the Secretary of State in relation to the discharge of any of their functions in relation to licences.

A licence may not be surrendered except in accordance with s. 39 of the Act (s. 35(9)) and a holder of a licence cannot transfer it though the WRA may (s. 35(10)).

A licence continues in force until it is entirely revoked by the WRA under s. 38 or it is surrendered and its surrender is accepted under s. 39.

Under s. 36(1) an application for a site licence (defined as that which authorises the treatment, keeping or disposal of waste in or on land) must be made to the WRA in whose area the land is situated, whereas an application for a mobile plant licence must be made to the WRA in whose area the operator of the plant has its principal place of business. By s. 36(2) a licence may not be issued for a use of land for which planning permission is required under the Town and Country Planning Act 1990 unless such planning permission is in force, or alternatively an established use certificate is in force under s. 192 of the Act.

Section 36(3) provides that, subject to the provisions of s. 36(2) and (4), a WRA must grant a licence if it is satisfied that the applicant is a fit and proper person (as defined by s. 74) unless it is satisfied that rejection is necessary for the purpose of preventing:

    (a)   pollution of the environment;
    (b)   harm to human health; or
    (c)   serious detriment to the amenities of the locality;

but paragraph (c) above is inapplicable where planning permission is in force in relation to the use to which the land will be put under the licence.

The Waste Management Licensing Regulations 1994 (SI 1994/1056) make provision for the application of a waste management licence. The regulations also make provision as to fit and proper persons in terms of s. 74 of the Environmental Protection Act 1990.

The WRA would have to be satisfied in an objective sense that the applicant is a fit and proper person (*Secretary of State for Education and Science* v *Tameside Metropolitan Borough Council* [1977] AC 1014). If the WRA proposes to issue a licence it is required to refer the proposal to the National Rivers Authority (NRA) and the Health and Safety Executive and consider any representations about the proposal which either body makes (s. 36(4)). Any disagreement between the WRA and the NRA about the granting of permission or conditions to be attached to the permission is to be determined by the Secretary of State (s. 36(5)). The section also gives the Nature Conservancy Council for England the right to be consulted where the relevant land has been notified under the Wildlife and Countryside Act 1981, s. 28(1) (protection for certain areas).

Variation, revocation and suspension of licences

It may happen that circumstances relevant to a licence change after it is granted. Section 37(1) of the Act therefore gives a WRA wide discretion to modify, on its own initiative, the conditions of any licence to any extent which, in the opinion of the authority, is desirable and is unlikely to require unreasonable expense on the part of the holder. Provision is also made to allow a licence holder to apply to the WRA for a modification of conditions of the licence. A WRA is placed by s. 37(2) under a duty (except in circumstances where it revokes the licence) to modify the conditions of a licence to the extent which, in the opinion of the authority, is required for the purpose of ensuring that the activities authorised by the licence do not cause pollution of the environment or harm to human health or become seriously detrimental to the amenities of the locality affected by the activities and to the extent required by any regulations in force under s. 35(6). Power is given to the Secretary of State to give the WRA directions as to the modifications which are to be made in the conditions of the licence either in relation to any variation the WRA brings about by its own initiative or in relation to any modification necessitated by environmental considerations.

The right under s. 36 of interested public bodies to be consulted in relation to the issue of a site licence applies, subject to certain minor exceptions, in relation to the modification of a licence under s. 37.

While normally the WRA will be able to secure the protection of the environment by simply modifying the conditions of a licence, it may be necessary for the authority to revoke the licence. Section 38(1) therefore provides that a WRA may revoke a licence which is in force if it appears to the authority:

    (a) that the holder of the licence has ceased to be a fit and proper person by reason of his having been convicted of a relevant offence; or

    (b) that the continuation of the activities authorised by the licence would cause pollution of the environment or harm to human health or would be seriously detrimental to the amenities of the locality affected; and

    (c) that the pollution, harm or detriment cannot be avoided by modifying the conditions of the licence.

Power is also given to the WRA to revoke a licence where it appears to the authority that the holder of the licence has ceased to be a fit and proper person by reason of the management of the activities authorised by the licence having ceased to be in the hands of a technically competent person (s. 38(2)). A licence may be revoked either in its entirety or in part (s. 38(3) and (4)). An entirely revoked licence ceases to have effect to authorise the carrying on of the activities specified in the licence. A partly revoked licence ceases to authorise the activities in respect of which it has been revoked. However, the revocation does not affect the requirements imposed by the licence which the WRA, in revoking the licence, specifies are to continue to bind the holder (s. 38(5)).

The revocation of a licence is a Draconian measure which will normally be used only as a last resort. However, a WRA is also given the power by s. 38(6) to suspend a licence wholly or in part if it appears to the authority:

    (a) that the holder of the licence has ceased to be a fit and proper person by reason of the management of the activities authorised by the licence having ceased to be in the hands of a technically competent person; or

    (b) that serious pollution of the environment or serious harm to human health has resulted from, or is about to be caused by, the activities to which the licence relates or the happening or threatened happening of an event affecting those activities; and

    (c) that the continuing to carry on those activities or any of those activities, in the circumstances will continue or, as the case may be, cause serious pollution of the environment or serious harm to human health.

There is no need for the holder of a licence to have been convicted of an offence before the licence can be suspended. It is sufficient that the licence holder ceases to become suitable by virtue of the management of the site ceasing to be in the hands of a technically competent person. Furthermore, in contrast to the position obtaining in respect of the revocation of licences, the harm from the relevant pollution must be serious before the licence can be suspended. There is also no requirement that the WRA must be of the opinion that the relevant pollution cannot be avoided by modifying the conditions of the licence. Any licence suspended under s. 38 ceases to have effect to authorise the conduct of the activities specified in the licence or the activities specified in the part of the licence that has been suspended (s. 38(8)). Where a licence is suspended under s. 38(6), the WRA may, when suspending it, or during the period it is suspended, require the holder of the licence to take appropriate measures to deal with existing or potential pollution or harm as the authority considers necessary (s. 38(9)). Section 38(10) makes it an offence for any person to fail to comply with any requirement imposed under s. 38(9) otherwise than in relation to special waste, which is dealt with later in the Act (see page 85).

Any revocation or suspension of a licence or imposition of a requirement during the suspension of a licence must be effected by notice served on the holder of the licence. The notice must state the time at which the suspension or requirement is to take effect. In the case of suspension, the WRA must specify the period at the end of which or the event on the occurrence of which, the suspension ceases (s. 38(12)).

Transfer of licences

A licence may be transferred to another person. Section 40 allows a licence to be transferred irrespective or whether the licence is partly revoked or suspended under any provisions of the Act. A licence holder wishing to transfer, and the proposed transferee, must apply to the WRA which granted the licence for a transfer of the licence. If the WRA is satisfied that the proposed transferee is a fit and proper person, the authority must effect the appropriate transfer.

Fees etc. for licences

Section 41 of the Act makes provision for the charging of fees by WRAs in respect of applications for licences and in respect of the holding of licences. Power is given to the Secretary of State to make, with the approval of the Treasury, a scheme for fees and charges.

Supervision of licensed activities

It is essential that an activity which is the subject of a licence is kept under constant supervision by the licensing authority. Section 42(1) therefore provides:

While a licence is in force it shall be the duty of the waste regulation authority which granted the licence to take the steps needed —

(a) for the purpose of ensuring that the activities authorised by the licence do not cause pollution of the environment or harm to human health or become seriously detrimental to the amenities of the locality affected by the activities; and

(b) for the purpose of ensuring that the conditions of the licence are complied with.

If it appears to a WRA that water is likely to be polluted by the activities to which a licence relates, the WRA must consult the NRA about the steps to be taken (s. 42(2)). Any officer of the WRA, authorised in writing for the purpose by the authority, may, if it appears to an officer of a WRA that, by reason of an emergency, it is necessary to carry out work on land, or in relation to plant or equipment on the land to which a licence relates, or in relation to the mobile plant to which a licence relates, he or she may (if authorised in writing for the purpose by the WRA) carry out the relevant work (s. 42(3)). Expenditure incurred on such remedial work can be recovered from the licence holder unless that person shows that there was no emergency requiring any work to be carried out or that the relevant expenditure was unnecessary (s. 42(4)).

If the conditions attached to a licence are not complied with, the WRA may, under s. 42(5), require the licence holder to comply with the condition within a specified time. If, in the opinion of the WRA, the licence holder has not complied with the condition within the specified time then the authority may exercise any of the powers specified in s. 42(6). That subsection empowers the WRA in the face of non-compliance on the part of a licence holder.

(a) to revoke the licence so far as it authorises the carrying on of the activities specified in the licence or such of them as the authority specifies in revoking the licence;

(b) to revoke the licence entirely; and

(c) to suspend the licence so far as it authorises the carrying on of the activities specified in the licence or, as the case may be, the activities specified by the authority in suspending the licence.

Where a licence is revoked or suspended under s. 42, subsections (5) or (8) and (9), (10) and (12) of s.38 apply with the necessary modifications as they do in relation to revocations or suspensions made under s. 38. The Secretary of State is empowered to give the WRA directions as to whether and in what manner, it should exercise its powers under s. 42.

Waste

Right to be heard and appeals

In common with other statutes which give local authorities etc. powers of licensing, the Environmental Protection Act 1990 makes provision for appeals to the Secretary of State against refusal or revocation of a licence etc. Section 43(1) of the Act provides:

> Where, except in pursuance of a direction given by the Secretary of State —
> (a) an application for a licence or a modification of the conditions of a licence is rejected;
> (b) a licence is granted subject to conditions;
> (c) the conditions of a licence are modified;
> (d) a licence is suspended;
> (e) a licence is revoked under sections 38 or 42 above;
> (f) an application to surrender a licence is rejected; or
> (g) an application for the transfer of a licence is rejected;
>
> then, except in the case of an application for a transfer, the applicant for the licence or, as the case may be, the holder or former holder of it may appeal from the decision to the Secretary of State and, in the case of an application for a transfer, the proposed transferee may do so.

An interesting issue, from a practical as well as theoretical viewpoint, is whether an applicant for a licence, or licensee etc. has a right to be heard by the WRA prior to its refusing or revoking the licence etc. Under general principles of administrative law, it would seem likely that the holder of a licence would have the right to be heard before it is revoked (*McInnes* v *Onslow-Fane* [1978] 1 WLR 1520). Since s. 36(3) places a duty on a WRA to grant a licence if satisfied that the applicant is a fit and proper person, it is probable, furthermore, that a fit and proper person applying for a licence would also have the right to be heard, since such a person would have a legitimate expectation of obtaining a licence (*R* v *Gaming Board for Great Britain, ex parte Benaim and Khaida* [1970] 2 QB 417). It is suggested that a WRA also has a duty to hear the licensee before suspending a licence unless the licence holder could not reasonably expect such a hearing (*Re Findlay* [1985] AC 318). For example, if the state of a site was such that it was patently clear that significant environmental harm could accrue from the continuation of the licensed activities, there would be no right to a hearing.

Another matter which should be briefly mentioned here in the context of natural justice and appeals, is the extent to which a failure to grant a hearing can be cured or negated by a subsequent hearing by the Secretary of State. This is a grey area of the law indeed. However, it is suggested that, as far as part II of the Act is concerned, an appeal to the Secretary of State would not rectify a former breach of natural justice by a WRA (see *Leary* v *National Union of Vehicle Builders* [1971] Ch 34).

On an appeal to the Secretary of State, any matter involved in the appeal may be referred to a person appointed by the Secretary of State for that purpose (s. 43(2)). For example, the Secretary of State could refer to a hydrologist questions concerning the likelihood of the site in question polluting water sources. Furthermore the Secretary of State may ask an appointed person to determine an appeal made under the section.

While an appeal is pending in a case falling within s. 43(1)(c) or (e), the decision in question, subject to subsection (6), becomes ineffective (s. 43(4)). If the appeal is dismissed or withdrawn the decision becomes effective from the day on which the appeal is dismissed or withdrawn. However, subsection (6) provides that subsection (4) does not apply to a decision modifying conditions of a licence under s. 37 (varying a licence) or revoking a licence under s. 38 or s. 42, where the notice effecting the modification or revocation includes a statement to the effect that, in the opinion of the authority, it is necessary for the purpose of preventing or, where that is not practicable, minimising pollution of the environment or harm to human health that subsection (4) should not apply.

Section 43(7) provides that where the decision under appeal is one falling under subsection (6) or is a decision to suspend a licence, and the Secretary of State or other person determining the appeal determines that the WRA acted unreasonably in excluding the application of subsection (4) or in suspending the licence then, if the appeal is still pending when the determination is made, subsection (4) is made to apply to the decision of the WRA from the end of the day that the determination by the Secretary of State etc. is made and, furthermore, the holder or former holder of the licence is entitled to compensation from the WRA.

The Waste Management Licensing Regulations 1994 (SI 1994/1056) make provision as regards appeals under s. 43.

Public registers

It is becoming increasingly common for statute to give members of the public access to information held by public authorities. This trend is particularly apparent in the field of environmental law. As far as waste is concerned s. 64 of the Environmental Protection Act 1990 places a duty on each WRA to maintain a register containing prescribed particulars of, or relating to, licences granted by the authority, applications made to the authority for a licence, the suspension or revocation of licences, and notices issued by the authority. Each WRA and WCA is required to ensure that its register is open to public inspection free of charge. However, under s. 65, no information may be included in a register if that information, in the opinion of the Secretary of State, would be contrary to the interests of national security. The Secretary of State is empowered to give the authorities maintaining registers directions specifying information which is to be excluded from the register or descriptions of information to be referred to the Secretary of State for determination. No information so referred may be included in the register until the Secretary of State determines that it should be included.

Section 66 of the Act provides that no information relating to the affairs of any individual or business may be included in a register maintained under s. 64, without the consent of that individual or the person for the time being carrying on that business, if and so long as the information is commercially confidential and is not required to be included in the register by virtue of directions made by the Secretary of State under the section. Information is not to be deemed commercially confidential unless it is determined to be so by the authority maintaining the register or, on appeal, by the Secretary of State. Section 66(2) allows a person who has furnished information to an authority for the purpose of an application for, or for the modification of, a licence, or complying with any condition of a licence or with a notice served under s. 71(2), to apply to the authority to have the information excluded from the register on the grounds that it is commercially confidential. If an authority considers that information it has obtained other than in circumstances falling under s. 71(2) might be commercially confidential, the authority is required to give the relevant person notice that the information is required to be included in the register unless excluded and give that person an opportunity of objecting to the inclusion of the information on the grounds of confidentiality (s. 71(4)).

If an authority determines that information is not confidential an appeal may be made to the Secretary of State against the decision (s. 71(5)). Information excluded from the register ceases for the purpose of the section to be commercially confidential after four years from the date it was excluded. However, the person who furnished it may apply to the authority for the information to remain excluded on the grounds that it is still confidential (s. 71(8)).

Closed landfills

Landfill sites which are no longer in use can sometimes continue to present an actual or potential danger to the environment especially from leachate emanating from the site. Section 61 therefore requires a WRA to cause its area to be inspected from time to time to detect whether any land is in such a condition that it may cause pollution of the environment or harm to human health from the concentration or accumulation in, and emission or discharge from the land of noxious gases or noxious liquids caused by deposits of controlled waste in the land (s. 61(2)). Powers of entry are given to the authority by s. 61(3) in relation to:

(a) land in or on which controlled waste has been deposited under the authority of a waste management licence or a disposal licence under the Control of Pollution Act 1974, s. 5,
(b) land where controlled waste has been deposited in the land at any time, or
(c) land where there are, or the authority has reason to believe there may be, concentrations or accumulations of noxious gases or liquids.

If pollution of water is likely to be caused by the state of the site, the WRA must consult the NRA (s. 61(5)).

The WRA is empowered to take appropriate remedial action to abate any state of affairs likely to cause pollution or harm to human health and, in most cases, recover the costs from the owner of the land (s. 61(7) and (8)). However, no costs may be recovered where the authority accepted the surrender under s. 39 of the waste management licence which authorised the activities in the course of which the waste was deposited.

COLLECTION OF CONTROLLED WASTE

It is of prime importance from the viewpoint of public health and adequate arrangements are made for the collection of household waste. Section 45(1) of the Environmental Protection Act 1990 provides:

It shall be the duty of each waste collection authority —
   (a) to arrange for the collection of household waste in its area except waste —

      (i) which is situated at a place which in the opinion of the authority is so isolated or inaccessible that the cost of collecting it would be unreasonably high, and
      (ii) as to which the authority is satisfied that adequate arrangements for its disposal have been or can reasonably be expected to be made by a person who controls the waste; and

   (b) if requested by the occupier of premises in its area to collect any commercial waste from the premises, to arrange for the collection of the waste.

If a WCA is requested by the occupier of premises in its area to collect any industrial waste from the premises, it may arrange for the collection of the waste provided it has the consent of the WDA for its area (s. 45(2)). No charge may be made for the collection of household waste except in cases prescribed in regulations made by the Secretary of State (s. 45(3)) but a reasonable charge must be made for the collection and disposal of waste other than for household waste (s. 45(4)). A WCA is empowered to contribute towards the cost incurred by another person in providing or maintaining plant or equipment intended to deal with commercial or industrial waste before it is collected.

Each WCA must make such arrangements for the emptying, without charge, of privies serving one or more private dwellings in its area as the authority considers appropriate (s. 45(5)). A privy is defined by the section as a latrine which has a moveable receptacle (for example, a chemical closet). A duty is also placed on each WCA, if requested by the person who controls a cesspool (defined as including a septic tank) serving any one or more private dwellings in its area, to empty the cesspool and remove such of the contents of the cesspool as the authority considers appropriate on payment of a reasonable charge, if the authority so requires (s. 45(5)). The WCA is empowered to empty any other privy or cesspool on the payment of a reasonable charge (s. 45(6)).

One means of conveying controlled waste from its place of production to the place of final disposal, is to have the refuse conveyed along pipes by means of either air pressure or water. The Garchey system is the most common of the latter. Power is given to the WCA to construct, lay and maintain within or outside its area, pipes and associated works for collecting waste, and to contribute towards the cost incurred by another person in providing or maintaining such pipes etc.

Receptacles for household waste

Section 46(1) provides that where a WCA has a duty to arrange for the collection of household waste from premises, it can, by notice served on the occupier of the premises, require the occupier to place the relevant waste in receptacles of a kind and number specified in the notice. As far as receptacles for the collection of household refuse is concerned, the local authority may, under s. 46(3):

(a) determine that they be provided by the authority free of charge;

(b) propose that they be provided, if the occupier agrees, by the authority on payment by him of such a single payment or such periodical payments as he agrees with the authority;

(c) require the occupier to provide them if he does not enter into an agreement under paragraph (b) above within a specified period; or

(d) require the occupier to provide them.

The WCA's notice may, under s. 46(4), make provision with respect to, *inter alia*, the size, construction and maintenance of the receptacles; the placing of the receptacles for the purpose of facilitating the emptying of them and access to the receptacles in question for that purpose; the placing of the receptacles for the same purpose on highways; the substances or articles which may or may not be put into the receptacles and the steps to be taken by occupiers of premises to facilitate the collection of waste from the receptacles. The WCA may not require the receptacles to be placed on a highway or a road unless the relevant highway authority or roads authority has given its consent to their being so placed and arrangements have been made as to the liability for any damage arising for any damage arising out of the receptacles being placed on the highway (s. 46(5)). Section 46(6) makes it an offence for a person, without reasonable excuse, to fail to comply with any requirements imposed by s. 46(1), (3)(c) or (d) or (4). An occupier of premises who is required under s. 46(1) to provide receptacles can, under s. 46(7), appeal to the magistrates' court against any requirement imposed under s. 46(1), (3)(c) or (d) or (4) on the ground that:

 (a) the requirement is unreasonable; or
 (b) the receptacles in which household waste is placed for collection from the premises are adequate.

If an appeal is brought under s. 46(7) against a requirement then the requirement has no effect pending the determination of the appeal, and the court may either quash or modify the requirement or dismiss the appeal. By s. 46(9), if an appeal is made, no requirement may be challenged for unreasonableness in any criminal proceedings under s. 46(6). In other words any person aggrieved by a requirement would be unable to attack its legality collaterally in criminal proceedings.

Receptacles for commercial or industrial waste

An important aspect of the work carried out by WCAs is the collection of commercial and industrial waste. Section 47(1) empowers a WCA, at the request of any person, to supply that person with receptacles for commercial or industrial waste which that person has requested the authority to arrange to collect. The WCA is required to make a reasonable charge for any receptacle supplied unless in the case of a receptacle supplied for commercial waste, the authority considers it appropriate not to make a charge. Under s. 47(2), if it appears to a WCA that there is likely to be situated on any premises in its area, commercial waste or industrial waste of a kind which, if the waste is not stored in receptacles of a particular kind, is likely to cause a nuisance or to be detrimental to the amenities of the locality, the authority may serve a notice requiring the occupier of the premises to provide at the premises receptacles for the storage of such waste of a kind and number specified. In making requirements under s. 47(2), the authority may make provision with respect to the size, construction and maintenance of the receptacles; the placing of the receptacles for the purpose of facilitating the emptying of them and access to the receptacles for that purpose; the substances or articles which may not be put into the receptacles and the precautions to be taken where particular substances or articles are put into them; and the steps to be taken by the occupiers of premises to facilitate the collection of waste from the receptacles (s. 47(4)).

Section 47(5) provides that no requirement may be made under subsection (2) for receptacles to be placed on a highway or road unless the relevant highway authority or roads authority has given its consent to the receptacles being so placed and arrangements have been made as to the liability for any damage arising out of their being so placed.

Any person who fails to comply with any requirements imposed under s. 47(2) or (4) commits an offence (s. 47(6)).

An occupier who is required to provide any receptacle under s. 47(2) can appeal to the magistrates' court within 21 days against any requirement imposed under the subsection on the ground that it is unreasonable or that the waste is not likely to cause a nuisance or be detrimental to the amenities of the locality (s. 47(7) and (8)). Where an appeal is made against a requirement, the requirement has no effect pending the determination of the appeal and the court may quash or modify the requirement or dismiss the appeal. Furthermore, where an appeal is made under the section, no question as to whether the requirement is unreasonable may be entertained in any proceedings for an offence under s. 47(6).

Disposal of waste

Section 48 makes provision in relation to the disposal of waste which is collected by a WCA. A duty is placed on each WCA to deliver for disposal all waste which it collects under s. 45 to such places as the WDA for its area directs unless the WCA decides to make arrangements for recycling the waste. A WCA must, as soon as reasonably practicable, inform its WDA in writing of any recycling arrangements which it proposes to make. Where a WDA has arranged for a waste disposal contract to recycle all or any household waste in its area or any part of its area, the WDA may, by notice served on the WCA, object to the WCA having the waste recycled. Where such an objection is made, the WCA is deprived of its power to have waste recycled, to the extent objected to by the WDA.

In order to facilitate the transport of waste which is to be recycled, power is given to a WCA to provide plant and equipment for the sorting and baling of waste (s. 48(6)). Subsection (6) does not apply to a WCA which is also a WDA but, in such a case, the WDA may make arrangements with a waste disposal contractor for the contractor to deal with the waste (s. 48(7)). The WCA may permit others to use plant etc. provided by it, but, if it does this, it is under a duty to make a reasonable charge unless the WCA considers it inappropriate to make such a charge. No charge may be made in relation to household waste.

Waste recycling plans

Local authorities in the United Kingdom have adopted the practice of recycling waste for many years. Ferrous metals and, to a lesser extent, textiles have been salvaged for re-use. Market forces have often determined the extent, if any, to which local authorities have been prepared to recycle waste. The Government is now committed to the principle of the recycling of waste (see *This Common Inheritance*, p. 187). The Environmental Protection Act 1990, therefore, is not simply content to empower a WCA to provide appropriate plant and equipment for the recycling of waste; rather it proceeds to place a duty on each WCA to formulate arrangements for the recycling of waste. Section 49(1) provides:

It shall be the duty of each waste collection authority, as respects household and commercial waste arising in its area —
(a) to carry out an investigation with a view to deciding what arrangements are appropriate for dealing with the waste by separating, baling or otherwise packaging it for the purpose of recycling it;
(b) to decide what arrangements are in the opinion of the authority needed for that purpose;
(c) to prepare a statement ('the plan') of the arrangements made and proposed to be made by the authority and other persons for dealing with waste in those ways;
(d) to carry out from time to time further investigations with a view to deciding what changes in the plan are needed; and
(e) to make any modification of the plan which the authority thinks appropriate in consequence of any such further investigation.

A duty is placed on a WCA, in preparing or modifying its waste recycling plan, to have regard to the likely effect of the plan on the amenities of any locality, and the likely cost or saving to the authority which would accrue from the arrangements (s. 49(2)). A WCA is also required, under subsection (3) to include in the plan information as to:

(a) the kinds and quantities of controlled waste which the authority expects to collect during the period specified in the plan;

(b) the kinds and quantities of controlled waste the authority expects to purchase during that period;
(c) the kinds and quantities of controlled waste which the authority expects to deal with under s. 49(1)(a);
(d) the arrangements which the authority expects to make during the relevant period with waste disposal contractors for them to deal with the waste;
(e) the plant and equipment which the authority expects to provide for the purposes of recycling; and
(f) the estimated costs or savings which would accrue from the methods of dealing with the waste in the ways provided for in the plan.

A WCA must send a copy of any plan in draft to the Secretary of State who will determine whether s. 49(3) has been complied with (s. 49(4)). The Secretary of State is empowered to give directions to the authority for securing compliance with s. 49(3) and it is the duty of the authority to comply with any directions made by the Secretary of State (s. 49(4)).

A WCA is placed under a duty to publicise its waste recycling plan in its area and have a copy for public inspection. It must also send a copy of the plan to the WDA and WRA for the area (s. 49(5)).

The Secretary of State may give any WCA directions as to the time by which the authority is to perform any duty imposed by s. 49. The WCA is placed under a duty to comply with any such directions (s. 49(7)).

Waste disposal plans

In order to be able to carry out its duties efficiently it is essential that a WRA makes formal arrangements for the disposal of waste. Section 50(1) therefore provides:

It shall be the duty of each waste regulation authority —
(a) to carry out an investigation with a view to deciding what arrangements are needed for the purpose of treating or disposing of controlled waste which is situated in its area and controlled waste which is likely to be so situated so as to prevent or minimise pollution of the environment or harm to human health;
(b) to decide what arrangements are in the opinion of the authority needed for that purpose and how it should discharge its functions in relation to licences;
(c) to prepare a statement ('the plan') of the arrangements made and proposed to be made by waste disposal contractors, or, in Scotland, waste disposal authorities and waste disposal contractors, for the treatment or disposal of such waste;

(d) to carry out from time to time further investigations with a view to deciding what changes in the plan are needed; and

(e) to make any modification of the plan which the authority thinks appropriate in consequence of any such further investigation.

An authority must have regard to the likely cost of its plan and its beneficial effects on the environment when drawing it up or modifying it (s. 50(2)).

Section 50(3) provides that the following must be included in a waste disposal plan:

(a) the kinds and quantities of controlled waste which the authority expects to be situated in its area during the period specified in the plan,

(b) the kinds and quantities of controlled waste which the authority expects to be brought into or taken for disposal out of its area during the relevant period,

(c) the kinds and quantities of controlled waste which the authority expects to be disposed of within its area during that period,

(d) the methods which are to be employed to treat controlled waste,

(e) the sites and equipment which persons are providing, and

(f) the estimated cost of the methods of disposal.

The importance the Act accords to the principle of recycling is illustrated in s. 50(4) which requires a WRA, when considering the methods to be employed in treating controlled waste, to have regard to the desirability, where reasonably practicable, of giving priority to recycling waste.

In preparing or modifying a waste disposal plan, a WRA is required to consult the NRA, the relevant WCA, or in Wales the county council, any other WRA, and, any persons engaged in refuse disposal or treatment the WRA considers it appropriate to consult (s. 50(5)). Before the plan is finally adopted it must be given adequate publicity and members of the public must be given an opportunity to make representations to the authority.

The WRA must also consider, in preparing the plan and making any modifications to it, what arrangements can reasonably be expected to be made for recycling waste and what provisions should be included in the plan for that purpose (s. 50(7)). Furthermore, the WRA may not finally determine the content of any plan where it is proposed to take waste into another WRA's area, except with the consent of the other WRA, or, if the WRA withholds its consent, with the consent of the Secretary of State (s. 50(8)).

A WRA must send a copy of any plan in draft to the Secretary of State who will determine whether s. 50(3) has been complied with. The WRA must comply with any direction given by the Secretary of State (s. 50(9)).

Adequate publicity must be given to the plan after its content has been finally determined, and a copy must be sent to the Secretary of State (s. 50(10)).

The Secretary of State may give directions to any WRA as to the time by which the authority is to perform any duties imposed by s.50 (s. 50(11)).

Functions of waste disposal authorities

The functions of a WDA are set out in s. 51(1). The main duties of a WDA are first, to arrange for the disposal of controlled waste collected in its area by the various WCAs and, secondly, for places to be provided at which persons resident in its area may deposit their household waste and for the disposal of waste so deposited. These arrangements are to be effected solely by means of arrangements with private waste disposal contractors in contradistinction to the authority itself carrying out the function. However, the Secretary of State is empowered by s. 32(2) to give directions to existing disposal authorities requiring them to form or participate in forming waste disposal companies and transfer to the companies so formed the relevant part of their undertakings. When a WDA proposes to enter into a contract for the keeping, treatment or disposal of waste, the authority is required to frame the terms and conditions so as to avoid undue discrimination in favour of one description of waste disposal contractor as against other descriptions of waste disposal contractors. The WDA is also required to have regard to environmental factors as well as those relating to public health (sch. 2, part II). In *R v Avon County Council, ex parte Terry Adams Ltd* (1994) *The Times*, 20 January, 1994, it was held on appeal that the relevant terms and conditions require to be reasonable in the *Wednesbury* sense. Furthermore the relevant terms must be formulated according to the honest judgment of the authority concerned. An authority is entitled to have a policy favouring one mode of disposal of waste but it is not entitled to close its mind to other means of disposal. It would be *ultra vires* therefore to flout the intention of the Environmental Protection Act.

As far as the duty to provide places for the deposit of household waste is concerned, each place must be situated either within the area of the authority or so placed as to be reasonably accessible to persons resident in its area. Each such place must also be available for the deposit of waste at all reasonable times. The facilities must be available free of charge to persons resident in the area, for the deposit of waste. However, the arrangements may restrict the availability of specified places to specified descriptions of waste (s. 51(2)). The WDA may permit the places used for the disposal of household waste free of charge to residents, to be used by others for the deposit of household or other controlled waste. The WDA may arrange for the provision, within or outside its area, of places at which waste disposed of at these points (whether household waste or other waste: s. 51(6)) can be treated or kept prior to its removal for treatment or disposal (s. 51(5)).

As far as the discharge of the duties of a WDA in connection with the disposal of controlled waste is concerned, s. 51(4) requires the WDA to give directions to the WCAs as to the persons to whom and places at which such waste is to be delivered. It may also arrange for the provision within or outside its area, by waste disposal contractors, of places at which such waste may be treated or kept prior to its removal for treatment or disposal. The WDA may also make available to waste disposal contractors plant and equipment for the purpose of enabling them to keep such waste prior to its removal for disposal, or to allow the waste to be treated (for example, compressed) to facilitate its transportation. The WDA may also acquire and/or make available to waste disposal contractors, land for the purpose of enabling them to treat, keep or dispose of waste in or on the land. Again, the WDA is empowered to contribute towards the cost incurred by persons who produce commercial or industrial waste, in providing and maintaining plant or equipment intended to deal with waste before it is collected. For example, a contribution could be made towards the cost of waste shredding or baling equipment. A contribution can also be made towards the cost incurred by persons who produce such waste in providing or maintaining pipes etc. connecting with the WDA's own refuse disposal pipes.

The WDA is empowered to own plant and equipment which is made available to waste disposal contractors for the purpose of enabling them to keep or treat household waste prior to its removal for disposal. Land may also be made available to waste disposal contractors to allow them to treat, keep or dispose of such waste in or on the land.

Payments for waste recycling and disposal

If a WCA decides to recycle waste in its possession a considerable saving could accrue to the relevant WDA. Section 52 therefore provides that where a WCA retains household or commercial waste for recycling, the WDA must make payments to the WCA representing the net saving of expenditure on the disposal of the waste to the WDA in respect of the waste so retained. Conversely, if, by virtue of the discharge of a WDA of its functions, waste arising in its area does not fall to be collected by a WCA, the latter is required to pay to the WDA, in relation to the waste that does need to be collected, amounts representing the net saving of expenditure to the WCA on the collection of the waste. Similarly, where a person other than a WCA collects waste which otherwise would have to be collected under s. 45 of the Act, the WDA is empowered to make payments to that person representing the net saving of expenditure on the disposal of the waste as the WDA determines. Again, where a person other than a WCA collects waste for recycling which would otherwise fall to be collected by a WCA, it may make to that person payments in respect of the waste so collected, such amounts representing the net saving on expenditure on the collection of the waste as the authority determines. See the Environmental Protection (Waste Recycling Payments) Regulations 1992 (SI 1992/462) made under s. 52.

Powers for recycling waste

A WDA may make arrangements with waste disposal contractors for them to recycle the waste which the authority has a statutory duty to arrange to dispose of under the Act or waste which the WDA has agreed to be disposed of or treated by another person (s. 55). Power is also given to a WDA to make arrangements with waste disposal contractors for them to use waste for the purpose of producing heat or electricity or both from it. Therefore, the waste could be employed, for example, in a district heating scheme. A WDA may buy or otherwise acquire waste with a view to its being recycled. It may also use, sell or otherwise dispose of waste as respects which it has a duty to arrange disposal of under the Act. It may also sell etc. anything produced from such waste.

A WCA may buy or otherwise acquire waste with a view to recycling it, or it may use or dispose of by way of sale or otherwise to another person, waste belonging to the authority or anything produced from the waste.

Power of Secretary of State over waste

An innovatory form or direct control which central government can exercise in relation to waste is contained in s. 57. The Secretary of State is empowered to direct the holder of any waste management licence to accept and keep or accept and treat or dispose of controlled waste at specified places on specified terms (s. 57(1)). Furthermore, a notice may be served on any person who keeps controlled waste on any land to deliver the waste to a specified person with a view to its being treated or disposed of by that person (s. 57(2)). A direction may impose a requirement as respects waste of any specified kind or as respects any specified consignment of waste. A direction made under s. 57(2) may require the person who is directed to pay the specified person reasonable costs for treating or disposing of the waste (s. 57(4)). It is an offence to fail to comply with a direction (s. 57(5)).

Interference with waste sites

Section 60 makes it an offence for anyone to interfere with anything dumped at an authorised waste site or anything deposited in waste receptacles provided by a WCA or waste disposal contractor. It is also an offence for anyone to interfere with the contents of a waste receptacle which has been placed on any highway.

SPECIAL WASTE AND NON-CONTROLLED WASTE

Section 62 of the Environmental Protection Act 1990 gives the Secretary of State power to make regulations in relation to waste which, by reason of its nature, is difficult to treat or keep or dispose of. The regulations may provide for the transport and storage of waste as well as the keeping of relevant records. Regulations made under s. 62 will replace the Control of Pollution (Special Waste) Regulations 1980 (SI 1980/1709) made under the Control of Pollution Act 1974, s. 17. These make provision for fairly detailed control over the transport and disposal of special waste, an expression which is defined in the regulations.

Power is also given to the Secretary of State by s. 63 to make regulations providing that certain provisions of part II of the Act have effect in a prescribed area. The relevant provisions would have effect as if references in the provisions to controlled waste included a reference to mine, quarry or agricultural waste.

It is an offence under s. 63(2), subject to certain exceptions, for anyone to deposit waste other than controlled waste, or knowingly cause or knowingly permit the deposit of any waste other than controlled waste, in circumstances where, if the waste were special waste and any waste management licence were not in force, the individual in question would be guilty of an offence.

The civil liability provisions of s. 73(6) (see page 63) apply to dumping in contravention of s. 63(2).

INSPECTORS

The Secretary of State is given power by the Environmental Protection Act 1990, s. 68(2), to appoint suitably qualified persons as inspectors. A similar power to appoint inspectors is given to WRAs. An inspector may not be liable in any civil or criminal proceedings for anything done in the purported performance of duties under ss. 69 or 70 of the Act which are discussed below (s. 68(4)).

Section 69 confers wide powers on inspectors appointed under the Act including the right:

(a) to enter premises at any reasonable time, or at any time if there is an immediate risk of serious pollution or serious harm to human health,

(b) to take such measurements and photographs and recordings as is considered necessary,

(c) to make such examination and investigation as may be necessary and to require any person whom the inspector has reasonable cause to believe to be able to give information relevant to the examination, to answer questions and sign a declaration of the truth of the answers,

(d) to take samples of any articles or substances found on any premises which the inspector has power to enter, and of the air, water or land in, on, or in the vicinity of, the premises,

(e) to dismantle, take possession of and detain any article or substance which appears to the inspector to have caused or be likely to cause pollution of the environment or harm to human health.

It is an offence for any person without reasonable excuse to fail to comply with any requirements imposed by s. 69 or intentionally to obstruct an inspector in the performance of his or her powers or duties.

Section 70 gives an inspector power to seize and render harmless any article or substance found on any premises which the inspector has power to enter, if the inspector has reasonable cause to believe it to be a cause of imminent danger of serious pollution of the environment or serious harm to human health. It is an offence intentionally to obstruct an inspector in the exercise of his or her powers under the section.

DEFAULT POWERS OF THE SECRETARY OF STATE

It may happen, for a variety of reasons, that a WRA fails to carry out its duties in terms of the Environmental Protection Act 1990. Section 72 therefore gives power to the Secretary of State, if satisfied that a WRA has failed to carry out any function under the Act, to make an order declaring the authority to be in default. The relevant order may direct the authority to perform any function specified in the order as well as specify the manner in which and the time or times within which, the function is to be performed by the authority. If the defaulting authority fails to comply with any directions contained in the relevant order the Secretary of State may, instead of enforcing the order by mandamus (that is to say, by way of an order of the High Court), take over any function of the authority specified in the order.

ADDITIONAL CONTROLS OVER THE DUMPING OF REFUSE, ABANDONED VEHICLES ETC.

Section 2 of the Refuse Disposal (Amenity) Act 1978 provides that an offence is committed by any person who without lawful authority:

(a) abandons on any land in the open air, or on any other land forming part of a highway, a motor vehicle or anything which formed part of a motor vehicle and was removed from it in the course of dismantling the vehicle on the land; or

(b) abandons on any such land any thing other than a motor vehicle, being a thing which he has brought to the land for the purpose of abandoning it there.

Section 6 gives a local authority power to remove anything in its area (other than a motor vehicle) which is abandoned without lawful authority on any land in the open air or on any other land forming part of a highway.

Section 3 places a duty on a local authority to remove any vehicle abandoned without lawful authority in its area on any land in the open air or on any land forming part of a highway. There is no duty to remove any vehicle situated otherwise than on a road if the cost of removing the vehicle to the nearest highway would be unreasonably high. Section 4 empowers the authority to dispose of vehicles which have been removed under s. 3.

Power is given to the Secretary of State by s. 99 of the Road Traffic Regulation Act 1984 to make regulations relating to the removal of vehicles which have been abandoned without lawful authority or which have broken down on a road. Regulation 5(1) of the Removal and Disposal of Vehicles Regulations 1986 (SI 1986/183) gives local authorities power to remove abandoned vehicles.

Section 34 of the Public Health Act 1961 empowers a local authority (which includes a county council) to remove rubbish from any land in the open air which appears to the authority to be seriously detrimental to the amenities of the neighbourhood.

LITTER

Part IV of the Environmental Protection Act 1990 makes special provision in relation to litter, which constitutes a perennial problem in modern society. Section 87 provides:

(1) If any person throws down, drops or otherwise deposits in, into or from any place to which this section applies, and leaves, any thing whatsoever in such circumstances as to cause, or contribute to, or tend to lead to, the defacement by litter of any place to which this section applies, he shall, subject to subsection (2) below, be guilty of an offence.

(2) No offence is committed under this section where the depositing and leaving of the thing was —

(a) authorised by law, or
(b) done with the consent of the owner, occupier or other person or authority having control of the place in or into which that thing was deposited.

The section applies to:

(a) any public open place (defined as a place in the open air to which the public are entitled or permitted to have access without payment; and any covered place open to the air on at least one side and available for public use) and,
(b) certain other places such as Crown land, land of any designated statutory undertaker and land of any educational institution.

Liability under the section is strict it is suggested.

Fixed penalties

There is a system of so-called 'on the spot' fines for litter offences under the Environmental Protection Act 1990. Section 88 provides that where on any occasion an authorised officer of a litter authority finds a person whom he or she has reason to believe has committed an offence the officer may give the person a notice offering that person the opportunity of discharging any liablity to conviction for that offence by payment of a fixed penalty.

Highway etc. and litter

Highways, roads etc. are particularly susceptible to defacement by litter. Section 89 of the Act places a duty on each local authority as respects any relevant highway; the Secretary of State as respects any trunk road which is a special road and any relevant highway or relevant road for which he is responsible; each principal litter authority as respects its relevant land, and the appropriate Crown authority as respects its relevant land, to ensure that the land is, so far as is practicable, kept clear of litter and refuse.

A duty is also placed on each local authority as respects any relevant highway or relevant road for which it is responsible, or the Secretary of State as respects any trunk road which is a special road and any relevant highway or relevant road for which he is responsible, to ensure that the highway or road is, so far as is practicable, kept clean.

The section provides that in determining what standard is required as respects any description of land, highway or road for compliance with the above provisions regard is to be had to its character as well as the measures which are practicable in the circumstances. See the *Code of Practice on Litter and Refuse,* 1991.

Litter control areas

Power is given to the Secretary of State by s. 90 to prescribe, by order, descriptions of land which may be either designated as, or part of, a litter control area. The relevant land may be described by reference to either the ownership or occupation of the land or the activities carried on in it. The Litter Control Areas Order 1991 (SI 1991/1325) designates, *inter alia*, public car parks, shopping precincts, industrial or trading estates, cinemas, theatres, inland beach or the seashore and any esplanade or promenade. A principal litter authority other than a county council or joint board may designate any land in its area as, or part of, a litter control area. However, no litter control order may be made unless the authority is of the opinion that by reason of the presence of litter or refuse the condition of the land is, and unless they make the appropriate order is likely to continue to be, such as to be detrimental to the amenities of the locality.

Summary proceedings by private individuals

It is unusual for statutes relating to the environment to give private individuals in contradistinction to public authorities the right to take proceedings before the courts. An exception which has already been noted to such an approach has been seen in relation to part III of the Control of Pollution Act 1974 which allows individuals discomfited by noise to enlist the aid of the courts. As far as litter is concerned, the Environmental Protection Act 1990, s. 91, gives a private individual the right to complain to a magistrates' court on the ground that he or she is aggrieved by the defacement by litter or refuse of, *inter alia*, any relevant highway, any trunk road which is a special road, any relevant land of a principal litter authority or any relevant Crown land. A complaint may also be made by any person on the ground that that person is aggrieved by the want of cleanliness of any relevant highway or any trunk road which is a special road. A principal litter authority is not to be treated as a person aggrieved for the purposes of the section. Proceedings instituted under the section must be brought against the person who has the duty to keep the land clear under s. 89(1) or keep the highway clean under s. 89(2).

If the magistrates' court is satisfied that the highway authority or land in question is defaced by litter or refuse or, in the case of a highway, is wanting in cleanliness, the court may, subject to certain exceptions, make a litter abatement order requiring the defendant to clear away the litter or refuse or clean the highway within a time specified in the order (s. 89(6)). It is an offence to fail to comply with a litter abatement order.

Litter abatement notices

Section 92 of the Environmental Protection Act 1990 allows a principal litter authority defined by s. 86(2) as including a county council, district council and London Borough Council (other than a county council, regional council or joint board) to serve a litter abatement notice if satisfied, as respects any relevant land belonging to the Crown, statutory undertaker, educational institution or land within a litter control area of a local authority, that the land is defaced by litter or refuse or that defacement of it by litter or refuse is likely to recur. The notice may require that the litter or refuse be cleared within the time specified in the notice and/or prohibit permitting the land from becoming defaced by litter or refuse. As far as litter etc. on land is concerned, the notice must be served on the occupier of the land or, if unoccupied, on the owner of the land. The person served with the notice may appeal against the notice to a magistrates' court. It is an offence to fail to comply with or contravene the terms of such a notice. The provisions of a code of practice made under s. 89(7) are admissible in evidence in any proceedings under s. 92.

In the event of the person on whom a litter abatement notice is served failing to comply with the requirement imposed by the notice, the authority is empowered to enter the land and clear the litter or refuse and recover the cost. This power does not apply to relevant Crown land or land belonging to statutory undertakers.

Street litter control notices

It is common for premises such as retail shops to generate a considerable amount of refuse which is deposited on the pavement or street adjoining the premises. The Environmental Protection Act 1990 addresses this problem. Section 93 allows a principal litter authority other than a county council, with a view to preventing the accumulation of litter or refuse in and around any street or open land adjacent to any street, to issue street control notices imposing requirements on occupiers of premises in relation to litter or refuse.

Under s. 93(2) if the authority is satisfied that, in respect of any premises which are of a description prescribed by the Secretary of State under s. 94(1)(a) and have a frontage on a street in its area, that:

(a) there is recurrent defacement by litter or refuse of any land, being part of the street or open land adjacent to the street, which is in the vicinity of the premises, or

(b) the condition of any part of the premises which is open land in the vicinity of the frontage is, and if no notice is served is likely to continue to be, detrimental to the amenities of the locality by reason of the presence of litter or refuse, or

(c) there is produced, as a result of the activities carried on on the premises, quantities of litter or refuse of such nature and in such amounts as are likely to cause the defacement of any part of the street, or of open land adjacent to the street, which is in the vicinity of the premises,

the authority may serve a street litter control notice on the occupier or, if the premises are unoccupied, on the owner of the premises.

The Street Litter Control Notices Order 1991 (SI 1991/1324) prescribes certain types of commercial and retail premises, as well as certain descriptions of land, for the purposes of s. 94.

A control notice may impose requirements relating to the clearing of litter or refuse from the area in question and may require the provision or emptying of receptacles for litter or refuse (s. 94(4)).

Public registers

The modern trend of making environmental information more accessible to the general public is continued in part IV of the Environmental Protection Act 1990. Section 95 places a duty, as far as England and Wales is concerned, on each principal litter authority other than a county council, to maintain a register containing copies of all orders made by the authority under s.90(3) of the Act as well as all street litter control notices issued under s. 93(1). The register must be made available at all reasonable times for inspection by the public free of charge.

Additional controls over litter

Brief mention can be made here of the Litter Act 1983 which has been partly repealed by the Environmental Protection Act 1990. Under s. 3 the Secretary of State is empowered to make grants to any body for the purpose of assisting the body to encourage the public not to deface places by litter. Section 4 places a duty on each county council as well as the other litter authorities whose areas are included in the county (and where the county includes land in a national park without a park board, the national park committee for that park) to consult both among themselves and with such voluntary bodies as they consider appropriate about the steps which the various bodies propose to take for the purpose of abating litter. Each county council must prepare and from time to time revise a statement of the steps proposed.

Section 5 confers a power on each litter authority (defined in s. 10 to include, *inter alia*, a county council, a district council, and a London borough council) in England and Wales to provide and maintain litter bins in any street or public place. Authorities must make arrangements for the regular emptying and cleansing of any litter bins they provide or maintain under the section.

TRANSPORT OF CONTROLLED WASTE

We have seen how the Environmental Protection Act 1990 lays down a detailed and sophisticated regime as far as the deposit of controlled waste is concerned. However, significant environmental harm can ensue from the improper transport of waste. It is important, therefore, that carriers of waste are subject to some form of statutory control. The Control of Pollution (Amendment) Act 1989 makes provision for the registration of carriers of controlled waste. Section 1 provides:

> (1) Subject to the following provisions of this section, it shall be an offence for any person who is not a registered carrier of controlled waste,

in the course of any business of his or otherwise with a view to profit, to transport any controlled waste to or from any place in Great Britain.

(2) A person shall not be guilty of an offence under this section in respect of —

(a) the transport of controlled waste within the same premises between different places in those premises;
(b) the transport to a place in Great Britain of controlled waste which has been brought from a country or territory outside Great Britain and is not landed in Great Britain until it arrives at that place;
(c) the transport by air or sea of controlled waste from a place in Great Britain to a place outside Great Britain.

The Controlled Waste (Registration of Carriers and Seizure of Vehicles) Regulations 1991 (SI 1991/1624), made under s. 1(3), exempt WCAs, WDAs and the producers of controlled waste from registration.

Liability under s. 1 is strict it is suggested. However, under s. 1(4) it is a defence to show that the waste was transported in an emergency of which notice was given as soon as practicable after it occurred to the relevant disposal authority. It is also a defence that the appropriate individual neither knew nor had reasonable grounds for suspecting that what was being transported was controlled waste and that the person in question took all reasonable steps to ascertain whether it was such waste. Lastly, it is a defence that the defendant acted under instructions from his or her employer.

The regulation authority is empowered to refuse an application for registration, *inter alia*, if the applicant or another relevant person (as defined in s. 3(5) has been convicted of a prescribed offence and in the opinion of the authority it is undesirable for the applicant to be authorised to transport controlled waste. The authority must give reasons to a carrier of controlled waste if it decides to revoke the registration (SI 1991/1624, reg. 10). The period of registration is three years (reg. 11).

Under s. 4 of the Act, appeals against either the refusal of an application for registration or the revocation of registration may be made to the Secretary of State who has complete powers of review.

The Transfrontier Shipment of Hazardous Waste Regulations 1988 (SI 1988/1562) make provision for the consignment of hazardous waste to both EC and non-EC countries. The regulations make provision for the notification of appropriate authorities as well as contents of relevant documentation.

RADIOACTIVE WASTE

The disposal of radioactive waste is now dealt with by the Radioactive Substances Act 1993 which repeals the Radioactive Substances Act 1960.

Section 13 makes it an offence for any person other than a person authorised in terms of the Act, to dispose of, or cause or permit to be disposed of, any radioactive waste on or from any premises where that person's business is carried on, if that person knows or has reasonable grounds for believing it to be radioactive waste. A person who is not authorised under the Act, who receives waste for the purpose of its being disposed of, must not dispose of, or cause or permit to be disposed of any of that waste which the person knows, or has reasonable grounds for believing to be, radioactive waste. Power is given to the minister to exclude particular types of radioactive waste from any of the provisions of s. 13 either absolutely or subject to limitations or conditions.

Section 40 precludes for the purposes of any statutory provision to which the section applies, any account being taken of any radioactivity possessed by any substance or article or by any part of any premises. The section applies, *inter alia*, to part III of the Environmental Protection Act 1990. Therefore, a local authority could not invoke its nuisance removal powers by virtue of an accumulation of waste being radioactive.

SIX
Water and sewerage

Water is a *sine qua non* of human existence. Its importance in public health terms cannot be overestimated. It is imperative therefore that the public are supplied with water which is wholesome. Enteric diseases such as cholera, which gravely afflicted our Victorian forebears, are often water-borne. Just as it is fundamental that the water we drink is pure in quality, it is equally important that it is available in sufficient quantity to meet all domestic and commercial requirements. Such a truism can readily be forgiven when one remembers that until the Victorian era was well advanced, many of our towns did not possess a constant supply of water. Rather, the water supply was intermittent. This was because there was a tendency for the bodies responsible for the distribution of water to supply only enough to meet the immediate needs of the population. By failing to take account of the greater demands an expanding community would have for water, such a policy inevitably resulted in a shortage of water for the community. This so called 'droplet' method of water supply epitomised the parsimony of the period as far as public health matters were concerned.

During the 19th century there was much debate, both Parliamentary and public, about whether the responsibility for supplying water to the community should be in the hands of local authorities or private companies. As the century progressed there was a tendency for municipal authorities to take over the private water companies which supplied water to their areas.

This chapter also deals with sewerage and drainage which are closely linked with water supply. Unless a community is adequately provided with an effective system of sewerage and drainage it is likely that the water supply system will become contaminated and disease will spread. Water-borne diseases such as cholera were spread in the 19th century largely because of imperfect and often non-existence municipal sewerage systems. Epidemics were often caused by contaminated sewage polluting the public water supply.

The chapter deals first with the modern law relating to water supply and then goes on to discuss sewerage.

WATER SUPPLY

The responsibility for providing water to the community has been a contentious issue since the 19th century at least. Essentially, debate has centred on whether the service should rest with local authorities or be in the hands of private companies. As far as the recent past is concerned, in accordance with Conservative Party policy, the water industry was privatised under the Water Act 1989. The legislation governing water supply is now contained in the Water Industry Act 1991, the main provisions of which are now discussed.

Duty to supply water

Each water undertaker must develop and maintain an efficient and economical system of water supply within its area and ensure that all necessary arrangements have been made for providing supplies of water to premises in that area and for making supplies of water available to persons who demand them (Water Industry Act 1991, s. 37). Each undertaker must also maintain, improve and extend water mains and pipes to the extent necessary to secure that the undertaker is, and continues to be, able to meet its obligations under the Act. The obligations imposed by s. 37 are enforceable by the Secretary of State who is empowered by s. 38 to make regulations for the purpose of making contraventions of requirements prescribed in the regulations a breach of the statutory duty imposed by s. 37. Regulations may also establish overall standards of performance.

The Director General of Water Services is required by s. 38A (inserted by the Competition and Service (Utilities) Act 1992 to collect information about the levels of overall performance achieved by water undertakers in connection with the provision of water supplies. Each water undertaker must take steps to inform its customers of the standards of overall performance established under s. 38 which are applicable to it and also to inform its customers of its level of performance in respect of the applicable standards (s. 38B).

Major supplies of water

It may happen that the public interest demands that one water undertaker be provided with water by another undertaker. For example, it may be desirable for one undertaking to derive water from a reservoir or other water source owned by another. Unfortunately the relevant parties may be unable to agree on the matter. The Water Industry Act 1991, s. 40 (as substituted by the Competition and Service (Utilities) Act 1992) therefore allows the Director General of Water Services to make an order, on the application of a water undertaker or a person who has applied to become a water undertaker, requiring another undertaker to give the applicant a supply of water in bulk, and on such terms and conditions as may be provided in the order, where it appears necessary or expedient for the purposes of securing the efficient use of water resources or the efficient supply of water that the other undertaker should give the supply to the applicant. Such an order can only be made if the Director is satisfied that the giving and taking of the supply cannot be secured by agreement. In exercising powers under the section the Director is placed under a duty, *inter alia*, to have regard to the desirability of facilitating effective competition within the water supply industry.

Requests to supply water

While the philosophy behind the Water Industry Act 1991 is to privatise the public water supply, it is obvious that simply giving water companies a free hand in choosing which premises should be served with water could be unacceptable, not least from a public health viewpoint. Section 41 therefore places a duty on a water undertaker to provide a water main to be used for providing such supplies of water to premises in a particular locality in its area as are sufficient for domestic purposes, if the undertaker is served with a notice by one or more persons, requiring the undertaker to provide the main. The relevant premises are premises consisting of buildings or parts of buildings, or premises which will so consist of these when appropriate building works are carried out. Therefore, a builder could make the relevant request in respect of a proposed development.

The obligation to supply a main is conditional on the requirements imposed by s. 42 being met. That section makes provision, *inter alia*, for the water undertaker to require the person who made the request, first, to give the undertaker such undertakings as appear reasonable and, secondly, to give such security as the undertaker may reasonably require if the person is not a local authority.

The classes of persons who are entitled to require the provision of a water main for any locality are specified in s. 41(2). They include the owner of any premises in that locality, the owner and occupier of any premises in that locality, and the local authority within whose area the whole or part of the locality is situated. Under s. 41(3) the duty imposed by the section to provide a water main is owed to the person who requries the provision of the main or each of the persons who joins in doing so. Where a duty is owed to any person, any breach of the duty which causes loss or damage becomes actionable at the suit of that person. In the absence of authority as to rules of remoteness of damage which should obtain in determining what loss is recoverable, it is suggested that the rule in *Re Polemis and Furness, Withy & Co. Ltd* [1921] 3 KB 560 would apply. Accordingly, all loss arising as a direct consequence of the breach in question would be recoverable even though such damage was not foreseeable.

Domestic connections

The owner or occupier of any premises which consists in the whole or in part of a building (or are premises on which any person is proposing to erect any building or part of a building) may serve notice on a water undertaker requiring it, for the purpose of providing a supply of water for domestic purposes, to connect a service pipe to those premises from the main (Water Industry Act 1991, s. 45). The undertaker must make the conection at the expense of the person serving the notice. The undertaker's duty arises only if the main with which the service pipe is required to be connected is neither a trunk main (as defined in s. 219) nor a water main which is, or is to be, used solely for the purpose of supplying water otherwise than for domestic purposes, and also any conditions which the undertaker may have imposed under s. 47 (e.g., as to security) have been satisfied. The duty to effect a connection arises whether or not the service pipe to which the notice relates has been laid when the notice is served.

In order to be able to connect a service pipe to the mains, ancillary works (such as excavation) may have to be carried out. The undertaker must do this at the expense of the person serving the notice (s. 46). The section specifically relates to the laying of so much of the service pipe to be connected with the water main as is necessary to make that connection in a street. Where the owner or occupier of any premises serves a connection notice on a water undertaker, the undertaker may require compliance with the requirements listed in s. 47. These include a requirement to the effect that the person who served the notice give the undertaker reasonable security, and, that a water meter be installed. It may also be required that a separate service pipe provided to each house or building on the relevant premises or where different parts of the building are separately occupied to each of those parts. Section 50 restricts the imposition of a condition requiring the provision of a separate service pipe to a house which has already been connected to the main and in respect of which a connection notice is served.

Domestic supplies

Section 52 of the Act places a duty on the undertaker as far as the domestic supply of water to any premises is concerned to supply those premises with water sufficient for domestic purposes and to maintain the connection between the undertaker's water main and the service pipe by which that supply is provided to those premises. The duty to supply the premises with water arises only if a demand for a supply of water for domestic purposes has been made in accordance with the provisions of the section or the premises were provided with water before 1 September 1989, and there has been no interruption of that supply since the demand was made or since 1 September 1989. Interruptions in the supply due to works being carried out are ignored but a disconnection by the undertaker ranks as an interruption.

Under s. 53, where a demand has been made to a water undertaker to supply water for domestic purposes, the undertaker may impose certain conditions, including one to the effect that where the supply has been disconnected as a result of non-payment, the amount owed must be paid plus the expenses reasonably incurred in cutting off the supply. Also an undertaker may impose a condition to the effect that there be no contravention of the regulations made under s. 74 in relation to the water fittings used in the premises. A duty imposed on a water undertaker under s. 52 is owed to the consumer (s. 54(1)), and any breach of the duty which causes the consumer loss or damage is actionable by the consumer (s. 54(2)).

Non-domestic water supplies

The Act imposes different duties on a water undertaker in respect of the supply of water for non-domestic purposes from those applicable to the supply of water for domestic purposes. Section 55 provides that there is a duty to provide a non-domestic water supply unless it would necessitate the undertaker incurring unreasonable expenditure in carrying out works in order to meet its existing and probable future obligations to supply water for domestic or other purposes, or would put at risk the ability of the undertaker to meet any of such obligations. No duty to provide a new non-domestic supply arises if there is a contravention of regulations made under s. 74 in relation to the water fittings used or to be used in connection with the supply of water to the premises, or the use of water in those premises.

Any terms or conditions governing a non-domestic supply which cannot be agreed between the parties concerned will be determined by the Director (s. 56). The Director is also empowered to determine any disputes arising between any person and a water undertaker in relation to s. 55(3) and (4) (i.e., whether a proposed supply would prejudice existing obligations or whether there would be a contravention in relation to the water fittings etc.).

Disconnections of water supply

Section 60 allows a water undertaker to disconnect a service pipe or otherwise cut off a supply of water to any premises if it is reasonable for the disconnection to be made or the supply to be cut off for the purpose of carrying out works. Section 61 allows disconnection for non-payment of charges for the supply of water. A disconnection may also be made at the request of the consumer (s. 62).

Means of supply

A water undertaker may, by virtue of s. 64(1) (as amended), require the provision of a separate service pipe (as defined in s. 219) to any premises which consist in a house or any other building or part of a building, being in the case of a building, a part which is separately occupied, and already supplied with water by the undertaker but without a separate service pipe. Where the supply of water to two or more houses is provided wholly or partly by the same service pipe, the water undertaker is not entitled to require the provision of a separate service pipe to those houses until any one of a number of conditions contained in subsection (2) are satisfied. Such conditions include: part of the service pipe belonging to someone other than the undertaker becoming so defective as to require renewal or no longer being sufficient to meet the requirements of the houses concerned; a payment in respect of the supply of water to any of those houses remaining unpaid; the houses being, by virtue of structural alterations to one or more of them, converted into a large number of houses.

Any dispute between a water undertaker and any other person as to whether any condition of a kind mentioned in subsection (2) has been met falls to be determined by the Director General of Water Services.

Under s. 64(3), if an undertaker serves notice on a consumer requiring the provision of a separate service pipe to the consumer's premises, the consumer is placed under a duty to lay, within three months after the service of the notice, so much of the required pipe as the undertaker is not under a duty to lay (in effect that part of the service pipe which is not owned by the undertaker). In the face of default on the part of the person on whom notice is served, the undertaker is empowered to carry out the works and recover expenses.

Duties in relation to water pressure etc.

Since Victorian times it has been traditional for Parliament to require public water suppliers to maintain a certain level of pressure in their water mains. Section 65(1) of the Water Industry Act 1991 places a duty on a water undertaker to cause the water in its mains which are used for providing supplies of water for domestic purposes, or have fire hydrants fixed on them, to be available constantly and at such a pressure as will cause the water to reach the top of the topmost storey of every building within the undertaker's area. However, the undertaker is not required to provide a water supply at a height greater than that to which it would flow by gravitation through its water mains from the service reservoir or tank from which the supply is taken.

The section goes on to make exceptions from the duty to provide the type of water supply described above, for example, if it is necessary to reduce the supply for the carrying out of any works. Furthermore, the Secretary of State is empowered by the section to make an order modifying the statutory duties in relation to any undertaker.

Power is given to a water undertaker by s. 66(1) to require the provision of a cistern fitted with a float-operated valve to be provided to any building or part of a building, the supply to which need not be constant (i.e., non-domestic premises) or houses to which water is required to be delivered at a level above a point 10.5 metres below the draw-off level of the service reservoir or tank from which the supply of water is being provided by the undertaker to the premises in question. The power to compel the provision of cisterns etc. in houses, only exists in relation to houses the erection of which was commenced after 1 September 1989. In the face of default on the part of the consumer in question, the undertaker is empowered to provide the cistern in question and recover expenses from the owner of the premises.

Water quality and prevention from contamination

Perhaps the most important requisite for any water supply concerns its wholesomeness. Section 67 of the Water Industry Act 1991 confers wide power on the Secretary of State to make regulations specifying standards as to wholesomeness (see the Water Supply (Water Quality) Regulations 1989 (SI 1989/1147) amended by SI 1991/1837 and the Private Water Supplies Regulations 1991 (SI 1991/2790).

Section 68 places a general duty on a water undertaker when supplying water to any premises for domestic or food purposes to supply only water which is wholesome at the time of supply and to ensure, so far as is reasonably practicable, that, in relation to each source or combination of sources from which that undertaker supplies water to premises for domestic or food production purposes, there is in general no deterioration in the quality of the water which is supplied from that source or combination of sources. The expression 'wholesome' is not defined in the Act. However, in *McColl* v *Strathclyde Regional Council* 1983 SC 225 it was held that 'wholesome' in the context of the Water (Scotland) Act 1980 meant that the water in question was free from contamination and pleasant to drink.

The duty imposed by s. 68 on the undertaker essentially consists of ensuring that the water is wholesome while the water is in the undertaker's pipes. However, the water is to be regarded as unwholesome if it has become so after it has left the pipes of the undertaker if it is still subject to pressure from a water main and has become unwholesome as a result of the undertaker's failure to take the necessary steps to secure the elimination, or reduction to a minimum, of any prescribed risk that the water would cease to be wholesome after leaving the undertaker's pipes. Therefore, for example, if the undertaker fails to take appropriate measures to secure compliance with a requirement imposed under s. 47(2)(g) to the effect that water fittings used in the appropriate premises be in confirmity with the provisions of s. 74 (which relates to the prevention of water contamination) the duty imposed by s. 68 would be breached.

Section 69 empowers the Secretary of State by regulations to require an undertaker to take such steps as may be prescribed for the purposes of securing compliance with s. 68.

Section 70 makes it an offence for a water undertaker to provide water which is unfit for human consumption. Liability under the section is strict it is suggested. However, the section provides a defence that the undertaker had no reasonable grounds for suspecting that the water would be used for human consumption, or that the undertaker took all reasonable steps and exercised all due diligence for securing that the water was fit for human consumption when it left the undertaker's pipes, or that the water was not used for human consumption.

Contamination and wastage

Section 72 makes it an offence for any person by whose act or neglect water in any waterworks, which is used or is likely to be used for human consumption or domestic purposes or for manufacturing food or drink for human consumption, is polluted or likely to be polluted. Liability under the statute is strict it is suggested. However, exceptions are made in relation to pollution caused by farming or by the reasonable use of oil or tar on public roads if the highway authority has taken all reasonable measures to prevent the oil or tar and any liquid or matter resulting from the use of oil or tar from polluting the water in any waterworks.

Section 73 makes it an offence for anyone who is the owner or occupier of premises to which a supply of water is provided by a water undertaker intentionally or negligently to cause or suffer any water fitting to be or to remain out of order, or to be so constructed or adapted or used that the water supply system, or the water supplied to the premises, is or is likely to be contaminated or wasted.

Since Victorian times, it has been customary for legislation to regulate the nature and efficiency of water fittings in premises, for example, cisterns and ball valves. Section 74 gives the Secretary of State power to make regulations for preventing the contamination of water supplies by the return of any substance from supplied premises to the main supplies; for securing that water which is in any pipe connected with any main or other pipe or which has been supplied to any premises by a water undertaker, is not contaminated, and that its quality and suitability for particular purposes is not prejudiced before it is used; and lastly for preventing water wastage.

Section 76 gives a water undertaker power in the face of a serious deficiency of water to prohibit or restrict the use of hosepipes for watering private gardens or washing private cars in the whole or part of its area. It is an offence for any person to contravene such a prohibition.

Local authority functions

A local authority must keep itself informed about the wholesomeness and sufficiency of water supplies provided to premises in its area (s. 77). It must notify any water undertaker of anything appearing to it to suggest that any supply by that undertaker of water for domestic or food production purposes in the area of the local authority is, has been, or is likely to become, unwholesome or insufficient for domestic purposes, or that the unwholesomeness or insufficiency of any supply is, was, or is likely to cause a danger to life or health (s. 78).

Private water supplies are more likely to become contaminated than public supplies. Section 80(1) provides that a local authority may serve a notice on the owner and/or occupier of premises served by a private water supply and/or the owner and/or occupier of the source of the supply and/or any person who exercises powers of management or control in relation to the source if it is satisfied:

(a) that any water which is being, has been or is likely to be supplied for domestic or food production purposes to those premises by means of that private supply is not, was not, or as the case may be, is likely not to be wholesome; or

(b) that that private supply is failing, has failed or is likely to fail to provide to any house on those premises such a supply of wholesome water as (so far as that house is concerned) is sufficient for domestic purposes.

The notice may designate the steps which are to be taken by the local authority itself as well as the person served. The local authority may require that a supply of water is provided by a water undertaker or other person to the premises. If it has specified that it intends itself to take certain remedial measures then it may exercise the appropriate powers contained in part VI of the Act (compulsory purchase powers and powers to lay pipes in streets) (s. 83).

In the face of default on the part of the person on whom notice is served, the local authority may under s. 82 itself take the necessary remedial action and recover from that person any expenses reasonably incurred.

Section 84 confers on any person designated for the purpose by a local authority the right to enter any premises in order to ascertain if there has been a contravention of s. 72 which relates to contamination of water sources. Power is given to carry out inspections, measurements and tests on premises entered.

Under the Public Health Act 1936, s. 140, if a local authority is of the opinion that the water from any well, tank or other source of supply not vested in it, being water which is, or is likely to be used for, domestic purposes or in the preparation of food or drink for human consumption, is or is likely to become so polluted as to be prejudicial to health, the authority may apply to a magistrates' court for an order closing the supply, either permanently or temporarily. The order may permit the supply to remain but restrict its use for certain purposes only.

Fluoridation

It has been known for some time that the addition of fluoride to the water supply has a beneficial effect on the teeth of children. The Water (Fluoridation) Act 1985 (now repealed) gave water authorities power to add fluoride to water supplies intended for human consumption. This Act was not universally welcomed. It was felt by some that the Act allowed, in effect, compulsory medication of the entire public served by the water supply in question for the benefit of those who could derive an appropriate dose of fluoride by other means. Section 87 of the Water Industry Act 1991 gives a district health authority power to apply in writing to a water undertaker for the water supplied within an area specified in the notice to be fluoridated. While the application is still in force, the fluoride content of the water may be increased by the undertaker only by the use of fluoride compounds mentioned in the section. Power is given to the Secretary of State to add to or remove any compound mentioned. Schedule 7 to the Act allows schemes for the fluoridation of water made before 1985 to be continued subject to certain conditions.

SEWERAGE

Just as water's importance cannot be overestimated, an adequate and sufficient sewerage system is essential to any community. Until recent years the responsibility of providing adequate sewers and drains has been that of the local authority. Now, since 1989, the duty falls to a private sewerage undertaker.

Duty to provide a sewerage system

Section 94(1) of the Water Industry Act 1991 places a duty on every sewerage undertaker:

(a) to provide, improve and extend such a system of public sewers (whether inside its area or elsewhere) and so to cleanse and maintain those sewers as to ensure that that area is and continues to be effectually drained; and

(b) to make provision for the emptying of those sewers and such further provision (whether inside its area or elsewhere) as is necessary from time to time for effectual dealing, by means of sewage disposal works or otherwise, with the contents of those sewers.

Section 94(2) provides that in performing its duty under s. 94(1) the undertaker is required to have regard:

(a) to its existing and likely future obligations to allow for the discharge of trade effluent into its public sewers; and

(b) to the need to provide for the disposal of trade effluent which is so discharged.

Section 219(1) defines the expression 'sewer' as including all sewers and drains within the meaning of the Act, which are used for the drainage of buildings and yards appurtenant to buildings. The expression 'drain' is defined as meaning a drain for the drainage of one building or of any buildings or yards appurtenant to buildings within the same curtilage.

In order to clarify whether any conduct by a sewerage undertaker amounts to a breach of its duties and to establish overall standards of performance in relation to the provision of sewerage services by an undertaker, s. 95 empowers the Secretary of State to make regulations which provide for contraventions of such requirements as may be prescribed to be treated as breaches of statutory duty. The regulations may provide that if a sewerage undertaker fails to meet a prescribed standard it is required to pay such amount as may be prescribed to any person who is affected by the failure and is of a prescribed description. The Water Supply and Sewerage Services (Customer Service Standards) Regulations 1989 (SI 1989/1159) amended by SI 1989/1383 have effect as if made under this section.

Performance of undertaker's duties by local authorities

Section 97 empowers a local authority, defined as including, *inter alia*, the Commission for the New Towns and a development corporation, to carry out sewerage functions on behalf of a sewerage undertaker in relation to the whole or part of the authority's area, together with parts of any adjacent areas of other authorities. The content of any agreement made may not, however, affect the right of any person to any remedy against the sewerage undertaker in respect of the carrying out of the undertaker's sewerage functions or of any failure to carry them out.

Provision of public sewers

The Water Industry Act 1991 establishes the principle that both the owner and occupier of domestic premises have a statutory right for the premises they occupy to be provided with a public sewer. Section 98 provides that each sewerage undertaker has a duty to provide a public sewer to be used for the drainage of domestic premises in its area if the undertaker is required to provide the sewer by a notice served on the undertaker. There is a duty to provide a public sewer only to premises on which there are buildings or, on which it is proposed to erect buildings. Those entitled to require the provision of a public sewer for any locality include:

(a) the owner of any premises in the locality;
(b) the occupier of any premises in that locality; and
(c) any local authority within whose area the whole or any part of that locality is situated.

A duty of care is owed by the undertaker to provide a public sewer to the person who required the provision of the sewer. Any loss or damage caused to the person who requested the provision of a sewer by the undertaker's failure to provide it is actionable at the suit of that person. However, in any proceedings brought against a sewerage undertaker it is a defence to show that the undertaker took all reasonable steps and exercised all due diligence to avoid the breach. Under s. 101 a sewerage undertaker does not breach a duty imposed by s. 98 in relation to any locality unless the period of six months beginning with the relevant day (as defined in s. 101) has expired and the sewerage undertaker has not, before the end of that period, laid a public sewer to enable drains and private sewers to be used for the drainage of premises in that locality by communicating with the public sewer.

Before providing a public sewer under s. 98, a sewerage undertaker can under s. 99, require the person or persons who made the request for the provision of the sewer to pay the undertaker the appropriate sum of money (which is calculated in accordance with the rules contained in ss. 99 and 100) and to give such security as is reasonably required.

Adoption of sewers and disposal works

In order to allow a sewerage undertaker to provide an effective sewerage system, s. 102 empowers it to acquire relevant sewers and sewage treatment works situated within its area. The undertaker is required to give notice of a proposal to acquire to the owner or owners of the sewer etc. In deciding if a sewer etc. should be acquired an undertaker is required to have regard to a variety of factors including whether the sewer etc. is required for any general system of sewerage or sewage disposal which the undertaker has provided, or proposes to provide.

Under s. 104 a sewerage undertaker is empowered to make an agreement with any person constructing any sewer or sewerage disposal works to the effect that the undertaker will acquire the works upon completion. Furthermore, the person (normally a builder) constructing or proposing to construct a sewer, may request the relevant sewerage undertaker to make an agreement under s. 104. Any such agreement made by a sewerage undertaker becomes enforceable against the undertaker by the owner or occupier for the time being of any premises served by the sewer.

Section 105 makes provision for appeals in relation to the adoption of sewers or sewage disposal works. The section gives the owner of any sewer or sewage disposal works the right to appeal to the Director General of Water Services if aggrieved by the proposal of a sewerage undertaker either to acquire or not to acquire the sewer or works.

Power to appeal to the Director is also given to a person constructing or proposing to construct a drain, sewer or sewage treatment works where the sewerage undertaker has refused an application under s. 104 or has offered to grant such an application on terms to which that person objects. The Director is given full powers of review in determining such an appeal.

Right to communicate with public sewers

The Water Industry Act 1991 establishes the principle that one has a general right to connect one's drains to a public sewer. Under s. 106 the owner or occupier of any premises or the owner of any private sewer which drains premises, is given the right to connect drains or sewers with the public sewer of a sewerage undertaker. The right extends to discharging foul and surface water from the premises or private sewer. However, the section does not confer any right to discharge either directly or indirectly into a public sewer any liquid from a factory, other than domestic sewage or surface or storm water, or any liquid from a manufacturing process or any liquid which is prohibited by or under any enactment. Furthermore, where separate public sewers are provided for foul water and for surface water, no right is conferred to discharge either directly or indirectly, foul water into any sewer provided for surface water and vice versa.

Any person who wishes to have drains connected with a public sewer must give notice to the sewerage undertaker who in turn may refuse to permit the communication to be made if it appears that the mode of construction or condition of the drain or sewer is such that the making of the communication would be prejudicial to the undertaker's sewerage system. An appeal may be made to the Director against an undertaker's refusal to permit connection. It is important that connections to a public sewer are effectively made, otherwise the flow in the public sewer could be impeded and the sewer could block. Section 107 therefore gives a sewerage undertaker the right to effect the communication of a private drain etc. with the public sewer. Power is given to the undertaker to require payment for the carrying out of the works.

It is an offence under s. 109 for any person to cause a drain or sewer to communicate with a public sewer in contravention of provisions of the Act. Liability under the section is strict it is suggested.

If a sewerage undertaker (or a person who has applied to be appointed a sewerage undertaker), wishes to have a sewerage system connected with another undertaker's system and the two cannot reach agreement then the Director can order connection on terms and conditions provided in the order (s. 110A).

Restrictions on use of sewers

The sewerage system is susceptible to misuse. Sewers can easily become blocked, for example, if large items such as building bricks and rubble enter the system either by accident or by reason of malice. Furthermore, the efficacy of sewage treatment works can be impaired if substances harmful to the biological process involved enter the works. In order to protect sewers, sewage treatment works and workers, s. 111(1) makes it an offence for any person to throw, empty or pass into any public sewer, or into any drain or sewer communicating with a public sewer:

(a) any matter likely to injure the sewer or drain, to interfere with the free flow of its contents or to affect prejudicially the treatment and disposal of its contents; or

(b) any such chemical refuse or waste steam, or any such liquid of a temperature higher than 110 degrees Fahrenheit, as by virtue of subsection (2) below is a prohibited substance; or

(c) any petroleum spirit or carbide of calcium.

Subsection (2) provides.

For the purposes of subsection (1) above, chemical refuse, waste steam or a liquid of a temperature higher than that mentioned in that subsection is a prohibited substance if (either alone or in combination with the contents of the sewer or drain in question) it is or, in the case of the liquid, is when so heated —

(a) dangerous;
(b) the cause of a nuisance; or
(c) injurious, or likely to cause injury, to health.

Liability under the section is strict it is suggested.

General sewerage schemes

Sometimes a builder may propose to construct a drain or sewer which could be integrated in a general sewerage system which a sewerage undertaker provides or proposes to provide. The drain or sewer however, may be of insufficient dimensions to be satisfactorily integrated in such a general sewerage system which the undertaker provides or proposes to provide. In such circumstances to avoid unnecessary duplication s. 112 empowers the undertaker to require the appropriate person to construct the drain or sewer in a different manner, as regards material or size of pipes, depth, fall, direction or outfall or otherwise. An appeal may be made to the Director against any requirements imposed under the section. The Director has complete powers of review in the matter.

A person on whom requirements are imposed by a sewerage undertaker must comply with those requirements. An undertaker which exercises the powers conferred by the section must repay the person constructing the drain or sewer the extra expenses reasonably incurred.

Power to alter drainage systems

Under s. 113 where any premises have a drain or sewer communicating with a public sewer or cesspool, but the system of drainage, though sufficient for the effectual drainage of the premises, is not adapted to the sewerage system of the area, or is, in the opinion of the sewerage undertaker for the area, otherwise objectionable, the undertaker may, at its own expense, close the existing drain or sewer, or fill up the cesspool, and carry out any work necessary for that purpose. The undertaker must first provide, in a position equally convenient to the owner of the premises in question, a drain or sewer which is equally effectual for the drainage of the premises and also communicates with a public sewer. The sewerage undertaker who proposes to carry out any work under the section, is required to give notice of its proposals to the owner of the premises in question who may refer the matter to the Director for determination.

Power to investigate a defective drain or sewer

Section 114 gives a sewerage undertaker the power to test any private drain or sewer connecting with a public sewer if there are reasonable grounds for believing: (a) that the drain or sewer is in such a condition as to be injurious, or likely to cause injury, to health or to be a nuisance, or (b) that the drain or sewer is so defective as to admit subsoil water. Power is given to open the relevant ground.

TRADE EFFLUENT

Effluent from industrial premises can have a profound detrimental effect on both sewers and sewage treatment works. Special controls therefore are needed to ensure such effluent does not pose potential harm to the sewerage system. The Water Industry Act 1991 therefore establishes a separate legal regime for the control of trade effluent.

Discharge of effluent into public sewer

Section 118 establishes the general principle that the occupier of any trade premises in the area of a sewerage undertaker may discharge any trade effluent proceeding from those premises into the undertaker's public sewers by means of a drain or sewer with the undertaker's consent. The section provides that the restrictions imposed by s. 106 (right to communicate with public sewer) and s. 111 (restriction on use of public sewer) have no effect in relation to trade effluent which is lawfully discharged in conformity with the provisions of the Act dealing with trade effluent. It is an offence to discharge trade effluent without the requisite consent. Liability under the section is strict it is suggested.

Consents etc.

In order to obtain consent to discharge trade effluent, notice must be served by owner or occupier on the undertaker (s. 119). The application must state the nature or composition of the trade effluent, the maximum quantity of the trade effluent which is proposed to be discharged on any one day, and the highest rate at which it is proposed to discharge the trade effluent.

Special category effluent

Special provision is made in relation to trade effluent of a potentially harmful nature. By s. 138(1) effluent is 'special category effluent' if:

> (a) such substances as may be described under this Act are present in the effluent or are present in the effluent in prescribed concentrations; or
> (b) the effluent derives from any such process as may be so prescribed or from a process involving the use of prescribed substances in quantities which exceed the prescribed amounts.

Under s. 120 if an application is made under s. 119 to discharge special category effluent then the undertaker must refer to the Secretary of State the question whether the discharges should be prohibited and whether, if they are not prohibited, any requirements should be imposed as to the conditions on which they are made. However, no duty to refer the application to the Secretary of State arises if the undertaker refuses to give consent to the application.

Conditions of consent
Wide power is conferred on a sewerage undertaker in relation to giving consent to the discharge of trade effluents into the public sewer. Section 121(1) gives power to the undertaker to give consent either conditionally or unconditionally. If conditions are imposed they can be imposed in relation, *inter alia*, to:

(a) the sewer or sewers into which the trade effluent may be discharged;

(b) the nature or composition of the trade effluent which may be discharged;

(c) the maximum quantity of trade effluent which may be discharged on any one day, either generally or into a particular sewer; and

(d) the highest rate at which trade effluent may be discharged, either generally or into a particular sewer.

Section 121(2) goes on to specify other conditions which an undertaker may impose in relation to the discharge of effluent from trade premises. These include:

(a) the period or periods of the day during which the trade effluent may be discharged from the trade premises into the sewer,

(b) the temperature of the trade effluent at the time when it is discharged into the sewer, and its acidity or alkalinity at that time,

(c) the payment by the occupier of the trade premises to the undertaker of charges for the reception of the trade effluent into the sewer and for the disposal of the effluent.

Appeals
Any person aggrieved by the refusal of a sewerage undertaker to give a consent to the discharge of trade effluent into a public sewer or the decision of an undertaker to attach conditions to consent may, under s. 122, appeal to the Director who has complete powers of review.

As far as an appeal concerning special category effluent is concerned, s. 123 provides that where no reference has been made to the Secretary of State by the undertaker, the Director is not allowed to determine the appeal otherwise than by upholding a refusal, unless, *inter alia*, the Director has referred the matter to the Secretary of State and copies of the reference have been served on the owner or occupier of the trade premises in question (according to whether the discharges to which the reference relates are to be by the owner or occupier), and also copies have been served on the undertaker.

Variation of consents

The nature, substance and quantity of trade effluent may change with the passage of time, necessitating different control measures on the part of the sewerage undertaker. Power is therefore given to a sewerage undertaker by s. 124 to vary the conditions which it has attached to any consent to discharge trade effluent. However, the conditions relating to a consent cannot be reviewed within two years from the date the consent was given without the agreement of the owner and occupier of the premises. Under s. 125 a variation can be made within two years if the sewerage undertaker considers it necessary to do so in order to provide proper protection for persons likely to be affected by the discharges. However, if a variation is made under s. 125, compensation is payable to the owner and occupier of the premises unless the undertaker is of the opinion that the variation is required because of a change of circumstances which has occurred since the consent was granted, the change which could not reasonably have been foreseen when the consent was granted. Compensation is not payable if the circumstances necessitating the variation have been brought about as a consequence of consents for discharges given after the beginning of the two year period.

An appeal against a variation of consent can be made under s. 126 to the Director who has complete powers of review in the matter.

Subject to certain conditions, consents relating to any special category effluent may be reviewed by the Secretary of State under s. 127. The Secretary of State may review whether the discharges authorised by the consent should be prohibited, and if they are not prohibited, whether any requirements should be imposed governing the discharge in question.

Agreements for the disposal of trade effluent

In certain circumstances it is desirable from the point of view of both the industrialist and the sewerage undertaker that they, in effect, enter into a commercial agreement for the disposal of trade effluent. Section 129 empowers a sewerage undertaker to enter into and carry into effect an agreement with the owner or occupier of any trade premises within its area for the reception and disposal by the undertaker of any trade effluent produced on those premises. The undertaker may also enter into an agreement with the owner and occupier of any premises to remove and dispose of substances produced in the course of treating any trade effluent on or in connection with those premises. Therefore, the undertaker could make an agreement to dispose of waste matter which has been extracted from trade effluent produced elsewhere than the premises in question.

Section 131 gives the Secretary of State power to review an agreement concerning special category effluent between a sewerage undertaker and the owner or occupier of any premises. The matters which can be reviewed are (a) whether the operations which, for the purposes of or in connection with the reception or disposal of the effluent, are carried out in pursuance of the agreement should be prohibited and (b), if not, whether any requirements should be imposed as to the conditions on which the operations are carried out. The section precludes the review of certain kinds of agreements.

Sewer maps

In order that members of the public have the opportunity to ascertain the location of public sewers and drains vested in a sewerage undertaker, s. 199 places a duty on every sewerage undertaker to keep records of the location of its sewers. The records are required to be made available to the public for inspection.

Defective drains etc.

Section 48 (as amended) of the Public Health Act 1936 empowers a local authority to examine and test a sanitary convenience, drain, private sewer or cesspool which is believed to be in such a condition as to be prejudicial to health or a nuisance. A local authority may also examine and test any drain or private sewer directly or indirectly communicating with a public sewer which it believes is so defective as to admit subsoil water.

Section 50 of the 1936 Act gives a local authority power to compel the remedying of leaking cesspools (defined by s. 90 as including septic tanks). An appeal may be made against a notice to a magistrates' court.

Section 17 of the Public Health Act 1961 gives power to a local authority to repair defective drains, sewers, water closets, waste pipes and soil pipes which can be sufficiently repaired at a cost not exceeding £250 (which can be increased by statutory instrument). The costs may be recovered from the owner or occupier of the premises concerned. In the case of a drain or private sewer the cost may be recovered from the owner of premises drained by means of it, and in the case of a sewer, the owner of the sewer. Power is also given to a local authority to serve notice on the owner or occupier of premises on which there appears to be a drain, private sewer, water closet, waste pipe or soil pipe which is stopped up to remove the defect within 48 hours from the service of the notice. If the notice is not complied with the local authority may carry out the works and recover costs from the person on whom the notice was served.

SEVEN
Public health control of food

The quality of the food we eat is of fundamental importance to our physical well-being. The legal control over the quality and composition of food therefore assumes a position of great significance in the field of environmental health. However, it was only in the second half of the Victorian era that Parliament deemed it appropriate to intervene and introduce legislation to secure the fitness of our food. The Adulteration of Food and Drugs Act 1872 (35 & 36 Vict c. 74) and the Sale of Food and Drugs Act 1875 represented a determined attempt to suppress mainly the deliberate adulteration of food and drink by food manufacturers, wholesalers and retailers. The 1875 Act laid the foundation of the modern law governing the public health control of food. This Act was amended over the years. The law was consolidated by the Food Act 1984. The 1980s witnessed a series of well-publicised incidents of food poisoning which attracted the sustained attention of the general public and the government, which decided that further legislation was necessary. The Food Safety Act 1990 comprises a comprehensive code intended to secure the purity of food as well as the control of food premises. The main provisions of the Act are now discussed.

FOOD SAFETY ACT 1990

Section 1(1) of the Food Safety Act 1990 gives a wide meaning to the expression 'food' which includes:

    (a)   drink;
    (b)   articles and substances of no nutritional value which are used for human consumption;

Public health control of food

(c) chewing gum and other products of a like nature and use; and
(d) articles and substances used as ingredients in the preparation of food or anything falling within this subsection.

Section 1(2), however, excludes certain things such as live animals, birds and fish, animal fodder and controlled drugs from the definition of 'food'.

The 1990 Act is intended in the main to control food which is sold, whether the sale is by a manufacturer, wholesaler or retailer. In some cases it is necessary for local authorities to have control over food which, though not sold, is dealt with in a commercial context. Section 2(1) therefore specifies that the supply of food otherwise than on sale in the course of a business is deemed to constitute sale of the food. Section 2(2) extends the scope of the Act to include food which is offered as a prize or reward or given away in connection with any entertainment to which the public are admitted as well as to food which, for the purpose of advertisement, is offered as a prize or given away in furtherance of any trade or business. The subsection also provides that the Act applies to food exposed or deposited in any premises for the purpose of being used by way of advertisement, prize etc.

Presumption that food is intended for human consumption

In order to circumvent practical and evidential problems in the enforcement of the Act s. 3(2) provides that if any food which is commonly used for human consumption is sold, offered, exposed or kept for sale then it is presumed, until the contrary is proved, to have been sold or intended for sale for human consumption. It is suggested that food, in order to come within the ambit of s. 3(2) need not be commonly used for human consumption in the United Kingdom. Any food commonly used for human consumption which is found on premises used for the preparation, storage or sale of that food, and any article of substance commonly used in the manufacture of food for human consumption which is found on such premises is to be presumed, until the contrary is proved, to be intended for sale or for manufacturing food for sale for human consumption (s. 3(3)). Any article or substance capable of being used in the composition or preparation of food commonly used for human consumption which is found on premises on which that food is prepared is to be presumed, until the contrary is proved, to be intended for such use (s. 3(4)).

Food authorities and enforcement of the Act

The public health control over food has traditionally been a local as opposed to a central government function. Section 5 of the Food Safety Act 1990 provides that the food authorities in England and Wales are the councils of the London boroughs, districts and non-metropolitan counties. Power is given to the Ministers' (namely, the Minister of Agriculture, Fisheries and Food and the Secretaries of State concerned with health in England and food and health in Wales) in cases where functions under the Act are exercisable concurrently by a non-metropolitan district and non-metropolitan county to be exercisable by only one of those authorities. Every food authority is required to enforce the provisions of the Act with the exception of those functions which are imposed on some other authority (s. 6). The Ministers may direct that, in relation to cases of a particular description or a particular case, any duty imposed on a food authority is to be discharged by the Ministers or a minister.

INJURIOUS FOOD

It is almost trite to state that it is essential that food production is conducted in a manner which secures the safety of the food. The Act therefore proscribes practices which have a deleterious effect on the safety of food. Section 7(1) provides:

> Any person who renders any food injurious to health by means of any of the following operations, namely —
>
> (a) adding any article or substance to the food;
> (b) using any article or substance as an ingredient in the preparation of the food;
> (c) abstracting any constituent from the food; and
> (d) subjecting the food to any other process or treatment,
>
> with intent that it shall be sold for human consumption, shall be guilty of an offence.

Paragraph (a) would cover a situation in which the dangerous article or substance is intentionally added to food (for example, icing added to cake) as an integral part of the manufacturing process.

Paragraph (d) covers a wide variety of improper modes of treating food. It would cover the irradiation of food carried out in such a way that the food is injurious to health. More commonly it could be invoked to control the ineffectual heat treatment of food during its production. Therefore the food manufacturer who fails to sufficiently raise the temperature of the retorts in which cans of meat are being processed, so that food poisoning pathogens are not destroyed, would commit an offence under the paragraph. While para. (d) would most commonly be invoked in the face of improper treatment of food during the manufacturing stage, it is suggested that the paragraph would also be relevant to a situation where food is improperly treated by others, for example, the retailer. Therefore the retailer who allows meat pies to remain in the ambient temperature of the shop so that food poisoning pathogens proliferate in the pies would, it is suggested, flout the paragraph.

Section 7(2) provides that in determining for the purposes of s. 7 whether any food is injurious to health regard must be paid not only to the probable effect on a person of consuming it but also that the probable cumulative effect of food of substantially the same composition on the health of a person consuming it in ordinary quantities. The appropriate time scale applicable can only be clarified by judicial decision but it is suggested that one would be entitled to take a whole human lifespan into account when determining if the appropriate food was injurious to health. Therefore the addition of a colouring ingredient or flavour enhancer which, if consumed over a period of 50 or 60 years, would have a detrimental effect on the liver would fall within the scope of s. 7(1). The expression 'injury' in relation to health includes any impairment whether permanent or temporary. Thus even trivial reactions to food would ground liability. The manufacturer of food which induces a mild headache on the part of the consumer would fall within the ambit of the Act therefore.

SUBSTANDARD FOOD

By the Food Safety Act 1990, s. 8(1), an offence is committed by any person who:

(a) sells for human consumption, or offers, exposes or advertises for sale for such consumption, or has in his possession for the purpose of such sale or of preparation for such sale; or

(b) deposits with, or consigns to, any other person for the purpose of such sale or of preparation for such sale,

any food which fails to comply with food safety requirements.

The section is aimed at most forms of commercial dealing with food. It should be noted here that there is a strong presumption in law that goods which are displayed in a shop window are not thereby offered for sale (see e.g., *Fisher* v *Bell* [1961] 1 QB 394; *Pharmaceutical Society of Great Britain* v *Boots Cash Chemists (Southern) Ltd* [1953] 1 QB 401). Such items of course, would be exposed for sale and therefore come within the ambit of the subsection.

As far as the meaning of the phrase 'has in his possession', is concerned, Erle J in *R* v *Smith* (1855) Dears CC 494, a case concerning receiving stolen property, described the meaning of 'possession' as 'that very vaguest of all vague matters'. The phrase simply bears its common everyday meaning. In other words the phrase is not a term of art (*Oliver* v *Goodger* [1944] 2 All ER 481). Whether or not unfit food is in the possession of the defendant is a question of fact (*Webb* v *Baker* [1916] 2 KB 753). Possession by an agent was held to constitute possession for the purposes of the Sale of Goods Act 1893, s. 24, in *City Fur Manufacturing Co. Ltd* v *Fureenbond (Brokers) London Ltd* [1937] 1 All ER 799. In *Towers and Co. Ltd* v *Gray* [1961] 2 QB 351 it was held that the owners of poultry did not divest themselves of possession of the poultry for the purposes of Merchandise Marks Act 1887 by depositing the poultry with a storage company under a contract of bailment since the company could withdraw the food on demand from the warehouse in which it was stored. In *Hooper* v *Petrou* (1973) 71 LGR 347 a restaurateur was successfully prosecuted for contravening the now repealed Food and Drugs Act 1955, s. 8, for being in possession of food unfit for human consumption notwithstanding the fact that the food concerned was not readily accessible in the restaurant. Food therefore found on food premises irrespective of the food's accessibility, would come within the scope of the Act.

Section 8(2) of the Food Safety Act 1990 provides that food fails to comply with food safety requirements if:

    (a) it has been rendered injurious to health by means of any of the operations mentioned in section 7(1) above;
    (b) it is unfit for human consumption; or
    (c) it is so contaminated (whether by extraneous matter or otherwise) that it would not be reasonable to expect it be used for human consumption in that state;
and references to such requirements or to food complying with such requirements shall be construed accordingly.

Whether food is unfit for human consumption is a question of fact (*Gateway Foodmarkets Ltd* v *Simmonds* (1978) 152 JP 11). Acting under the spirit of the Act, the court would be disposed towards interpreting the term unfit 'food' widely in order to bring that which is passed off for food within the ambit of the Act. For example, in *Meah* v *Roberts* [1977] 1 WLR 1187 a customer who was in a restaurant run by the defendant ordered lemonade for his children. The waiter brought the children two glasses of caustic soda. The proprietor of the restaurant was charged with selling food which was unfit for human consumption contrary to the Food and Drugs Act 1955, s. 8 (now repealed). It was held that an offence had taken place since the waiter had wished to provide food in the form of lemonade although something quite different was provided. In *Knight* v *Bowers* (1885) 14 QBD 845, which was cited with approval in *Meah* v *Roberts*, a herbalist was charged with selling the drug savin instead of saffron as demanded by the purchaser. The substance supplied was in its natural state and not mixed or compounded with any other drug of ingredient. The learned judge stated:

> I think that the legislature intended to protect purchasers from impositions of this kind. . . . One can imagine many instances – as when chicory is supplied instead of coffee, or lard instead of butter – in which the object of the legislature would not be attained [if it were correct that an offence is committed only by supplying an adulterated form of what was demanded].

The Food Safety Act 1990 does not define the expression 'unfit'. It is not a term of art. Rather, it is suggested, it bears its ordinary everyday meaning. Food may be rendered unfit by a variety of means. Food could be contaminated by pathogenic bacteria, chemicals or even radioactivity. Food could be unfit by virtue of putrefaction or deterioration. Food could be unfit because it is mouldy (*Walker* v *Baxter's Butchers Ltd* (1977) 76 LGR 183) or because it contains extraneous matter, though it has been held that an item of food containing a single extraneous item is not necessarily unfit for human consumption (*Turner and Son Ltd* v *Owen* [1956] 1 QB 48). The judgment of the Lord Justice-Clerk in *Kyle* v *Laird* 1951 JC 65 is worthy of note in the present context. His judgment concerned the fitness of milk but it is suggested that it is of general applicability. He stated:

> What makes milk unfit for the food of man seems to me to be very much a question of circumstances . . . and these circumstances must be infinitely varied. . . . This is the sort of thing to be looked at in a practical, common-sense way.

It would seem therefore that whether food is unfit for human consumption is a question of fact. Food need not pose a threat to human health before it can be categorised as unfit (*David Greig Ltd* v *Goldfinch* (1961) 59 LGR 304; *Guild* v *Gateway Foodmarkets Ltd* 1990 JC 277).

Section 8(2)(c) is innovatory. It would obviously cover a situation where food is contaminated to such an extent as to render it unpalatable. Dough which has been contaminated by sand would fall within the scope of s. 8(2)(c). While s. 8(2)(c) undoubtedly covers contamination of food by solid matter, to what extent contamination by liquid and gaseous matter falls within its scope is unclear. It is suggested that such contamination could bring the food within the scope of s. 8(2)(c). For example were baker's confectionery filling to become contaminated by the non-toxic but powerful aroma of (say) fish which was lying in the vicinity of the filling, it would then come within the scope of the paragraph.

In the absence of authority it is suggested that there is no need for food to be obviously or manifestly contaminated. It would be sufficient that the hypothetical consumer, on being informed that the food was contaminated, would refuse to consume it.

Is it necessary to prove knowledge of possession in order to secure a conviction under s. 8(1)(a)? The authority on this point may be derived from the interpretation of 'possession' under the Drugs (Prevention of Misuse) Act 1964, s. 1(1) (repealed by the Misuse of Drugs Act 1971), which made it an offence to have certain types of controlled drug in one's possession. However, the case law should be treated with caution as far as its applicability to the 1990 Act is concerned since some case law under the former legislation may be result orientated.

In *Warner* v *Metropolitan Police Commissioner* [1969] 2 AC 256 the defendant was accused of being in possession of controlled drugs. He claimed that he believed the parcels in which the drugs were found contained scent and he therefore lacked the relevant *mens rea*. It was held however, that liability under the section was absolute. He was therefore guilty of an offence under the 1964 Act. While it was not necessary that the defendant knew he had a controlled drug in his possession, it was necessary that he knew he was in possession of something. The judgment of Lord Reid (at p. 271) is worthy of repetition in the present context:

> If a person sets up as say a butcher, a publican, or a manufacturer and exposes unsound meat for sale, or sells drink to a drunk man, or certain parts of his factory are unsafe, it is no defence that he could not by the exercise of reasonable care have known or discovered that the meat was unsound, or that the man was drunk or that his premises were unsafe.

In *Blaker* v *Tilstone* [1894] 1 QB 345, which was cited with approval in *Warner* v *Metropolitan Police Commissioner*, the accused was charged with selling unsound meat contrary to the Public Health Act 1875, s. 117 (now repealed). It was held to be unnecessary to show that the accused had personal knowledge of the condition of the meat concerned. Therefore in the context of the Food Safety Act 1990, s. 8(1)(a) it would seem necessary for the prosecution to prove that the accused knew he had some article in his possession. It would not, however, be necessary to prove he knew it was food which failed to comply with food safety requirements.

Bulk quantities etc.

Section 8(3) of the Food Safety Act 1990 provides that where any food which fails to comply with food safety requirements is part of a batch, lot or consignment of food of the same class or description, it is presumed for the purposes of ss. 8 and 9 (which deals with the inspection and seizure of suspected food), until the contrary is proved, that the entire consignment fails to comply with the requirements. The words 'batch', 'lot' and 'consignment' are not defined in the Act. It is suggested therefore that they should be given their everyday meaning. One of the main practical consequences of this provision is that if, for example, an authorised officer discovered among a consignment of tins of ham, that one tin was blown, the whole consignment could be seized under s. 9. In order to avoid any doubt about the soundness of meat which may not have been slaughtered in hygienic conditions, s. 8(4) provides, as far as Scotland is concerned, that any part of, or product derived wholly or partly from an animal which has been slaughtered in a knacker's yard or of which the carcase has been brought into a knacker's yard, is deemed to be unfit for human consumption.

Inspection and seizure of suspected food

In order that the provisions of the Food Safety Act 1990 can be adequately enforced, wide power is given to authorised officers to inspect and seize food which fails to comply with food safety requirements. Under s. 9(1) an authorised officer of a food authority may at all reasonable times inspect any food intended for human consumption which:

(a) has been sold or is offered or exposed for sale; or
(b) is in the possession of, or has been deposited with or consigned to, any person for the purpose of sale or of preparation for sale.

Subsections (3) to (9) apply where, on such an inspection, it appears to the authorised officer that any food fails to comply with food safety requirements. The provisions also apply, if it appears to an authorised officer, otherwise than during the course of such an inspection, that any food is likely to cause food poisoning or any disease communicable to human beings.

Procedure for dealing with suspected food etc.
Under s. 9(3), an authorised officer who has found food not complying with food safety requirements may either:

(a) give notice to the person in charge of the food that, until the notice is withdrawn, the food or any specified portion of it —

(i) is not to be used for human consumption; and
(ii) either is not to be removed or is not to be removed except to some place specified in the notice; or

(b) seize the food and remove it in order that it can be dealt with by a justice of the peace.

The subsection goes on to provide that any person who knowingly contravenes the requirements of a notice under s. 9(3)(a) commits an offence.

If the authorised officer decides to serve notice under s. 9(3)(a), it is suggested that the person in charge of the food would not be entitled to a hearing before the notice is served, since it appears to be the legislature's intention in s. 9 to confer a right to a hearing only when food is seized by the officer in order to have it dealt with by a justice of the peace and then only to persons liable to be prosecuted under the Act.

If the authorised officer decides to seize the food under s. 9(3)(b), there would be no immediate requirement for a hearing since adequate provision for this is made later in s. 9.

Under s. 9(4) if the authorised officer decides to exercise powers under s. 9(3)(a) a decision must be taken about whether the food complies with food safety requirements as soon as is reasonably practicable, and in any event, within 21 days. If the officer is satisfied that the food complies with food safety requirements, the notice must be withdrawn forthwith. If the officer is not so satisfied then the food must be seized in order that it may be dealt with by a justice of the peace. Any persons who may be liable to prosecution in relation to the food are given the right to be heard before the justice of the peace before whom the food is brought. Witnesses may be called. In practice such witnesses would be expert witnesses such as food scientists. It should be noted here that the section gives an express right to be heard etc. only to individuals who could be prosecuted under the Act. No similar right is conferred on the person simply in charge of the food such as a warehouseman or carrier who could be substantially inconvenienced by the seizure.

Under general principles of natural justice a person who has a right to be heard under s. 9(4) must be given adequate time to prepare a case (*R v Thames Magistrates' Court, ex parte Polemis* [1974] 1 WLR 1371). Since the justice of the peace occupies a quasi-judicial position he or she must act impartially and therefore must not hear one side in the absence of the other (*R v Birmingham City Justice, ex parte Chris Foreign Foods (Wholesalers) Ltd* [1970] 1 WLR 1428).

If it appears to the justice of the peace that the food fails to comply with food safety requirements, the justice must condemn the food and order it to be destroyed or to be disposed of so as to prevent it from being used for human consumption (s. 9(6)). Any such order is deemed sufficient evidence in any proceedings under the Act of the failure of the food to comply with food safety requirements. Finally, any expenses reasonably incurred in connection with the destruction or disposal of the food can be recovered from the owner (s. 9(6)(b)).

IMPROVEMENT, PROHIBITION NOTICES AND CONTROL ORDERS

Sections 10 and 11 of the Food Safety Act 1990 give authorised officers, as well as the courts, special powers to deal with premises which fail to comply with regulations which make provision for requiring, prohibiting or regulating the use of any process or treatment in the preparation of food or for securing the observance of hygienic conditions and practices in connection with the carrying out of commercial operations with respect to food or food sources.

Improvement notices

Under s. 10(1) an authorised officer who has reasonable grounds for believing that the proprietor of a food business is failing to comply with the regulations is empowered to serve an improvement notice on the proprietor. The notice may:

(a) state the officer's grounds for believing that the proprietor is failing to comply with the regulations;
(b) specify the matters which constitute the proprietor's failure so to comply;
(c) specify the measures which, in the officer's opinion, the proprietor must take in order to secure compliance; and
(d) require the proprietor to take those measures, or measures which are at least equivalent to them, within such period (not being less than 14 days) as may be specified in the notice.

Any person aggrieved by a decision of an authorised officer to serve an improvement notice may appeal to the magistrates' court (s. 37(1)). Any person who fails to comply with an improvement notice commits an offence (s. 10(2)).

Prohibition orders

A prohibition order is more draconian than an improvement notice. There are two types of prohibition order. One type may be made under s. 11(1), if the proprietor of a food business is convicted of an offence under the regulations and the court before which the proprietor is convicted is satisfied that the health risk condition is fulfilled in relation to the premises. Section

11(2) states that the health risk condition is fulfilled if any of the following involves risk or injury to health.

    (a)   the use for the purposes of the business of any process or treatment;
    (b)   the construction of any premises used for the purposes of the business, or the use for those purposes of any equipment; and
    (c)   the state or condition of any premises or equipment used for the purposes of the business.

What is prohibited by an s. 11(1) prohibition order depends on which paragraph of s. 11(2) the case falls within:

    (a)   if it is within para. (a) then the order will prohibit the use of the process or treatment for the purposes of the particular food business;
    (b)   if it is within para. (b) then the order will prohibit the use of the premises or equipment for the purposes of the particular food business or any other food business of the same class or description;
    (c)   if it is within para. (c) then the order will prohibit the use of the premises or equipment for the purposes of any food business.

The other type of prohibition order may be made under s. 11(4) when a proprietor or manager of a food business is convicted of an offence under the regulations and it prohibits that person from participating in the management of any food business, or any food business of a class or description specified in the order.

The Act introduces a novel device as far as UK environmental health law is concerned. Section 11(5) places an obligation on the part of an enforcing authority to serve a copy of a prohibition order on the proprietor and, if the order is made under s. 11(1), to affix a copy of the order in a conspicuous position on such premises used for the purposes of the business as the authority considers appropriate. There is no need therefore that the order be affixed to the premises where the relevant offence took place. In order to give maximum publicity to the order, therefore, the enforcing authority could attach it to a window or wall of premises likely to be seen by most people. The possibility of the display of the order bringing adverse publicity no doubt is intended by Parliament to encourage food proprietors to ensure their premises and food practices conform to the law.

A prohibition order made under s. 11(1) ceases to have effect on the issue by the enforcement authority of a certificate to the effect that it is satisfied that the proprietor has taken sufficient measures to ensure that the health risk condition is no longer satisfied in relation to the business (s. 11(6)). A prohibition order made under s. 11(4) ceases to have effect on the relevant

Public health control of food

court giving a direction to that effect. The enforcement authority must issue a certificate under s. 11(6) within three days of being satisfied that the health risk condition is no longer satisfied in relation to the business. On the application by the proprietor of the business the authority must determine as soon as reasonably practicable and, in any case, within 14 days whether or not it is so satisfied. If the authority is not so satisfied the proprietor must be informed of the reasons for the authority's decision. As far as a prohibition order relating to a food hygiene offence is concerned, the court must, on the application of the proprietor, give a direction to the effect that the prohibition order ceases to have effect if the court thinks it proper to do so having regard to all the circumstances of the case, including in particular the conduct of the proprietor since the making of the order. However, no such application may be entertained within six months after the making of the prohibition order or within three months after the making by the proprietor of a previous application for such a direction.

Emergency prohibition notices and orders

A considerable period may elapse between a potentially dangerous state of affairs being discovered by an authorised officer and the trial of those responsible. The Food Safety Act 1990 therefore gives the appropriate officer power to take the necessary prophylactic action unilaterally, that is to say, without the intervention of the courts. Under s. 12(1) if an authorised officer of an enforcement authority is satisfied that the health risk condition is fulfilled in relation to any food business, the officer may serve an emergency prohibition notice on the proprietor of the business. Such a notice may be served only if the food business concerned presents an imminent risk of injury to health (s. 12(4)).

As soon as practicable after the service of an emergency prohibition notice on the initiative of an enforcement authority officer, the authority is required to affix a copy of the notice in a conspicuous position on such premises used for the purposes of the business as it considers appropriate (s. 12(5)). Any person who knowingly contravenes such a notice commits an offence.

Instead of serving an emergency prohibition notice on the proprietor, the authorised officer may make application to a magistrates' court for an emergency prohibition order. In any case an emergency prohibition notice ceases to have effect if no application is made for an emergency prohibition order within three days after service of the notice. If such application is in fact made, the notice ceases to have effect on the determination or abandonment of the application (s. 12(7)).

Where an emergency prohibition notice is served on the proprietor of a business, the enforcement authority is required to compensate the proprietor in respect of any loss suffered by reason of his complying with such a notice unless an application for an emergency prohibition order is made within the period of three days beginning with the service of the notice and the court is satisfied that the health risk condition was fulfilled with respect of the business at the time the notice was served. It is therefore in the interest of the appropriate authority to make such application. Any disputed question as to the right or to the amount of compensation payable requires to be settled by arbitration (s. 12(10)).

As soon as practicable after the making of an emergency prohibition order by a magistrates' court, the enforcing authority is required to serve a copy of the order on the proprietor of the business and affix a copy in a conspicuous position on such premises used for the purposes of the business as the authority considers appropriate (s. 12(6)). Any person who knowingly contravenes the order commits an offence (s. 12(6)).

An emergency prohibition notice or order ceases to have effect on the issue by the enforcement authority of a certificate to the effect that it is satisfied that the proprietor has taken sufficient measures to secure that the health risk condition is no longer fulfilled in relation to the business (s. 12(8)). Such a certificate must be issued within three days of the authority being so satisfied. On application by the proprietor for such a certificate, the authority is required to determine as soon as reasonably practicable, and in any event within 14 days, whether it is so satisfied. If it decides that it is not satisfied, notice must be given to the proprietor of the reasons for that decision (s. 12(9)).

Emergency control orders

Whereas food control can normally be effectively administered at local level, sometimes it is desirable, if not essential for the sake of expediency, that the public health control of food be exercised centrally. Section 13 of the Food Safety Act 1990 gives wide power to the minister to prohibit by order the carrying out of commercial operations in relation to food, food sources or contact materials of any class or description which involves or may involve, imminent risk of injury to health. The power could be used, for example, to prohibit the commercial catching of fish from polluted streams as well as the use of types of food packaging material known to be deleterious to human health. Any person who knowingly contravenes an emergency control order commits an offence.

A degree of flexibility is introduced by s. 13(3) which gives the minister power to give consent either conditionally or unconditionally to the doing of anything prohibited by an emergency control order. For example, if an emergency control order were to prohibit the commercial collecting of molluscs from a certain area of the coast, the Minister could use the power contained in s. 13(3) to allow such collection to take place subject to the molluscs being cleansed in tanks afterwards.

The minister may give such directions as appear necessary or expedient for the purpose of preventing the carrying out of commercial operations with respect to any food, food sources or contact materials to which the minister believes on reasonable grounds an emergency control order applies (s. 13(5)). Any person who fails to comply with a direction under the subsection commits an offence.

CONSUMER PROTECTION

Section 14(1) of the Food Safety Act 1990, which essentially repeals and re-enacts the Food Act 1984, s. 2, provides:

> Any person who sells to the purchaser's prejudice any food which is not of the nature or substance or quality demanded by the purchaser shall be guilty of an offence.

Liability under the section is strict (*Smedleys Ltd* v *Breed* [1974] AC 839). There is no need, therefore, to prove intention or, perhaps more appropriately, negligence, on the part of the defendant.

It seems that the words 'nature or substance or quality' should be construed disjunctively, that is to say, each word in the phrase should be construed as having a distinct meaning (*Bastin* v *Davies* [1950] 2 KB 579; *Moore* v *Ray* [1951] 1 KB 98). However, it should be stressed that in many of the reported cases the judgments do not clearly indicate whether the offence is being dealt with as one of nature, substance or quality (see, e.g., *Robertson* v *McKay* 1924 JC 31). Whether the food concerned falls within the scope of the section is a question of fact (*Goldup* v *John Manson Ltd* [1982] QB 161) to be determined by the court (*Webb* v *Knight* (1877) 2 QBD 530). It should be stressed here that while for the purpose of discussion it is helpful to deal with the relevant case law under the headings 'nature', 'substance' and 'quality', the courts have failed to define the terms clearly. It seems from the decided cases that each term is not distinct from the other: there is some overlap as far as meaning is concerned.

'Nature'
Food which is not of the composition demanded by the purchaser would fall under this rubric (*Breed* v *British Drug Houses Ltd* [1947] 2 All ER 613). Food can rightly be regarded as being not of the nature demanded, even if it is in pristine condition, provided it does not meet the purchaser's demand. In *Meah* v *Roberts* [1977] 1 WLR 1187 a customer in a restaurant ordered lemonade. Caustic soda was served instead of lemonade. It was held that an offence had been committed under the Food and Drugs Act 1955, s. 2, which corresponds to the section under discussion.

Food may be not of the nature demanded because it contains extraneous matter, even if it poses no risk to human health (*Greater Manchester Council v Lockwood Foods Ltd* [1979] Crim LR 593; see also *J. Miller Ltd v Battersea Borough Council* [1956] 1 QB 43).

Substance
Food which is not of the composition demanded by the purchaser is not of the substance demanded (*Hall v Owen-Jones* [1967] 1 WLR 1362; see also *Goldup v John Manson Ltd* [1982] QB 161). Food may also come under this rubric if it contains extraneous matter (*J. Miller Ltd v Battersea Borough Council* [1956] 1 QB 43 at p. 48) or if it fails to conform to the composition normally associated with the food in the appropriate trade or profession (*White v Bywater* (1887) 19 QBD 582). However, if the food is sold under a generic title it does not contravene the section provided its substance conforms to the standard normally associated with food of that description. In *Anderson v Britcher* (1913) 110 LT 335 sugar was sold as demerara sugar. It did not come from Demerara. It was held that the expression 'demerera' simply implied that the sugar bore certain particular attributes. Provided the sugar in question possessed such physical qualities, no offence was committed. (Quaere 'Scotch' whisky.)

Quality
'Quality' means commercial quality (*McDonald's Hamburgers Ltd v Windle* (1986) 151 JP 333). In *Barber v Co-operative Wholesale Society Ltd* (1983) 81 LGR 762, which concerned the presence of a straw in a milk bottle, it was held that an offence was committed if the relevant food was not of such a quality as the purchaser was entitled to expect. In determining this question it is necessary to consider if a reasonable purchaser would object to the presence of the extraneous article. The case is also illustrative of the point that the courts measure such expectation objectively, that is to say, in terms of the expectation of a hypothetical purchaser possessed of the knowledge of the purchaser in question. The case shows that the mere presence of an extraneous article in food may render it not of the quality demanded (see also *Newton v West Vale Creamery Co. Ltd* (1956) 120 JP 318).

The nature etc. of the food demanded by the purchaser and sold by the seller is determined, in accordance with the norms of contract law, at the time of sale. Therefore any representations made by the seller at that time can be taken into account when determining if s. 14 has been breached (*Kirk v Coates* (1885) 16 QBD 49). Similarly the contents of a notice concerning the physical attributes of the food in question, may be taken into account by the court, provided the notice is drawn to the attention of the purchaser at the time of sale (*Rodbourn v Hudson* [1925] 1 KB 225). It is immaterial if

Public health control of food

the purchaser fails to comprehend the physical effect of consuming the food in question provided its ingredients have been accurately described (*Williams* v *Friend* [1912] 2 KB 471). The notice must be seen by the purchaser in question (*Sandys* v *Small* (1878) 3 QBD 449). However, where statute prescribes the nature, substance or quality of the food, the purchaser's demand is determined by such standard (*Roberts* v *Leeming* (1905) 69 JP 417; *Skinner* v *MacLean* 1979 SLT (Notes) 35).

Falsely describing etc. food

The Food Safety Act 1990 adopts a holistic approach to food. Therefore the Act also deals with what could conveniently come under the rubric 'deceit', as far as the description, labelling etc. of food is concerned. Section 15(1) provides:

> Any person who gives with any food sold by him, or displays with any food offered or exposed by him for sale or in his possession for the purpose of sale, a label, whether or not attached to or printed on the wrapper or container, which —
>
> (a) falsely describes the food; or
> (b) is likely to mislead as to the nature or substance or quality of the food, shall be guilty of an offence.

It would seem that liability under s. 15(1) is strict (*Kat* v *Diment* [1951] 1 KB 34). The defendant would not therefore have to know that the label was false for liablity to lie. It is suggested, in the absence of authority, that whether or not the label falsely describes the food or is likely to mislead is a question of fact.

A statement may be false not simply because it is *ex facie* so, but also by virtue of what it conceals or omits to state (*R* v *Lord Kylsant* [1932] 1 KB 442). Whether the statement is likely to mislead must be determined by considering whether the statement would have misled a hypothetical ordinary individual (*Concentrated Foods Ltd* v *Champ* [1944] KB 342).

It is the intention of Parliament to prohibit adverts about food which are misleading. Section 15(2) therefore provides:

> Any person who publishes, or is a party to the publication of, an advertisement (not being such a label given or displayed by him as mentioned in subsection (1) above) which —
>
> (a) falsely describes any food; or
> (b) is likely to mislead as to the nature or substance or quality of any food, shall be guilty of an offence.

The act of publishing an advertisement (which is defined in s. 53(1)) is simply making its contents known to another person (*Dew* v *Director of Public Prosecutions* (1920) 89 LJ KB 1166). The liability of the publisher is strict. It need not be shown that there was an intention to publish the misleading advert. It is also unnecessary to prove that the publisher was negligent in not ascertaining that the advertisement was misleading (*Paterson Zochonis and Co. Ltd* v *Merfarken Packaging Ltd* [1983] 3 All ER 522). For someone to be party to the publication of an advertisement would require some active role in the relevant publication (see *Thorne* v *Heard and Marsh* [1895] AC 495). However, the degree of participation necessary to ground liability under the section, is uncertain.

It is an offence for a person to sell, offer, expose for sale or have in one's possession for the purpose of sale, any food the presentation of which is likely to mislead as to its nature, substance or quality (s. 15(3)).

In proceedings for an offence under s. 15(1) or (2) the fact that a label or advertisement contains an accurate statement of the composition of the food does not preclude the court from finding that an offence was committed under the Act (s. 15(4)). Therefore a label which falsely describes food but gives an accurate description of its composition would infringe the Act. If Canadian whisky was described as 'Scotch' whisky the Act would be infringed, notwithstanding the composition of the beverage was correctly described. Section 15(4) also implicitly recognises the proposition mentioned above that the label is interpreted through the eyes of a hypothetical ordinary individual. Thus if the words in a label are couched in esoteric, albeit accurate, language, likely to mislead such a person as to the composition of the food, an offence would be committed. Furthermore, if the commercial quality of food were wrongly described, it would be no defence that the composition of the food was accurately stated.

SUBORDINATE LEGISLATION

Wide power is given to the Ministers under s. 16 to make regulations relating to food safety and consumer protection. Regulations may, under s. 16(1), make:

(a) provision for requiring, prohibiting or regulating the presence in food or food sources of any specified substance, or any substance of any specified class, and generally for regulating the composition of food;

(b) provision for securing that food is fit for human consumption and meets such microbiological standards (whether going to the fitness of the food or otherwise) as may be specified by or under the regulations,

(c) provision for requiring, prohibiting or regulating the use of any process or treatment in the preparation of food,

(d) provision for securing the observance of hygienic conditions and practices in connection with the carrying out of commercial operations with respect to food or food sources,

(e) provision for imposing requirements or prohibitions as to, or otherwise regulating, the labelling, marking, presenting or advertising of food, and the descriptions which may be applied to food; and

(f) such other provision with respect to food or food sources, including in particular provision for prohibiting or regulating the carrying out of commercial operations with respect to food or food sources, as appears to them to be necessary or expedient —

(i) for the purpose of securing that food complies with food safety requirement or in the interests of the public health; or

(ii) for the purpose of protecting or promoting the interests of consumers.

Under s. 16(2) regulations may be made:

(a) for securing the observance of hygienic conditions and practices in connection with the carrying out of commercial operations with respect to contact materials which are intended to come into contact with food intended for human consumption;

(b) for imposing requirements or prohibitions as to, or otherwise regulating, the labelling, marking or advertising of such materials, and the descriptions which may be applied to them; and

(c) otherwise for prohibiting or regulating the carrying out of commercial operations with respect to such materials.

It was Parliament's intention to make the 1990 Act a comprehensive food statute not solely concerned with the immediate deleterious effect of certain food on human health. Section 16(4) therefore allows ministers when making regulations under s. 16(1) to address their minds to the desirability of restricting, so far as reasonably practicable, the use of substances of no nutritional value.

The European influence

Section 17(1) of the Act gives power to the Ministers to make regulations on the subject of food, food sources or contact materials necessitated by any Community obligation. Normally such an obligation will take the form of a Directive which will not have direct effect in the UK. In relation to legislation which is directly enforceable, such as Regulations made by the Commission, s. 17(2) gives power to the ministers to make regulations to ensure that such legislation is adequately administered etc. under the 1990 Act.

REGISTRATION AND LICENSING OF FOOD PREMISES

It has been common since Victorian times to allow local authorities to license or register premises or activities which could redound to the public detriment if they are not conducted properly. Offensive trades have traditionally been controlled this way. Section 19(1)(a) of the Food Safety Act 1990 gives the ministers power to make regulations for the registration by enforcement authorities of premises used, or proposed to be used, for the purposes of a food business, and for prohibiting use for those purposes of premises which are not registered in accordance with the regulations (see the Food Premises (Registration) Regulations 1991 (SI 1991/2825). Under s. 19(1)(b) the ministers may make regulations for the issue of licences by enforcement authorities in respect of food businesses and for prohibiting the use for those purposes of any premises except in accordance with a licence issued under the regulations. Licensing regulations may be made only where it appears necesssary or expedient for the purpose of securing that food complies with food safety requirements or in the interests of public health or for the purpose of protecting or promoting the interests of consumers.

In administrative law there is a distinction between licensing and registration. An enforcing authority has wide discretion (subject to the norms of administrative law) as to whether or not to grant a licence but as long as a person seeking registration complies with the relevant law, the enforcing authority would be under a legal obligation to make the registration.

DEFENCES

Fault of some other person

In common with the provisions of other public health statutes, liability under the Food Safety Act 1990 is strict, that is to say the prosecution need not prove intention or fault on the part of the defendant. This rule could lead to injustice. For example, a retailer who sells food which has been contaminated by the negligence of the manufacturer would automatically commit an offence under the Act. It is Parliament's intention, however, that proceedings be taken against the individual at fault. Section 20 of the Act therefore provides that where the commission by any person of an offence is due to an act or default of some other person, that other person is guilty of the offence and may be charged with and convicted of the offence under the section whether or not proceedings are taken against the first person.

Section 20 would normally allow the manager of a supermarket company to be prosecuted instead of, or in addition to, the company, provided the manager had not been delegated all management powers the company itself possessed, since, in such a case, the manager would be regarded as 'another person' in terms of the section (*Tesco Supermarkets Ltd* v *Nattrass* [1972] AC 153; see also *Woodhouse* v *Walsall Metropolitan Borough Council* [1994] Env LR 30). The act or default of the other person must itself be unlawful (*Noss Farm Products Ltd* v *Lilico* [1945] 2 All ER 609). However, such an act may satisfy the requirement of illegality simply by virtue of being an offence of strict liability (*Lamb* v *Sunderland and District Creamery Ltd* [1951] 1 All ER 923; see also *Fisher* v *Barrett and Pomeroy (Bakers) Ltd* [1954] 1 WLR 351).

Reasonable precautions and due diligence defence

In order to mitigate further the potential injustice which could be brought about by the automatic operation of the strict liability rule, s. 21(1) provides that it is a defence for a person charged with an offence under part II to prove that he took all reasonable precautions and exercised all due diligence to avoid commission of the offence by himself or by a person under his control.

There is little authority on the substantive difference between the standard governed by the expressions 'reasonable precautions' and 'due diligence'. In the absence of authority it is suggested that the requirement of reasonable precautions is satisfied by the accused taking positive prophylactic action, for example, by adopting a recognised system of work to prevent breaking the law, whereas the latter may be fulfilled by appropriate passive inaction. There is no difference in the appropriate standard of care in relation to either head (*Texas Homecare Ltd* v *Stockport Metropolitan Borough Council* (1987) 152 JP 83).

Whether or not the accused has exercised due diligence is a question of fact (*R. C. Hammett Ltd* v *Crabb* (1931) 145 LT 638) to be determined on the particular facts of the case (*Riverstone Meat Co. Pty Ltd* v *Lancashire Shipping Co. Ltd* [1960] 1 QB 536). On existing authority it seems that passive reliance on a certificate furnished by a wholesaler or manufacturer as to the quality of goods will not be sufficient to make out the defence, especially where it would have been possible for the accused to have the relevant goods sampled (*Taylor* v *Lawrence Fraser (Bristol) Ltd* [1978] Crim LR 43). The courts will be unwilling to allow the defence of due diligence to succeed if a simple test performed by the accused would have indicated that the relevant goods failed to comply with the law (*Sherratt* v *Gerald's the American Jewellers Ltd* (1970) 68 LGR 256). When the performance of tests on the goods is left to agents of the accused, the courts require the latter to ensure such tests are effectively carried out. Simple reliance on the assurances of such agents is not enough (*Hicks* v *Sullam* (High Court 4

February 1983 unreported). However, it has been held that it may be sufficient to rely on the known accuracy of a machine to secure compliance with the relevant law (*Bibby-Cheshire* v *Golden Wonder Ltd* [1972] 1 WLR 1487). In *Turtington* v *United Co-operatives Ltd* [1993] Crim LR 376 it was held that mere instructions given by the accused to his own employees about how to ascertain the presence of a batch number on a product, which allowed the origin of the product to be traced, was insufficient to allow the defence of due diligence to succeed. It was incumbent on the accused to take further measures to check their origin.

Section 21(2) provides that without prejudice to the generality of s. 21(1) a person charged with an offence under s. 8 (selling food which fails to comply with safety standards), s. 14 (selling food not of the nature, substance or quality demanded) or s. 15 (falsely describing or presenting food), who neither prepared the relevant food not imported it into Great Britain, is to be deemed to have established the defence provided by s. 21(1) if the requirements of subsections (3) or (4) are satisfied.

Subsection (3) provides that the defence is established if the accused proves:

    (a) that the commission of the offence was due to an act or default of another person who was not under his control, or to reliance on information supplied by such a person;

    (b) that he carried out all such checks of the food in question as were reasonable in all the circumstances, or that it was reasonable in all the circumstances for him to rely on checks carried out by the person who supplied the food to him; and

    (c) that he did not know and had no reason to suspect at the time of the commission of the alleged offence that his act or omission would amount to an offence under the relevant provision.

Subsection (4) provides that the defence is established if the accused proves:

    (a) that the commission of the offence was due to an act or default of another person who was not under his control, or to reliance on information supplied by such a person;

    (b) that the sale or intended sale of which the alleged offence consisted was not a sale or intended sale under his name or mark; and

    (c) that he did not know, and could not reasonably have been expected to know, at the time of the commission of the alleged offence that his act or omission would amount to an offence under the relevant provision.

The defence provided by subsection (3) is most apposite to a situation where food contravenes the provisions of the Act by virtue of the negligence of the manufacturer or wholesaler prior to the food being delivered to the retailer. The defence would also be applicable where, for example, the retailer has been given incorrect information as to the correct temperature at which the food should be stored as a result of which the food has become contaminated. The subsection could be invoked by a food manufacturer who was supplied with contaminated meat (which was apparently sound) from a supplier who had negligently allowed the meat to become contaminated. How scrupulous the courts will require the defendant to be can not be predicted with certainty. For example, will the courts require retailers and manufacturers to have a certain proportion of all produce (especially sealed produce) analysed before the defence can be invoked or will checks capable of being personally performed (such as visual inspection, palpation etc.) suffice? These issues can only be answered in the light of judicial decision.

The defence provided by s. 21(4) would be available, for example, to a food distributor who is normally reliant on a food processor for the quality of food distributed. The subsection would also provide a defence to a retailer who infringes the Act because of the negligence of the manufacturer. In contrast to the requirements of subsection (3) there is no express requirement that the accused should have carried out checks on the food. Furthermore there is on requirement that the accused perform any positive act, for example examining the food, before the defence can be invoked.

PROMOTION OF FOOD SAFETY

Food hygiene training

It is well known that most food poisoning incidents emanate from the improper handling of food. It is therefore of prime importance that individuals who handle food receive appropriate training. The Food Safety Act 1990, s. 23, allows a food authority to provide either inside or outside its area training courses on food hygiene for persons who are or intend to become involved in the food business. It is now common for environmental health departments in the United Kingdom to provide food hygiene courses which follow syllabi prepared either by the Institute of Environmental Health Officers, the Royal Environmental Health Institute of Scotland, or the Royal Society of Health.

Shellfish cleansing facilities

There is a tendency for shellfish in the United Kingdom to be gathered from coastal waters polluted by raw sewage which provides the shellfish with nutrients. This poses an obvious potential risk to human health especially if the shellfish are eaten raw or partially cooked. Pathogenic viruses as well as bacteria have traditionally been associated with shellfish. Shellfish fortunately have the capacity to cleanse themselves readily if they are allowed to remain in clean water. The Food Safety Act 1990, s. 24, allows a local authority to provide such cleansing facilities either within or outside its area. The section expressly precludes the construction of cleaning tanks on the foreshore (which belongs to the Crown) unless such works are approved by the Secretary of State.

Sampling and analysis of food

An important feature of any statute aimed at securing the quality of products concerns the rights of enforcing authorities to sample such products. Section 29 of the Food Safety Act 1990 confers wide powers on an authorised officer in relation to sampling. Such an officer may:

(a) purchase a sample of any food, or any substance capable of being used in the preparation of food;

(b) take a sample of any food, or any such substance, which —

(i) appears to him to be intended for sale, or to have been sold, for human consumption; or

(ii) is found by him on or in any premises which he is authorised to enter by or under section 32 below;

(c) take a sample from any food source, or a sample of any contact material, which is found by him on or in such premises;

(d) take a sample of any article or substance which is found by him on or in any such premises and which he has reason to believe may be required as evidence in proceedings under any of the provisions of this Act or of regulations or orders made under it.

See the Food Safety (Sampling and Qualifications) Regulations 1990 (SI 1990/2463). A purchase of goods must be by way of a contract of sale (i.e., normally an offer to buy coupled with an acceptance of that offer (*Southwell v Ross* [1945] 2 All ER 590). It has been held that an officer can purchase a sample through an agent or messenger (*Stace v Smith* (1880) 45 JP 141; *Macaulay v Mackirdy* (1893) 20 R 58). The officer in question must purport to exercise the powers under s. 29. In *McLeod v Morton* 1981 SLT (Sh Ct) 107 it was held that the receipt of a bottle of milk by an officer from a complainant did not constitute the exercise of such power and therefore the bottle in question could not be regarded as a sample. In *Grimsby Borough Council v Louis C. Edwards and Sons (Manufacturing) Ltd* [1976] Crim LR

512 it was held that only food picked out indiscriminately from among similar substances with the object of making a random test could constitute a sample.

Emergency controls

It is sometimes necessary for speedy legislative action to be taken to protect the public from contaminated food. Section 1 of the Food and Environment Protection Act 1985 (as amended) empowers the Minister of Agriculture or the Secretary of State to make an order by statutory instrument designating any area of land in the United Kingdom or sea within the British fishery limits, or both such area of land and sea from which anything is derived which is or may become unfit for human consumption. The order may contain emergency prohibitions. It is made an offence to contravene such prohibitions. To date the powers conferred by the section have been invoked to proscribe the gathering of shellfish in parts of northern Scotland and also the use of the meat of sheep and cattle affected by the Chernobyl accident. Under s. 3 either of the ministers may waive conditionally or unconditionally anything prohibited by an emergency prohibition order. Officials known as 'investigating officers' under the Act, are given wide powers of inspection under s. 4.

FOOD HYGIENE REGULATIONS

It has already been mentioned that enteric diseases, especially diarrhoeal diseases, constantly afflicted Victorian Britain. The young were more seriously affected. Infant mortality during the summer months was especially severe. While the causes of such disease were manifold, the main cause was probably the unhygienic condition of food supplied by retail shops. In the complete absence of food hygiene legislation, meat and dairy produce, for example, would normally be left exposed for sale at ambient temperature which allowed pathogens to flourish. One of the most important functions of the modern environmental health departments in local government is the enforcement of food hygiene legislation. In England and Wales, the current law relating to food hygiene is contained in the Food Hygiene (General) Regulations 1970 (SI 1970/1172) as amended, the main provisions of which are now discussed.

General requirements

Under reg. 6 no food business may be carried on at any insanitary premises, or at any premises or place the condition, situation or construction of which is such that food is exposed to the risk of contamination. Regulation 7 makes provision for the cleanliness of articles and equipment with which food comes into contact in the course of a food business, which is defined as a business consisting wholly or partly of the supply of food intended by the supplier for immediate consumption. With the exception of non-returnable containers, articles and equipment must be constructed of such materials and kept in such order as to enable them to be thoroughly cleaned, to prevent, so far as is reasonably practicable, any matter being absorbed by them and any risk of contamination of the food. In determining whether any article or equipment is clean, regard must be paid to the use, nature and packing of the food for which the article or equipment is required and to the use which is made of the article or equipment.

Regulation 8 restricts the giving out of food for preparation or packing by another person at any domestic premises other than those of the person carrying on the business.

Food handlers

Many food poisoning outbreaks are directly attributable to food becoming contaminated by the food operative. It is therefore fundamentally important that strict controls exist. Under reg. 9 a person who engages in the handling of food is required to take all steps reasonably necessary to protect the food from any risk of contamination. Food while exposed for sale or during delivery must also be protected from the risk of contamination. In order to contravene the regulation the risk of contamination must be of such a nature that there is a risk to public health (*MacFisheries (Wholesale and Retail) Ltd* v *Coventry Corporation* [1957] 1 WLR 1066). Regulations 10 and 11 make provision for the personal cleanliness, mode of dress and hygienic practices of food handlers. Regulation 13 requires any person engaged in the handling of food who becomes aware that he or she is suffering from or is the carrier of typhoid, paratyphoid or any other salmonella infection or amoebic or bacillary dysentery or any staphylococcal infection likely to cause food poisoning, to inform the person carrying on the food business. That person is required to inform the appropriate medical officer of health on pain of penalty.

Food premises

The regulations make detailed provision as to hygienic requirements for food premises. Regulation 12 requires every sanitary convenience situated in or regularly used in conjunction with food premises to be kept clean and in efficient order and placed so that no offensive odours can penetrate into a food room. Any room or other place containing a sanitary convenience must be suitably lighted and ventilated and kept clean. There is also prohibited the use of a room as a food room which contains a sanitary convenience.

No room or other place which contains a sanitary convenience may communicate directly with a food room.

Under reg. 17 the water supply provided to any food premises must be clean and wholesome as well as constant.

All food premises must be provided with suitable and sufficient number of wash-hand basins. The basins must be provided with both hot and cold water. Whether a wash-hand basin is conveniently accessible is a question of fact to be determined on the particular facts of the case. In *Adams v Flook and Flook* [1987] BTLC 61, it was held that a wash-hand basin in the living quarters of an employer which had to be approached by stairs was conveniently accessible to the food handlers in question. The basin must be kept clean and in good working order and must be supplied with soap and clean towels or other drying facilities. Failure to supply one or more of these items creates separate offences under the Food Safety Act 1990.

Food premises must also be supplied with washing facilities suitable and sufficient for any necessary washing of food and equipment used in the food business. Such washing facilities must be provided with an adequate supply of hot and cold water or of hot water of suitably controlled temperature. Cold water only suffices for washing fish, fruit or vegetables or for washing with a suitable bactericidal agent only drinking vessels or ice cream formers or servers. Every such sink must be kept clean and in good working order (reg. 21).

Food premises must be suitably lit and ventilated, except where humidity and temperature are controlled (reg. 22).

Regulation 25 provides that the walls, floors, doors, windows, ceiling, woodwork and all other parts of the structure of every food room must be kept clean and in good working order, repair and condition so as to enable them to be effectively cleaned and prevent, so far as reasonably practicable, the entry of birds and any risk of infestation by rats, mice, insects or other pests. Failure to keep the structure of every food room clean, and failure to keep the structure of every food room in good order, repair and condition so as to prevent any risk of infestation etc. constitute separate offences under the 1990 Act (*George v Kumar* (1981) 80 LGR 526).

It is of prime importance that food is not exposed to the risk of contamination by virtue of the layout of food premises. Regulation 26 provides that the layout of food premises must be such as to provide adequate space, suitably sited, for the removal of waste from food and the separation of unfit food from other food, and the storage of any such waste and unfit food prior to disposal.

Temperature control of food

Pathogenic micro-organisms can grow rapidly at certain temperatures. It is therefore important that the temperature of food is controlled. Regulation

27 prescribes maximum temperatures of 8°C and 5°C for chilled foods and a minimum of 63°C for hot foods. The 5°C control became effective from 1 April 1993. The temperature requirements apply to food during production, during transport, and while at a retail or catering outlet. Food sent by mail order or courier to the final consumer is currently exempt from temperature control. Types of food to which the temperature requirements apply include:

(a) meat,
(b) fish,
(c) eggs,
(d) cheese,
(e) cereals,
(f) pulses,
(g) vegetables,
(h) smoked or cured fish,
(i) smoked or cured meat,
(j) prepared vegetable salad,
(k) cooked pies,
(l) cooked sausage rolls,
(m) sandwiches and filled rolls.

Certain foods, such as bread, biscuits, cakes, pastry, and dehydrated and canned food, are exempt from the temperature control requirements as are food in certain circumstances such as food in a food room during a period of two hours from the conclusion of its preparation, provided certain conditions are met. Furthermore, the regulations allow the temperature control requirements to be exceeded by 2°C in other circumstances.

Exemptions

The relevant authority can exempt food premises from certain provisions of the regulations if compliance cannot reasonably be required with respect to any activities carried on in the premises. The provisions are reg. 17 (water supply); reg. 20 (accommodation for clothing etc.) and reg. 24 (food room not to communicate with bedroom).

Food markets, stalls etc.

The Food Hygiene (Markets, Stalls and Delivery Vehicles) Regulations 1966 (SI 1966/791) make similar provision in relation to markets, vehicles etc. as do the 1970 regulations in relation to food premises.

Proposals for reform

It is likely that the Food Hygiene (General) Regulations 1970 will be replaced during 1994 by new regulations (which will apply to the UK as a whole) to implement the EC Food Hygiene Directive (93/43/EEC).

MILK AND DAIRIES

Milk hygiene

Milk is an ideal medium for the transmission of disease. In the 19th century, tuberculosis and other diseases such as scarlet fever as well as enteric diseases were often caused by milk being derived from cattle which were kept in grossly insanitary conditions. It is imperative, therefore, that special legislative attention is given to milk and dairies. There are a fairly large number of regulations governing milk hygiene, composition and labelling. No attempt here can be made even to summarise them. However, brief mention can be made of the current legislative controls governing the production of milk from the point of view of hygiene, which are mainly contained in the Milk and Dairies (General) Regulations 1959 (SI 1959/277) which now takes effect as if made under the Food Safety Act 1990.

Registration of dairy premises etc.
The Minister of Agriculture, Fisheries and Food must keep a register of persons carrying on the trade of dairy farmer and also of dairy farms (reg. 6). Permission to register may be refused if the provisions of the regulations cannot be complied with. Registration may also be cancelled for similar reasons.

Whereas the duty to register dairy premises falls on central government, the responsibility for registering distributors of milk falls on the local authority (reg. 8).

Inspection of cattle etc.
Power is given to the minister to cause inspections to be made of cattle (reg. 9). It is an offence for a person to sell, offer or expose for sale for human consumption the milk of a cow which the person knows or suspects is affected with, *inter alia*, tuberculosis of the udder, acute mastitis or suppuration of the udder.

Buildings, water supply
Part 5 of the regulations deals with the structure of and water supply to dairy buildings etc. Generally speaking such premises require to be adequately lit

and ventilated and constructed in such a way as to be easily cleaned and also provided with a suitable and sufficient supply of water.

Hygienic handling of milk
Part 6 addresses, *inter alia,* a very important issue as far as the hygienic quality of milk is concerned, namely, the milking process, and makes provision for the general cleanliness of the place where cows are milked as well as the handling of milk.

Impure milk etc.
Part 7 of the regulations makes provision for the protection of milk from infection. Power is given to the medical officer of health of the appropriate district to examine dairy workers and stop the distribution of milk which is, in his or her opinion, infected.

Contamination of milk
Parts 8 and 9 of the regulations make provision as to the protection of milk against contamination of infection and the cleansing and storage of milk vessels and utensils.

Types of milk

The Milk (Special Designation) Regulations 1989 (SI 1989/2383) make provision as to special designations applicable to the sale of milk. Any person using such a designation is required to hold a licence permitting the use of such a designation. The designations currently in use are 'Untreated', 'Pasteurised', 'Sterilised' and 'Ultra Heat Treated'. Special conditions apply to the grant of each type of licence. Milk producers require to hold a licence granted by the Minister of Agriculture, Fisheries and Food, whereas dealers in milk are required to be in possession of a licence granted by a local authority.

EIGHT
Health and safety at work

This chapter deals with the general principles of the law relating to health and safety at work. Here we consider the control of the employee's immediate working environment in contrast to the wider environment which has been the focus of attention of the book thus far. In a work of this nature only the main provisions of the relevant statutes can be discussed. This is an area where the principal Acts have generated a plethora of subordinate legislation. Furthermore, EC influence in this area of law has been fairly substantial. No attempt will be made here to discuss, or even mention, the existence of such legislation. Only brief mention can be made of the common law duties owed by employer to employee as far as the latter's health and safety is concerned. The chapter therefore divides into three sections, namely;

(a) The common law controls over the working environment.
(b) The Health and Safety at Work etc. Act 1974.
(c) Other statutory controls.

COMMON LAW CONTROLS OVER THE WORKING ENVIRONMENT

The common law rules governing employers' duties to employees were crystallised during the 19th century. The common law rules are examined here briefly, first for the sake of completeness and, secondly, because Parliament has drawn heavily on common law concepts to frame certain of the statutory provisions which will be discussed later in the chapter. Therefore sometimes there is an overlap between the common law and statute. For example, the case law concerning certain concepts such as systems of work, which is found in both legal regimes, is mutually interchangeable.

The main duties which an employer owes an employee at common law are discussed in turn. These are a duty to provide:

(a) safe plant and machinery,
(b) a safe place of work,
(c) a safe system of work,
(d) competent staff.

Safe plant and machinery

An employer is under a common law duty to take reasonable steps to ensure that employees are provided with plant and equipment which is safe (*Lovell v Blundells and T. Albert Crompton and Co. Ltd* [1944] KB 502). The duty extends to ensuring that the plant etc. is maintained in a safe condition while it is used by the employee. It should be noted that the employer is only required to do that which is reasonable. The duty imposed by the common law therefore is not absolute or strict. It may sometimes happen, however, that an employee is injured by reason of equipment which has been negligently manufactured and therefore potentially dangerous, yet the danger is not apparent on reasonable inspection. If common law rules were to obtain the employer would escape liability. However, under the Employer's Liability (Defective Equipment) Act 1969 an employer is deemed personally liable for any injury suffered by an employee if the injury is caused by a latent defect in any plant or equipment, if the defect is caused by the negligence of a third party. The expression 'equipment' is construed widely. In *Knowles* v *Liverpool City Council* [1993] 1 WLR 1428 it was held that a flagstone was equipment within the meaning of the Act.

Safe place of work

An employer is under a duty to take reasonable measures to ensure that an employee has a safe place of work (*Naismith* v *London Film Productions Ltd* [1939] 1 All ER 794). Such a duty is non-delegable. If, therefore, the employee is sent to work away from premises under the immediate control of the employer, the duty of care remains (*Wilson* v *Tyneside Window Cleaning Co.* [1958] 2 QB 110). However, the duty owed by the employer in such circumstances is lower. If the premises do not present an obvious risk to the safety of the worker, there is no duty on the employer to inspect the premises to ascertain if they are safe (*Wilson* v *Tyneside Window Cleaning Co.*). For example, if an employer were to send an employee, a joiner, to fit a new gutter on the roof of a house and the joiner was to be injured by falling from a ladder which had been resting on a fascia which disintegrated because of dry rot, the employer would not be liable. However, if the building to which the employee was sent was known or ought to have been known by the employer to be in a dangerous state, the employer would be liable at common law. The scope of the duty an employer owes to an employee who has been sent to work in premises situated in a foreign country was considered recently in *Cook* v *Square D Ltd* [1992] ICR 262, in which the case law dealing generally with the situation where an employee has been sent to work in premises not occupied by the employer was discussed. In *Cook* v *Square D Ltd*, the respondent had been sent by the appellants to work in premises situated in Saudi Arabia. The respondent was injured when his foot became jammed in a hole situated in the floor of the premises. He sued his employers, claiming that they had breached their common law duty to ensure that his place of work was safe. It was held by the Court of Appeal that the common law duty had not been breached. In so deciding the Farquharson LJ stated (at p. 268):

> ... in determining an employer's responsibility one has to look at all the circumstances of the case, including the place where the work is to be done, the nature of the building on the site concerned (if there is a building), the experience of the employee who is so despatched to work at such a site, the nature of the work he is required to carry out, the degree of control that the employer can reasonably exercise in the circumstances, and the employer's own knowledge of the defective state of the premises.

In the instant case, the company which controlled the premises in which the respondent was injured was reliable and was aware of its responsibility in relation to its own employees. The court was of the opinion, however, that in certain circumstances, an employer which sends an employee to work in a foreign country may be under a duty to inspect the premises to ensure that they are safe. This would be the case, for example, where a number of employees are sent to work on a foreign site, or where one or two employees are sent to work for a very considerable period of time.

Safe system of work

An employer must ensure that the various systems of work the employee performs in the course of his or her duties are reasonably safe (*Speed* v *Thomas Swift and Co. Ltd* [1943] KB 557). The courts have unfortunately been unable to provide a satisfactory definition of the expression 'system of work'. The expression seems wide in scope. In *Speed* it was held that the phrase included the physical layout of the job, the sequence in which the work is to be carried out, as well as the provision, where necessary, of warnings, notices and instructions. A system of work may not be confined to the duties which the employee is expressly instructed to carry out by the employer. In *Davidson* v *Handley Page Ltd* [1945] 1 All ER 235 it was held that 'system of work' covers all acts which are normally and reasonably incidental to the day's work. Therefore, for example, if an employer instructed an employee to dredge a canal bed, and the only way of disposing of the relevant detritus was by way of dumping it along the canal bank, the process of dumping the waste matter would be a system of work. Accordingly, such a process would have to be safe at common law.

There has been some judicial discussion of the extent to which an employer is under a duty to warn an employee of dangers and ensure that such warnings are put into effect by the employee.

As far as the duty on the employer simply to warn is concerned, if the danger to the employee is readily apparent, there is no duty on the employer to warn the employee of the danger especially if the employee is experienced (*Baker* v *T. Clarke (Leeds)* [1992] PIQR P262). If, however, the risk is insidious, which would seem to be a question of fact and degree, there is a duty to warn the employee. For example, in *Pape* v *Cumbria County Council* [1992] ICR 132 it was held incumbent on the employer of a cleaner to warn her of the danger of dermatitis by her failure to wear gloves when applying certain cleaning agents.

The extent to which the law requires an employer to ensure by affirmative action that an employee takes the necessary prophylactic measures is dependent upon the nature and gravity of the risk. If the employee in question is relatively inexperienced the employer is under a greater duty to ensure that warnings etc. are implemented than would be the case if the employee had considerable experience (*Qualcast (Wolverhampton) Ltd* v *Haynes* [1959] AC 743 at p. 755). If the risk of an accident occurring is small but there is a high probability of injury being serious if an accident did in fact occur, then there is a duty to ensure that the warnings etc. are put into effect (*Nolan* v *Dental Manufacturing Co. Ltd* [1958] 1 WLR 936). Furthermore, if the potential injury would have graver consequences for a particular employee than it would in respect of a normal able-bodied employee, the employer needs to take greater precautions in respect of that particular employee (*Paris* v *Stepney Borough Council* [1951] AC 367).

It is, however, important to reiterate here the caveat made by Lord Denning in *Qualcast (Wolverhampton) Ltd* v *Haynes* [1959] AC 743 at p. 759 to the effect that in determining whether a particular employer has breached a duty of care to an employee, one should not elevate judicial decisions based on the facts of particular cases, into propositions of law for general application. The sole question which requires to be determined is whether the employer in question took reasonable care in the circumstances.

The courts seem unwilling to allow an employer to be absolved of the responsibility to provide a safe system of work by entering into a labour-only contract with a third party. This point was illustrated in *Morris v Breaveglen Ltd* [1993] ICR 766 where the first employer sent an employee to work under a labour-only contract for the second employer. The plaintiff was required to drive a dumper. He was not suitably trained to drive the vehicle in a safe manner. The vehicle overturned while he was driving it. He was injured. It was held that the first employer was liable since it was that employer's duty to provide a safe system of work and the duty was non-delegable.

Competent staff

An employer is under a common law duty to exercise reasonable care to select a reasonably competent workforce (*Butler v Fife Coal Co. Ltd* [1912] AC 149). The duty remains during the entire period of the employment (*Hudson v Ridge Manufacturing Co. Ltd* [1957] 2 QB 348). The main import of this is that if a worker is injured because of the intrinsic inability on the part of a fellow employee to perform his or her duties, the injured worker can sue the employer. The duty is not based on vicarious liability. The duty in question is one which is directly owed by the employer to the employee. Therefore an employer would be liable for the injury caused to a fellow worker by someone known to the employer to be a practical joker (*Hudson v Ridge Manufacturing Co. Ltd*). It would be immaterial that the conduct in question was outside the scope of the latter's course of employment.

STATUTORY CONTROLS OVER WORK AND WORKPLACES

One of the most undesirable consequences of the industrial revolution was the degrading and often dangerous conditions factory workers were forced to endure. Indeed, one of the most striking images which seems to epitomise the plight and helplessness of the working classes in early Victorian Britain, is that of the overcrowded, poorly lit factory, manned by a ragged, emaciated, grim-faced workforce. Graphic accounts of such conditions by authors such as J.P. Kay, *The Moral and Physical Condition of the Working Classes employed in the Cotton Manufacture in Manchester* (1832), P. Gaskell, *The Manufacturing Population of England. Its Moral, Social and Physical Condition* (1833) and C. Thackrah, *The Effects of the Principal Arts, Trades and Professions, and of Civic States and Habits of Living on Health and Longevity* (1831) fuelled the factory reform movement which demanded that more humane conditions should obtain in Britain's factories. This movement gathered momentum in the 1830s and led to the passing of the Factory Act 1833 which introduced a State inspectorate for factories. A number of other Factory Acts were passed during the 19th century. That century also saw the passing of legislation dealing with working conditions in mines as well as in shops. As the 20th century progressed, more and more legislation was made for factories, mines, shops etc. The primary legislation governing such workplaces begot a plethora of secondary legislation. Indeed industrial safety probably became the most highly regulated branch of environmental health law. To further obfuscate matters, the enforcement of health and safety law was split between a number of different inspectorates, such as those of the mines and quarries and factories, and the local authorities. The whole system was a hotchpotch which called for radical change.

The statutory control of industrial safety law was examined by the Robens Committee which reported in 1972 (Cmnd 5034). Its main recommendations were implemented by the Health and Safety at Work etc. Act 1974 the main provisions of which are now discussed.

Health and Safety at Work etc. Act 1974

The Health and Safety at Work etc. Act 1974 (HASAWA) constitutes a landmark in the law governing health and safety at work. The main feature of the HASAWA is that it gives statutory protection to all those who are 'at work' (subject to certain exceptions) irrespective of where the work is taking place. The Act is as applicable to the office worker as it is to the farm labourer. The phrase 'at work' is defined in s. 52(1) which provides that, for the purposes of part I of the Act:

(a) 'work' means work as an employee or as a self-employed person;

(b) an employee is at work throughout the time when he is in the course of his employment, but not otherwise; and

(c) a self-employed person is at work throughout such time as he devotes to work as a self-employed person.

It can be seen therefore that the expression 'at work' covers not only those who are at work under a contract of service, but also those who are self-employed. For the purposes of the Act, the distinction between an employee (or servant) and an independent contractor is unimportant since both would fall within its scope. However, the case law relating to the issue of whether an employee is or is not acting in the course of his or her employment is of relevance in this context. This will be found in the standard textbooks on tort.

Health and safety regulations and relevant statutory provisions

The HASAWA is a statute which sets out general requirements in relation to safety at work. It is the intention of Parliament to supplement the provisions of the HASAWA with detailed regulations and codes of practice to deal with particular work situations and practices. Section 15(1) empowers the Secretary of State to make regulations for any of the general purposes of part I of the Act except as regards matters relating exclusively to agricultural operations. Section 15(2) allows regulations to be made for the purposes listed in sch. 3 to the Act. The power contained in s. 15(2) does not derogate from the general power conferred by s. 15(1). A large number of regulations have been made under this section. No attempt can of course be made here to list, far less discuss, all of the regulations. However, a brief explanation is given of several important regulations at the end of the chapter. Of further importance is s. 15(3), which allows health and safety regulations to repeal and modify any of the 'existing statutory provisions', that is, the existing enactments which are listed in sch. 1 to the Act and which include the Offices, Shops and Railway Premises Act 1963 and the Factories Act 1961.

In the HASAWA, 'relevant statutory provisions' comprise the provisions of part I of the Act and of any health and safety regulations plus the existing statutory provisions.

General duties of employers

A fundamental characteristic of the HASAWA is that all persons who are at work are given statutory protection. Section 2(1) therefore provides:

> It shall be the duty of every employer to ensure, so far as is reasonably practicable, the health, safety and welfare at work of all his employees.

It is an offence to fail to discharge this duty (s. 33).

Essentially s. 2 simply imports into statute law that which obtains at common law. The employer is under a duty to do only that which is reasonably practicable. In other words the duty the section imposes on the employer is not strict. The leading case on the meaning of the phrase 'reasonably practicable' is *Edwards* v *National Coal Board* [1949] 1 KB 704, in which Asquith LJ stated that in order to ascertain if an employer had done that which was reasonably practicable, the quantum or magnitude of risk associated with the duty in question had to be weighed against the measures necessary to avert the danger. Such a computation had to be made before the occurrence of the accident in which it was alleged that a breach of duty had taken place. A similar interpretation was adopted by the House of Lords in *Marshall* v *Gotham Co. Ltd* [1954] AC 360. Lord Oaksey stated that whether something was reasonably practicable depended upon '... whether the time, trouble and expense of the precautions are disproportionate to the risk involved' (at p. 370). If the preventative measures outweigh the risk involved, the employer is under no obligation to take the measures. In *Austin Rover Group Ltd* v *HM Inspector of Factories* [1990] 1 AC 619, Lord Goff of

Chieveley considered the degree of likelihood of the accident occurring was an important element in the equation.

The types of risk that the employer is under a duty to guard against are almost infinite in nature and range from protecting the employee from dangerous machinery (*Belhaven Brewery Co.* v *McLean* [1975] IRLR 370) to protecting the employee against the effect of noxious fumes (*Cartwright* v *GKN Sankey Ltd* (1973) 14 KIR 349), and even against the risk of armed robbery (*West Bromwich Building Society Ltd* v *Townsend* [1983] ICR 257).

Subsection (2) of s. 2 specifies the nature of the duty the employer owes in relation to the employee. It provides:

Without prejudice to the generality of an employer's duty under the preceding subsection, the matters to which that duty extends include in particular —

(a) the provision and maintenance of plant and systems of work that are, so far as is reasonably practicable, safe and without risks to health;

(b) arrangements for ensuring, so far as is reasonably practicable, safety and absence of risks to health in connection with the use, handling, storage and transport of articles and substances;

(c) the provision of such information, instruction, training and supervision as is necessary to ensure, so far as is reasonably practicable, the health and safety at work of his employees;

(d) so far as is reasonably practicable as regards any place of work under the employer's control, the maintenance of it in a condition that is safe and without risks to health and the provision and maintenance of means of access to and egress from it that are safe and without such risks;

(e) the provision and maintenance of a working environment for his employees that is, so far as is reasonably practicable, safe, without risks to health, and adequate as regards facilities and arrangements for their welfare at work.

As far as para. (a) is concerned the expression 'plant' is given a wide meaning by the courts. In *Haigh* v *Charles W. Ireland Ltd* [1974] 1 WLR 43, Lord Morris of Borth-y-Gest stated (at p. 47) that 'plant' should be regarded as 'a somewhat general [word] covering the equipment or the apparatus or the gear or the implements or the appliances or the machinery which anyone would expect to find in a factory'. In *Bolton Metropolitan Borough Council* v *Malrod Insulations Ltd* [1993] ICR 358 it was held that the employer's duty to provide and maintain safe plant and equipment extended to ensuring the safety of employees who did not use the equipment in question. A breach of s. 2 occurred when unsafe plant was made available although it was not being used and had not been used. Furthermore, the duty to provide safe equipment did not only arise when employees were actually at work

As far as para. (c) is concerned, the employer's common law duty to warn and instruct the employee (see page 146) would be relevant here. Moreover, in *R* v *Swan Hunter Shipbuilders Ltd* [1981] ICR 831 it was held that the duty of an employer to provide a safe system of work for the employer's own employees extended in certain cases to giving information and instruction relating to potential dangers to employees of a subcontractor who worked alongside the employer's own workforce.

As far as (d) is concerned the leading case on the employer's duty to provide a safe means of access to work is *Taylor* v *Coalite Oils and Chemicals Ltd* (1967) 3 KIR 315 in which Diplock LJ stated (at p. 319):

> A working place is 'safe' if there is nothing there which might be a reasonably foreseeable cause of injury to anyone working there, acting in a way in which a human being may reasonably be expected to act, in circumstances which may reasonably be expected to occur.

He continued (at p. 321):

> How frequently it is reasonably practicable to inspect a particular place in a factory must depend upon all the circumstances and involve a computation in which the quantum of risk is placed in one scale and the sacrifice involved in the inspection (in money, time and trouble) is placed in the other.

In other words the court has to weigh the probability or likelihood of a given state of affairs generating a danger to the workforce against the preventative measures necessary to combat the risk. It is suggested that whether adequate preventative measures have been taken in any instance is a question of fact which falls to be determined on the particular circumstances of the case. It is inappropriate, therefore, to found general propositions on issues decided in reported cases. By way simply of illustration, therefore, in *Darby* v *GKN Screws and Fasteners Ltd* [1986] ICR 1, the plaintiff, while entering the premises of his employer, slipped and fell on frozen snow which had fallen the previous evening. It was held that the employer had not breached his statutory duty to provide a safe means of access to his premises. Peter Pain J stated that the law would not require the employer to have a substantial body of men permanently ready to deal with snow whenever it might fall there (p. 2). (See also *Hunter* v *British Steel Corporation* 1980 SLT 31.) Whereas there is probably no legal obligation on the employer to warn the employee of dangers in relation to access to the employee's place of work where such dangers are readily apparent, such a duty does exist in relation to those which are not (*Ashdown* v *Samuel Williams and Sons Ltd* [1957] 1 QB 409).

As far as (e) is concerned, the working environment, that is, the workplace itself, must be kept in a safe condition. Whereas it could be argued that the ambit of the paragraph would include the activities taking place at work as well as the workplace as a static entity, it was held in *Evans* v *Sant* [1975] QB 626 that one had simply to determine the safety of the place of work as a static entity. Therefore since the only thing rendering the premises in the case unsafe was the use of defective equipment brought on to it, the premises were not unsafe within the meaning of the subsection.

The Management of Health and Safety at Work Regulations 1992 (SI 1992/2051) make provision for each employer to assess the risks to the health and safety of employees to which they are exposed whilst they are at work (reg. 3). A duty is also placed on the employer to make and give effect to such arrangements as are appropriate, having regard to the nature of the employer's activities and the size of the undertaking, for the effective planning, organisation, control, monitoring and review of preventive and protective measures (reg. 4).

Written safety policy

An innovative feature of the HASAWA is the requirement placed on the employer by s. 2(3) to prepare a written statement of the employer's general policy with respect to the health and safety at work of employees and the organisation and arrangements for the time being in force for carrying out that policy, and to bring the statement to the notice of all employees. To date there is no judicial authority on either the form or the content of a safety policy. The Employer's Health and Safety Policy Statements (Exception) Regulations 1975 (SI 1975/1584), reg. 2, waives the requirement to have a written safety policy statement in relation to an undertaking in which fewer than five people are employed at any one time. The regulations do not define the expression 'undertaking'. An obvious question of practical importance therefore is whether an employer who carries on a business at a number of premises has a number of separate undertakings within the meaning of the regulations, in which case, if there are fewer than five persons employed at any one site, the exception applies. In *Osborne* v *Bill Taylor of Huyton Ltd* [1982] ICR 168 the appellant owned and controlled 31 betting shops. In one shop fewer than five people were normally employed. The appellant was prosecuted for failing to provide a safety policy statement on the ground that the appellant's undertaking comprised all the betting shops and so the exception provided in reg. 2 did not apply. On appeal, Ormrod LJ was of the opinion (at p. 174) that in order to ascertain if the shop in question was a separate undertaking one should consider whether the employer was carrying on 31 separate businesses or whether the employer was carrying on a single undertaking in 31 shops. It was a question of fact as to which category the relevant premises fell into. On the separate issue of whether, for the purposes of reg. 2, two people who, at different times, stood in for off-duty personnel, could be counted, the court was of the opinion that they could not on the basis that the phrase 'for the time being' in reg. 2 meant at any one time.

General duties of employers to others

It is the intention of the HASAWA to ensure the general safety not only of persons at work but also of the public in general. This holistic approach is well illustrated by s. 3. Subsection (1) provides:

> It shall be the duty of every employer to conduct his undertaking in such a way as to ensure, so far as is reasonably practicable, that persons not in his employment who may be affected thereby are not thereby exposed to risks to their health or safety.

It is an offence to fail to discharge this duty (s. 33).

Again this does no more than reproduce the common law. The building contractor who carries out demolition work near a public place in such a way as to endanger passers-by, would commit an offence under s. 3(1). In *R v Board of Trustees of the Science Museum* [1993] 1 WLR 1171 it was held that the word 'risk' as used in s. 3(1) implied the possibility of danger and that it is not necessary for the prosecution to prove that any non-employees had in fact sustained any injury.

In *RMC Roadstore Products Ltd v Jester, The Times*, 8 February 1994, it was held that in certain circumstances the work of an independent contractor could fall within the scope of an employer's undertaking in terms of s. 3(1) of the Act. However, for this to occur it is necessary for the employer either to exercise actual control over the activity of the independent contractor or be under a duty to do so. Complete control is not necessary.

A similar duty is placed by s. 3(2) on the self-employed to ensure that others are not placed at risk.

Section 3(3) places a duty on every employer and every self-employed person, in prescribed cases, to give persons (other than employees) who may be affected by the undertaking, the prescribed information about the aspects of the undertaking which might affect their health or safety. To date no regulations have been made under this subsection.

In *Aitchison v Howard Doris Ltd* 1979 SLT (Notes) 22 it was held that s. 3 relates solely to protection from danger accruing from the conduct of the undertaking. The section was not therefore applicable to an individual's access to a place of work.

The general duty placed on the employer by s. 3(1) has been held to extend to the need to give, in appropriate situations, relevant information to persons other than employees to protect their safety and health. Section 3(3) therefore does not derogate from the general duty imposed on employers by s. 3(1). In *Carmichael* v *Rosehall Engineering Works Ltd* [1983] IRLR 480 two youths, who were involved in a work experience programme but were not employed by the defender, were burned when their overalls, which were impregnated with paraffin, caught fire. It was held on appeal that the defenders could rightly be convicted of infringing s. 3(1) by virtue of failing to provide relevant information to persons who were not employees about the dangers of using paraffin.

The scope of s. 3(1) is wide. For example, in *Sterling-Winthrop Group Ltd* v *Allan* 1987 SLT 652 it was held that a chemical company owed a duty to a customer to give that customer information about the unstable nature of chemicals the company had supplied. The duty was owed to the employees of the customer and possibly to members of the public outwith the company's premises.

Duties of controllers of premises to persons who are not their employees

It has already been emphasised that the HASAWA is a holistic statute which in essence seeks to give the worker a safe working environment. It has already been observed that the employer is placed under a general duty to ensure the safety of employees. However, a person at work may be injured or placed at risk by virtue of the acts or omissions of persons other than the employer. An obvious situation in which a person at work could be injured is when the employee is working on premises which are controlled by persons other than the employer. Section 4 therefore places a duty on persons in relation to those who:

(a) are not their employees; but
(b) use non-domestic premises made available to them as a place of work or as a place where they may use plant or substances provided for their use there,

and applies to premises so made available and other non-domestic premises used in connection with them.

Section 53 of the Act defines the expression 'domestic premises' as premises occupied as a private dwelling (including any garden, yard, garage, outhouse or other appurtenance of such premises which is not used in common by the occupants of more than one such dwelling), and 'non-domestic premises' is to be construed accordingly.

The nature of the s. 4 duty is set out in s. 4(2):

> It shall be the duty of each person who has, to any extent, control of premises to which this section applies or of the means of access thereto or egress therefrom or of any plant or substance in such premises to take such measures as it is reasonable for a person in his position to take to ensure, so far as is reasonably practicable, that the premises, all means of access thereto or egress therefrom available for use by persons using the premises, and any plant or substance in the premises or, as the case may be, provided for use there, is or are safe and without risks to health.

It is an offence to fail to discharge this duty (s. 33).

The scope of s. 4 is wide. The ambit of the section was succinctly explained by Lord Jauncey of Tullichettle in *Austin Rover Group Ltd v HM Inspector of Factories* [1990] 1 AC 619 at p. 635:

> The ambit of section 4 is far wider than that of sections 2 and 3. It applies to anyone who is in occupation of non-domestic premises and who calls in tradesmen to carry out repairs, it applies to those tradesmen in relation to the employees of others, and it applies to anyone who makes the premises available on a temporary basis for others to carry work out in. Thus organisations varying from multinational corporations to the village shop are brought under the umbrella of the section.

Section 4(2) recognises the fact that more than one person may have control of the premises in question. Whether or not someone has control over premises would be a question of fact, which would centre on the person's right to exclude others from the premises. The learning, which, it is suggested, is applicable derives from the law relating to the occupation of land (see, e.g., *Telfer v Glasgow Corporation* 1974 SLT (Notes) 51).

It seems from the decision in *T. Kilroe and Sons Ltd v Gower* [1983] Crim LR 548, that the measure of control exercised by the occupier over the premises in order to come within the scope of the section must be such as to reasonably expect the occupier to take the appropriate measures to abate the relevant danger. One would adopt an objective test to ascertain if the person in control had done all that was reasonable in the circumstances; in other words one would juxtapose a hypothetical reasonable occupier with the occupier in question and ascertain which precautions the former would have taken. In *Austin Rover Group Ltd v HM Inspector of Factories* [1990] 1 AC 619, Lord Jauncey was of the opinion that in determining if premises were unsafe and without risks to health, one is required to determine the safety of the premises in the light of the use to which they were put at any time, and not simply at the time when they were first made available for non-employees to work in.

Whereas s. 3 deals with dangers to others arising from the undertaking as a dynamic enterprise, s. 4 is principally directed to ensure the safety of those who enter the workplace. To what extent, if any, there is any overlap between ss. 3 and 4 is uncertain. In *Aitchison* v *Howard Doris Ltd* 1979 SLT (Notes) 22 the High Court of Justiciary, on appeal, did not decide whether ss. 3 and 4 are mutually exclusive. It seems, however, that the courts are prepared to construe the expression 'non-domestic premises' widely. For example, in *Westminster City Council* v *Select Management Ltd* [1985] 1 WLR 576 an improvement notice was served on the occupiers of the common parts of a block of flats which contained a lift on the basis that the lift equipment was dangerous and posed a risk to lift engineers, electricians, repairers etc. It was held by a majority of the Court of Appeal that the lift was to be considered as separate entity and therefore constituted non-domestic premises within the meaning of the Act.

Duties of manufacturers of equipment for use at work

While the manner in which an employer manages the business is of great importance to the safety of the worker, the safety of the equipment which the worker has to use is equally important. The HASAWA again draws on the common law (in this case the so-called 'narrow rule' in *Donoghue* v *Stevenson* [1932] AC 562, in which it was held that a manufacturer of goods owes a duty of care to persons who could foreseeably be affected by defects in those goods) for the provisions of s. 6 (as amended). Under s. 6(1)(a) a duty is placed on 'any person who designs, manufactures, imports or supplies any article for use at work to ensure, so far as is reasonably practicable, that the article is so designed and constructed as to be safe and without risks to health when properly used'. Section 6(2) goes on to place a duty on those who design or manufacture articles for use at work to carry out necessary research with a view to eliminating or minimising risks to health or safety which may arise from the design of the article. Section 6(4) places a similar duty on manufacturers of substances for use at work. The word 'substance' is defined by s. 53 as 'any natural or artificial substance, whether in solid or liquid form or in the form of a gas or vapour'.

It is an offence to fail to discharge any of these duties (s. 33).

Mention should also be made here of the Supply of Machinery (Safety) Regulations 1992 (SI 1992/3073) which makes provision concerning the supply of certain types of machinery.

Duties of employees at work

The safety of those at work as well as that of others can be prejudiced not only by the acts or omissions of the employer but also by the conduct (whether intentional or accidental) of employees themselves. Section 7 of the HASAWA therefore provides:

It shall be the duty of every employee while at work —

(a) to take reasonable care for the health and safety of himself and of other persons who may be affected by his acts or omissions at work; and
(b) as regards any duty or requirement imposed on his employer or any other person by or under any of the relevant statutory provisions, to cooperate with him so far as is necessary to enable that duty or requirement to be performed or complied with.

Again here the HASAWA simply draws on the common law which places similar responsibilities on the employee to the public as well as his or her fellow workers. Section 8 complements this section by providing:

No person shall intentionally or recklessly interfere with or misuse anything provided in the interests of health, safety or welfare in pursuance of any of the relevant statutory provisions.

It is an offence to fail to fulfil the s. 7 duty or to contravene s. 8 (s. 33).

Health and Safety Commission and Health and Safety Executive

The HASAWA establishes two bodies corporate, namely, the Health and Safety Executive and the Health and Safety Commission (ss. 10–14). Both bodies (in effect quangos) carry out their functions on behalf of the Crown. The statutory duties the Act places on both the Executive and the Commission are wide. However, the main responsibility of both is to implement the HASAWA in the United Kingdom.

Codes of practice

The use of codes of practice is becoming increasingly popular in environmental health law, for example in the field of food law (see page 114). As far as the HASAWA is concerned, s. 16 allows the Health and Safety Commission to approve and issue codes of practice to facilitate compliance with ss. 2 to 7 of the HASAWA or existing statutory provisions (for example, the Factories Act 1961 or the Offices, Shops and Railway Premises Act 1963). The Commission may not approve a code of practice without the consent of the Secretary of State (s. 16(2)). Before seeking that consent it must consult with the appropriate government department or other body that appears appropriate. The Secretary of State may also direct the Commission to consult particular government departments or other bodies.

Codes of practice and criminal proceedings

A code of practice made under the HASAWA is simply a guide to good practice, and a contravention of a code does not carry any civil or criminal sanction (s. 17). However, if, in any criminal proceedings, a party is alleged to have committed an offence by reason of a contravention of any provision of ss. 2–7 of the HASAWA, or of health and safety regulations, or of any existing statutory provisions (for example, the Factories Act 1961 or the Offices, Shops and Railway Premises Act 1963) and the provisions of a code of practice are relevant to the breach in question, then failure to comply with the code will result in a finding that the statutory provision had been breached unless the court is satisfied that the provision had been complied with in some other way. The significance of codes of practice under s. 17 can be illustrated by the following example. Suppose there was a code of practice relating to the storage of goods in warehouses which stated that such goods should be stacked and de-stacked by means of a movable guarded platform. If a warehouseman chose instead to provide the employees who stacked goods with stepladders, and the warehouseman was thereafter prosecuted under s. 2(2)(a) of the HASAWA for failing to provide a safe system of work for the employees, the warehouseman would be deemed by s. 17(2) to have breached s. 2(2)(a). The onus of proving that the actual system of work complied with s. 2(2)(a) would then rest on the employer.

Enforcement of health and safety legislation

The HASAWA places the main responsibility for the enforcement of statutory provisions on the Health and Safety Executive. Section 18(1) places a duty on the executive to make adequate arrangements for enforcement except to the extent that some other body is made responsible. The Secretary of State is empowered to make regulations making local authorities responsible for such enforcement or enabling responsibility for enforcement of the regulations to be transferred from the Executive to local authorities or vice versa. Regulation 3 of the Health and Safety (Enforcing Authority) Regulations 1989 (SI 1989/1903) provides that where the main activity carried on in non-domestic premises falls within the scope of sch. 1 to the regulations, the appropriate local authority, as opposed to the Executive, is responsible for the implementation of the relevant provisions. The schedule includes premises used for the sale of goods or storage of goods for retail or wholesale distribution, for office activities, for catering and for the provision of permanent or residential accommodation.

Appointment and powers of inspectors

Section 19 of the HASAWA empowers every enforcing authority to appoint inspectors to enforce health and safety legislation. No qualification is prescribed for such inspectors. It is up to the enforcing authority to determine the appropriate qualification, if any, for its inspectors to possess. Each appointment must be in writing. In *Campbell* v *Wallsend Slipway and Engineering Co. Ltd* [1978] ICR 1015 it was held that the presumption of regularity of appointment was applicable to persons appointed under the section.

The document conferring authority on a person appointed must specify the statutory powers the inspector possesses.

The powers conferred by s. 20 on an inspector are wide. An inspector has power under s. 20(2), *inter alia*:

(a) to enter premises at any reasonable time in order to inspect those premises (s. 20(2)(a)),

(b) to take measurements and photographs (s. 20(2)(f)),

(c) to take samples of any articles or substances found in any premises which the inspector has power to enter and of the atmosphere in and in the vicinity of the premises (s. 20(2)(g)),

(d) to cause any article or substance likely to cause danger to health or safety to be dismantled or subjected to any process or test (s. 20(2)(h)),

(e) in the case of any article or substance mentioned in (d) above, to take possession of it and detain it for so long as is necessary for the purpose of, *inter alia*, examining it or ensuring that it is available for use as evidence in proceedings (s. 20(2)(i)).

An inspector who takes possession of any article or substance found in any premises must either leave there, with a responsible person, or, if that is impracticable, fix in a conspicuous position, a notice giving particulars of the article or substance sufficient to identify it and stating that it has been taken under the Act (s. 20(6)). When taking possession of a substance, an inspector must, if practicable, take a sample and give a portion of the sample to a responsible person at the premises. In *Laws* v *Keane* 1983 SLT 40 the accused had required his workmen to carry out demolition work in conditions which rendered the workers liable to inhale asbestos dust. The inspector took samples of broken pipe lagging which contained asbestos and which formed part of the environment of the workforce. It was held on appeal that the inspector did not have to comply with the provisions of s. 20(6), which are only applicable only when an inspector takes possession under s. 20(2)(i) but not under s. 20(2)(g). According to the court, the assumption of s. 20(2)(i) is that the *whole* of the article or substance is taken.

Section 20(6) had therefore no relevance to sampling carried out under s. 20(2)(g), that is to say when only *part* of that which was considered to be deleterious, was seized.

Improvement and prohibition notices

One of the outstanding features of the health and safety legislation which preceded the HASAWA, from the point of view of enforcement, was the general inability on the part of officials to have unsatisfactory work situations redressed without court proceedings. The HASAWA gives such officials the right in certain circumstances, by way of service of improvement and prohibition notices, to secure compliance with the law. Sections 21 and 22 deal with improvement and prohibition notices respectively. They are now dealt with in turn.

The main purpose of the improvement notice procedure is to allow inspectors to redress breaches of health and safety legislation. Section 21 allows an inspector to serve an improvement notice if the inspector is of the opinion that a person:

(a) is contravening one or more of the relevant statutory provisions; or
(b) has contravened one or more of those provisions in circumstances that make it likely that the contravention will continue or be repeated.

An improvement notice specifies the provision or provisions which the inspector believes is being, or has been, contravened, states the reasons why the inspector is of that opinion, and requires the person served to remedy the contravention or the matters occasioning it within a specified period. It should be noted that the inspector must be of the opinion that a statutory provision is being breached before an improvement notice can be served.

The issue of a prohibition notice under s. 22 is a more drastic measure. A prohibition notice can be served if the relevant activities involve a risk of serious personal injury. A prohibition notice states that the inspector is of that opinion and must specify the matters which give rise or will give rise to the risk. If any of those matters involves, or will involve, a contravention of the relevant statutory provisions, particulars must be given of why the inspector is of that opinion. A prohibition notice directs that the activities to which it relates must not be carried on by or under the control of the person on whom the notice is served unless the matters specified in the notice have been remedied. Such a direction takes immediate effect if the inspector is of the opinion that the risk of serious personal injury is imminent. In any other case the notice becomes effective only at the end of the period specified in the notice.

Under s. 23 both improvement and prohibition notices may, but need not, include directions as to the measures to be taken to remedy any contraventions or matters to which the notice relates. Any such directions may be framed by reference, in whole or in part, to any approved code of practice, and, furthermore, provide the person on whom the notice is served with different ways of remedying the contraventions or matters. The person on whom either an improvement or prohibition notice is served can appeal under s. 24(2) to an industrial tribunal which has complete powers of review in that it can cancel, affirm or modify the notice. If such an appeal is made, it has the automatic effect of suspending the operation of an improvement notice until the appeal is finally disposed of or withdrawn. However, in the case of a prohibition notice the bringing of an appeal has the effect of suspending the operation of the notice if, and only if, the tribunal so directs.

Under s. 33 it is an offence to contravene the provisions of an improvement or prohibition notice. Liability for contravention is strict. It is irrelevant for the purposes of liability that it is impracticable to comply with the terms of the notice (*Deary* v *Mansion Hide Upholstery Ltd* [1983] ICR 610).

Criminal offences under the Act

The *raison d'être* of the HASAWA is to bring all those at work within the protection of the law. Generally speaking, non-compliance with the main provisions of the Act attracts penal sanctions. Section 33 provides that it is an offence to contravene the provisions of ss. 2–9 or health and safety regulations made under the Act.

Section 40 provides that in any proceedings for an offence under any relevant statutory provisions, consisting of a failure to comply with a duty or requirement to do something, so far as is practicable, or to use the best practicable means, it is for the accused to prove that it was not practicable or not reasonably practicable, or that there was no better practicable means than that which was used. This reverses the normal rule in criminal law that the prosecution must prove all elements of the offence in question (see *Garner* v *John Thompson (Wolverhampton) Ltd* (1968) 6 KIR 1).

FACTORIES ACT 1961

Factories were among the first workplaces to be given special legislative attention in the 19th century. A number of statutes governing safety in factories were passed during that century. The trend continued in the 20th century. The most recent statute dealing with factories is the Factories Act 1961 which repeals and replaces the statute of the same name of 1937.

Before embarking on a general discussion of the provisions of the Factories Act 1961 it is desirable to look at the expression 'factory' as defined in the Act. Section 175(1) provides that 'factory' means:

> ... any premises in which, or within the close or curtilage or precincts of which, persons are employed in manual labour in any process for or incidental to any of the following purposes, namely—
>
>   (a) the making of any article or of part of any article; or
>   (b) the altering, repairing, ornamenting, finishing, cleaning, or washing or the breaking up or demolition of any article; or
>   (c) the adapting for sale of any article; ...
>
> being premises in which, or within the close or curtilage or precincts of which, the work is carried on by way of trade or for purposes of gain and to or over which the employer of the persons employed therein has the right of access or control.

Paragraphs (d) and (e) of subsection (1) bring slaughterhouses and animal lairages within the meaning of the expression 'factory'.

A condition precedent to premises falling within the definition of a factory is that persons are employed therein in 'manual labour', an expression which is not defined in the 1961 Act. A leading case on the meaning of the phrase 'manual labour' is *J. and F. Stone Lighting and Radio Ltd* v *Haygarth* [1968] AC 157. There, the appellants were occupiers of a shop with an adjoining workroom. A television sale and hire business was conducted in the workroom where a radio and television engineer was employed. The question the House of Lords had to consider was whether the work the engineer was engaged in constituted manual labour. This question was answered in the affirmative. Lord Morris of Borth-y-Gest stated (at p. 175):

> My lords, I cannot think that if someone spends all his time, or at least the greater part of it, doing work with his hands he is not to be regarded as employed in manual labour merely because he needs knowledge to do this work.

Lord Upjohn, in attempting to provide a rough guide to which category the relevant premises fell, stated (at p. 186):

> that to determine whether a person was employed in manual labour you look at a particular job and find out what is the dominant feature which he is required to do and if the brain governs the hand he is not doing manual labour.

It seems, then, that for any given situation one attempts to ascertain if the predominant feature of the tasks performed require brain rather than brawn. This indeed is a crude test, and one can envisage a number of situations in which it would be difficult to apply, for example, where the work is of an intricate nature.

It is suggested that whether the work being performed on the premises constitutes manual labour is a question of fact. It is sufficient that only one person is employed on the premises (*Griffith* v *Ferrier* 1952 JC 56).

By way simply of illustration of the types of premises which have fallen within the definition of s. 175(1) mention should be made of two decided cases. In *Bromwich* v *National Ear, Nose and Throat Hospital* [1980] ICR 450, it was held that a hospital workshop, used from time to time for mechanical and electrical repairs was a 'factory'. In *Paul Popper Ltd* v *Grimsey* [1963] 1 QB 44, premises where photographic negatives were developed were held to be a factory.

It should be noted that by virtue of the provisions of s. 175(1) the entire premises within the close or curtilage of which manual labour takes place are a factory (*Newton* v *John Stanning and Son Ltd* [1962] 1 WLR 30; see also *T. Kilroe and Sons Ltd* v *Gower* [1983] Crim LR 548). However, the premises need not possess a boundary or fence. For example, in *Barry* v *Cleveland Bridge and Engineering Co. Ltd* [1963] 1 All ER 192 it was held that two unbordered areas in a quay, which were used for the purposes of steel storage and erection, constituted a factory.

In *Findlay* v *Miller Construction (Northern) Ltd* 1977 SLT (Sh Ct) 8 it was held that a building was not an article within the meaning of s. 175 and accordingly the site within which the building was contained was not a factory in terms of the Act. Furthermore, in *R* v *AI Industrial Products plc* [1987] ICR 418 it was held that the conduct of building works on a site did not constitute a process within the meaning of s. 175(1). In *Norse* v *Morganite Crucible Ltd* [1989] 1 AC 692 it was held that the word 'process' as used in the Asbestos Regulations 1969 (SI 1969/690) meant an activity with some degree of continuity and repetition of a series of acts.

An incidental process need not be an industrial activity. For example, in *Newton* v *John Stanning and Son Ltd* [1962] 1 WLR 30, a pump house within the curtilage of, and supplying water to, a factory was itself held to be a factory. Similarly in *Powley* v *Bristol Siddeley Engines Ltd* [1966] 1 WLR 729, it was held that an administration block within a factory complex was itself part of the factory and therefore came within the scope of the section.

General provisions

Parts I and II of the Factories Act 1961 contain general provisions relating to the working environment in factories. Factories are required by s. 1 to be kept in a clean state (see the Factories (Cleanliness of Walls and Ceilings) Order 1960 (SI 1960/1794) amended by SI 1974/427) and in a satisfactory sanitary condition (see SR & O 1938/611 amended by SI 1974/426). Section 2 provides that no factory is to be overcrowded to the extent that persons employed therein are exposed to the risk of injury. The section also requires that the amount of cubic space allowed for each worker must be not less than 400 cubic feet.

Section 3 provides that a reasonable temperature must be maintained in each workroom. A minimum of 60°F (15.5°C) is prescribed.

Section 4(1) requires that effective and suitable provision is made 'for securing and maintaining by the circulation of fresh air in each workroom the adequate ventilation of the room'.

In *Cartwright* v *GKN Sankey Ltd* (1972) 12 KIR 453, (1973) 14 KIR 349, the plaintiff was employed as an electrician and welder. During the course of his employment he was exposed to prolonged inhalation of low concentrations of fumes including oxides of nitrogen, by reason of which he contracted chronic bronchitis and emphysema. It was held that before the employer could be held liable, it would have to be shown that the employer had actual or constructive knowledge of the relevant danger and had failed to keep abreast of current medical and other scientific knowledge, discoveries and warning (see also *Wallhead* v *Ruston and Hornsby Ltd* (1973) 14 KIR 285).

Section 5(1) requires that effective provision be made for securing and maintaining:

> sufficient and suitable lighting, whether natural or artificial, in every part of a factory in which persons are working or passing.

In *Davies* v *Massey Ferguson Perkins Ltd* [1986] ICR 580, it was held that s. 5(1) imposes an absolute duty. It was quite irrelevant, therefore, that the defendants were not negligent in failing to provide suitable lighting. See also *Lane* v *Gloucester Engineering Co. Ltd* [1967] 1 WLR 767. In *Thornton* v *Fisher and Ludlow Ltd* [1968] 1 WLR 655 it was held that a roadway within the curtilage of a factory is covered by s. 5(1).

Sections 6 and 7 deal respectively with the drainage of floors and sanitary conveniences.

Fencing of machinery

It is fundamental to the safety of the employee that machinery which has the capacity to injure is securely fenced. The Factories Act 1961, s. 14(1), threfore provides:

Every dangerous part of any machinery, other than prime movers and transmission machinery, shall be securely fenced unless it is in such a position or of such construction as to be as safe to every person employed or working on the premises as it would be if securely fenced.

The expression 'machinery' is defined by s. 176 as including any driving belt. As the law stands it is uncertain whether vehicles can be construed as machinery within the meaning of the section. In *Cherry* v *International Alloys Ltd* [1961] 1 QB 136, it was held that a truck which was used in a factory to transport materials was not machinery but in *British Railways Board* v *Liptrot* [1969] 1 AC 136, a mobile crane employed in a scrapyard was held to be machinery notwithstanding the fact that the crane was mounted on a chassis fitted with four rubber-tyred wheels, the crane being able to move from place to place under its own power. It seems therefore that there is no requirement that the equipment in question be fixed to the premises concerned for it to fall within the scope of s. 14. However, the courts seem unwilling to give a comprehensive definition of machinery and each case will depend on its own facts. From the decision in *TBA Industrial Products* v *Lainé* [1987] ICR 75, the phrase 'any machinery' does include machinery being modified and tested on the premises concerned.

Under s. 15, in determining whether the dangerous part of any machinery is safe to those employed or working at the premises, no account is to be taken of any person carrying out an examination of the machinery, or lubricating or adjusting the machinery, if such activity can only take place while the machinery is in motion. Liability imposed by the section is strict. In other words, the mere fact that the relevant dangerous part is unfenced grounds liability (*Simpson* v *Hardie and Smith Ltd* 1968 JC 23; *McGuiness* v *Key Markets Ltd* (1972) 13 KIR 249).

In determining whether any given part of machinery is dangerous, one must consider if it is reasonably foreseeable that a danger is presented to the workforce by virtue of the state of the machine (*Ballard* v *Ministry of Defence* [1977] ICR 513; see also *Close* v *Steel Co. of Wales Ltd* [1962] AC 367). In the leading case of *Wearing* v *Pirelli Ltd* [1977] 1 WLR 48, the defendants employed the plaintiff to work on a machine which consisted of a revolving drum. The drum was not fenced. The plaintiff was injured while working at the machine. In holding the defendants liable Lord Edmund-Davies quoted the judgment of Wills J in *Hindle* v *Birtwistle* [1897] 1 QB 192 at p. 195:

[Parts of machinery] are dangerous if in the ordinary course of human affairs danger may be reasonably anticipated from the use of them without protection. ... In considering whether machinery is dangerous, the contingency of carelessness on the part of the workman in charge of it, and the frequency with which that contingency is likely to arise, are matters that must be taken into consideration. It is entirely a question of degree.

See also *F. E. Callow (Engineers) Ltd* v *Johnson* [1971] AC 335; *Millard* v *Serck Tubes Ltd* [1969] 1 WLR 211; the judgment of Lord President Cooper in *Mitchell* v *North British Rubber Co. Ltd* 1945 JC 69 is also worthy of study.

Sometimes when considering whether machinery is dangerous the courts have taken into account considerations of cost (see, e.g., *Belhaven Brewery Co.* v *McLean* [1975] IRLR 370). It is suggested that questions of cost have no relevance in relation to the section.

On the authority of *Foster* v *Flexile Metal Co. Ltd* (1967) 4 KIR 49, s. 14(1) should be read as if the words implied that fencing must be provided during all the normal workings of the machine in question, which includes preparation of the machine for normal use, and during any alterations or adjustments which could reasonably be foreseen. However, the section does not impose a duty on the employer to fence any part of machinery against a tool (as opposed to part of the body of a person) coming into contact with the machine (*Sparrow* v *Fairey Aviation Co. Ltd* [1964] AC 1019; see also *Pearce* v *Stanley-Bridges Ltd* [1965] 1 WLR 931). Furthermore, it seems that the section protects all those working at premises who could foreseeably be injured by machinery on the premises. Individuals acting outside the scope of their employment could therefore be protected by the section (*Uddin* v *Associated Portland Cement Manufacturers Ltd* [1965] 2 QB 582).

In certain situations it is inevitable that operatives are exposed to danger while carrying out remedial works to a machine. Section 15 therefore provides that in determining for the purposes of s. 14 whether any part of machinery is in such a position as to be as safe to every person employed or working on the premises as it would be if securely fenced, no account is to be taken of any person carrying out an examination of the machinery or lubricating the machinery etc. if such work can only be carried out while the machinery is in motion.

Section 16 requires fencing and safeguards provided by way of compliance in respect of s. 14 to be:

> of substantial construction, and constantly maintained and kept in position while the parts required to be fenced or safeguarded are in motion or use, except when any such parts are necessarily exposed for examination and for any lubrication or adjustment shown by the examination to be immediately necessary.

There are a number of decided cases on when a machine is in motion for the purposes of s. 16. In *Richard Thomas and Baldwins Ltd* v *Cummings* [1955] AC 321, it was held by the House of Lords that a machine, which was normally powered by electricity, was not in motion for the purposes of s. 16 if the machine was being rotated by hand. Lord Reid stated: 'The phrase "in motion" appears to be more apt to describe a continuing state of motion lasting, or intended to last, for an appreciable time'. (See also *Mitchell* v *W. S. Westin Ltd* [1965] 1 WLR 297.) If the machine is simply going slowly, it is still in motion (*Joy* v *News of the World* (1972) 13 KIR 57). However, if the machine is being moved by hand for the purposes of cleaning, it is not 'in motion' (*Finnie* v *John Laird and Son Ltd* 1967 SLT 243). Nor is the machine in motion if it is being moved intermittently, albeit under mechanical power (*Mitchell* v *W. S. Westin Ltd*). In considering whether a machine is in motion, one should look at the character of what was being done and the circumstances in which it was being done (per Sellars LJ in *Mitchell* v *W. S. Westin Ltd*). The case law therefore is not particularly helpful. Indeed the judicial reasoning would undoubtedly invoke the censure of a logician. The approach can at best be described as pragmatic. By way of conclusion, it seems that the test of whether a machine is in motion depends on whether the machine is being put to, or is being prepared for, normal use, and also whether the movement of the machine is continuous. If both conditions are met, the courts would be disposed to regard the machine as being in motion for the purposes of the section.

Floors, passages etc.

Often those employed in factories are required to transport heavy loads from one part of the factory to another. Vision may be partially obscured by the bulk of the load being transported. It is essential, therefore, that factory floors, passageways etc. are kept free from obstruction. The Factories Act 1961, s. 28(1), accordingly provides:

> All floors, steps, stairs, passages and gangways shall be of sound construction and properly maintained and shall, so far as is reasonably practicable, be kept free from any obstruction and from any substance likely to cause persons to slip.

The words 'floors', 'steps', 'stairs', 'passages' and 'gangways' are not defined in the Act. In *Thornton* v *Fisher and Ludlow Ltd* [1968] 1 WLR 655 it was held that a roadway within the curtilage of a factory was not a 'passage' or a 'gangway' within s. 28(1). However, in *Harper* v *Mander and Germain Ltd* (1992) *The Times*, 28 December 1992 it was held that a duckboard was a floor or at least a passage or gangway within the meaning of the section.

There have been a number of cases on the meaning of 'obstruction' in s. 28. A pragmatic approach was adopted by Lord Denning MR in *Pengelley* v *Bell Punch Co. Ltd* [1964] 1 WLR 1055 at p. 1058: '... an "obstruction" is something on the floor that has no business to be there, and which is a source of risk to persons ordinarily using the floor'. In *Jenkins* v *Allied Ironfounders Ltd* [1970] 1 WLR 304 it was held that a piece of metal lying on a factory floor constituted an obstruction but in *Marshall* v *Ericsson Telephones Ltd* [1964] 1 WLR 1367 it was held that a trolley negligently left in a factory gangway did not. The Court of Appeal in *Marshall* v *Ericsson Telephones Ltd* held that the section did not purport to penalise the existence of that which was there by virtue of the ordinary course of work for the movement of goods. Danckwerts LJ expressed this point forcefully in the following terms: 'The Factories Act 1961 is not dealing with a model of a factory in a museum but with an actual working factory in practical conditions' (at p. 615).

From *Jenkins* v *Allied Ironfounders Ltd* it seems that whether an item can rank as an obstruction within the meaning of s. 28(1) would depend on whether it is extraneous to the usual state of affairs encountered in the particular workplace. It is immaterial that the obstruction is created inadvertently (*Bennett* v *Rylands Whitecross Ltd* [1978] ICR 1031).

The word 'substance' in s. 28(1) was given a purposive construction in *Taylor* v *Gestetner Ltd* (1967) 2 KIR 133 where it was held to include water which was covering a factory floor. *McCart* v *Queen of Scots Knitwear Ltd* 1987 SLT (Sh Ct) 57 further illustrates this point. There it was held that a plastic bag negligently left lying on a factory floor contravened s. 28(1) by virtue of being a substance. In *Williams* v *Painter Brothers Ltd* (1968) 4 KIR 487, it was accepted that in certain circumstances the presence of grease on a factory floor, could fall within the scope of s. 28(1).

Safe means of access and safe place of employment etc.

It is of fundamental importance that the workplace is inherently safe and furthermore that a safe means of access is provided and maintained to every place of work. The Factories Act 1961, s. 29(1), therefore provides:

> There shall, so far as is reasonably practicable, be provided and maintained safe means of access to every place at which any person has at any time to work and every such place shall, so far as is reasonably practicable, be made and kept safe for any person working there.

On the authority of *Dexter* v *Tenby Electrical Accessories Ltd* [1991] Crim LR 839 liability under the section is strict (see also *Larner* v *British Steel plc* [1993] ICR 551). In *McFaulds* v *Reed Corrugated Cases* 1993 SLT 670 it was held that a fork-lift truck was not a place for the purposes of s. 29(1). In *Harkins* v *McCluskey* 1987 SLT 289, it was held that a path in a factory was not a place and it was held that s. 29 did not cover activities taking place in the factory, as opposed to the workplace as a static entity. Therefore a place

Health and safety at work

of work in a factory which is intrinsically safe cannot be rendered unsafe in terms of the section simply by the way it is used.

Section 29(2) requires the provision of a secure foothold and, where necessary, a secure handhold where any person has to work at a place from which he is liable to fall a distance more than 6 feet (1.82 m).

Lifting heavy weights

According to the Health and Safety Commission's Annual Report for 1991/92, the most common cause of accident which occasioned an employee's absence from work for more than three days related to handling (p. 90). It is imperative therefore that the employee is protected from carrying anything of a weight which could cause injury. The Factories Act 1961, s. 72(1), provides, therefore:

> A person shall not be employed to lift, carry or move any load so heavy as to be likely to cause injury to him.

In determining whether a given load is likely to cause injury to an employee, one must take into account the personal physical characteristics of that employee. However, an employer cannot be held liable if it could not reasonably be expected that the employer would know of the physical idiosyncrasy which rendered the employee likely to sustain injury by lifting a particular weight. 'Likely' simply means probable (*Whitfield* v *H and R Johnson (Tiles) Ltd* [1991] ICR 109).

It sometimes happens that it is left up to the employee whether to lift a particular weight. If the employee does in fact lift it and it is likely to injure him or her, the employer would be liable under s. 72(1) (*Brown* v *Allied Ironfounders Ltd* [1974] 1 WLR 527). It is suggested that liability would only lie in such a situation where it was reasonable for the employee to lift the load in question.

OFFICES, SHOPS AND RAILWAY PREMISES ACT 1963

As far as health, safety and welfare of employees is concerned, attention has traditionally tended to be concentrated on factories and mines. Offices and shops, however, also require to be regulated since a variety of activities which take place in these types of premises could place the employee at risk. The current Act regulating safety in such premises is the Offices, Shops and Railway Premises Act 1963 (OSRPA 1963), the main provisions of which are now discussed.

Under s. 1(2), the expression 'office premises' means a building or part of a building, being a building or part the sole or principal use of which is as an office or for office purposes. In *Westwood* v *Post Office* [1974] AC 1, the courts were prepared to give the definition a wide meaning. There it was held that a lift motor room within a telephone exchange was office premises. The expression 'office purposes' is defined by s. 1(2)(b) as including, the 'purposes of administration, clerical work, handling money and telephone and telegraph operating'.

The expression 'shop premises' includes shop premises where the sole or principal use is the carrying on of retail trade and premises where goods are kept for sale wholesale by a wholesale dealer (s. 1(3)(a)) but not a warehouse belonging to the owners, trustees or conservators of a dock, wharf or quay (see *Fisher* v *Port of London Authority* [1962] 1 WLR 234). The expression also includes business premises to which members of the public deliver items for repair or themselves carry out repairs and also premises for storing solid fuel for sale.

The expression 'railway premises' is defined by s. 1(4) as premises used for the purposes of a railway undertaking, but not including office or shop premises, or living accommodation or hotels.

Exception for certain premises

It sometimes happens that a very small number of persons are employed in a shop or office premises. This is more likely to be the case in premises where those working are all members of one family. It was the intention of Parliament to exclude such premises from the provisions of the OSRPA 1963. Section 2 therefore excludes premises which would otherwise have fallen within the scope of the Act where those employed in the premises include only the husband, wife, parent, grandparent, son, daughter, grandchild, brother or sister of the employer. It is suggested that such an exclusion is unwarranted since all those employed to work in office or shop premises should enjoy the protection the Act affords. The section also excludes a dwellinghouse which would be within the Act by reason only that a person who lives there, and is employed by a person who does not live there, does work (for example, clerical work) in the house in fulfilment of a term of the employment contract.

Section 3 exempts all premises in which the total hours worked each week does not normally exceed 21. It should be noted that in calculating the number of hours worked on the premises for the purposes of s. 3, one is required to take into account the number of hours worked by the relatives (mentioned in s. 2) of the employer.

Cleanliness

Section 4 of the OSRPA 1963 requires all furniture, furnishings and fittings in premises to which the Act applies to be kept clean.

Overcrowding

Accidents are more likely to occur in premises which are overcrowded. The OSRPA 1963, s. 5(1), therefore provides that no room to which the Act applies may be overcrowded to such an extent as to cause risk of injury to the health of persons working therein. Whether a given room is overcrowded is a question of fact. In determining whether a room is overcrowded one is required to take into account, the space occupied by furniture, furnishings, fittings etc. The number of persons habitually employed at any one time to work in any room, must be allocated not less than 40 square feet (about 3.72 square metres) in terms of floor area and 400 cubic feet (about 11.33 cubic metres) in cubic capacity, on average (s. 5(2)). The requirements imposed by s. 5(2) are in addition to the general requirements imposed by s. 5(1). However, s. 5(2) does not apply to rooms to which members of the public are invited to resort.

Temperature

An important factor governing the comfort of employees is the ambient temperature of the workplace. The OSRPA 1963, s. 6, requires that a reasonable temperature be maintained in every workroom. Whether the temperature is reasonable is a question of fact. By s. 6(2) a temperature of not less than 60.8°F (16°C) must be attained and maintained after the first hour in rooms where the work done does not involve severe physical effort. The temperature requirement does not apply to rooms to which members of the public are invited to resort and in which the maintenance of this temperature is not reasonably practicable. Rooms in railway or shop premises in which the maintenance of the required temperature is not reasonably practicable or would cause deterioration of goods, are also exempt. However, in such cases there must be provided conveniently accessible facilities to enable employees to warm themselves. Furthermore the employer must afford employees reasonable opportunity to warm themselves.

Ventilation and lighting

It is a vital requirement for human health that offices and shops are suitably lit and ventilated. Sections 7 and 8 respectively of the OSRPA 1963 make provision for the effective and suitable ventilation and lighting of premises. No standards are prescribed.

Sanitary conveniences and washing facilities

Suitable and sufficient sanitary conveniences must be provided for the use of persons employed in premises subject to the OSRPA 1963 and must be conveniently accessible to them (s. 9). Whether conveniences are suitable and sufficient is a question of fact. In *A. C. Davis and Sons* v *Environmental Health Department of Leeds City Council* [1976] IRLR 282 two women were employed in a shop. An arrangement was made by the occupiers of the shop with the tenants of the flat upstairs that the employees of the shop could use the toilet situated in the flat. There was a condition in the lease of the flat, requiring its tenants to give access to the occupiers of the shop at all times. It was held that the toilet was 'conveniently accessible' as required by s. 9. The Sanitary Convenience Regulations 1964 (SI 1964/966) lay down detailed requirements relating to the number and types of conveniences which require to be provided.

Section 10 requires suitable and sufficient washing facilities to be provided at places conveniently accessible to persons employed in premises subject to the Act. The Washing Facilities Regulations 1964 (SI 1964/965) lay down requirements as to the number and type of basins etc. to be provided. Washing facilities must be effectively lit and kept in a clean and orderly condition (OSRPA 1963, s. 10(2)). All apparatus installed in such facilities must be kept clean and properly maintained. In *South Surbiton Co-operative Society* v *Wilcox* [1975] IRLR 292, it was held that a wash-basin was not being properly maintained as required by the section because it was cracked.

Accommodation for clothing

Office, and especially shop, workers are often required to wear uniform when carrying out their duties. The OSRPA 1963, s. 12, therefore provides that suitable and sufficient provision must be made for enabling clothing of employees which is not being worn by them during working hours, to be hung up or otherwise accommodated. The facilities must allow the clothing to be dried. Accommodation must also be provided for clothing worn by employees during work but not taken home afterwards.

Seating

It is a fundamental requirement to the comfort and health of employees that they have adequate sitting facilities and are allowed to use them. The OSRPA 1963, s. 13, requires that where persons who are employed to work in premises covered by the Act have in the course of their work reasonable opportunity for sitting without detriment to it, there must be provided at suitable places for their use, and conveniently accessible to them, suitable facilities for sitting sufficient to allow them to take advantage of such opportunity. Whether any employee can sit without detriment to his or her work is a question of fact. As far as shop premises are concerned, seats must be provided in the ratio of at least 1 to 3.

Under s. 14, a seat must be provided for an employee whose work, or a substantial part of it, can or must be done sitting. Such a seat must be of a design, construction and dimensions suitable for the employee. If the employee's feet cannot comfortably be supported without a footrest then a footrest must be provided. In determining whether the seat is suitable, one is required to take into account the type of work the employee does. For example, in *Tesco Stores Ltd* v *Edwards* [1977] IRLR 120 an industrial tribunal held that a supermarket checkout employee required a chair which incorporated a swivelling action.

Eating facilities

It is sometimes customary for persons who are employed in shop premises to eat their meals on the premises. Where employees do in fact eat meals on the premises, the OSRPA 1963, s. 15, requires suitable and sufficient facilities for eating the meals to be provided. In the absence of authority it is suggested that in order to comply with the section it would be necessary for the relevant facilities to afford the employees some degree of privacy.

Floors, passages and stairs

It is fundamentally important that the employee is able to move about the workplace in safety. The OSRPA, s. 16(1), therefore provides:

> All floors, stairs, steps, passages and gangways comprised in premises to which this Act applies shall be of sound construction and properly maintained and shall, so far as is reasonably practicable, be kept free from obstruction and from any substance likely to cause persons to slip.

Westwood v *Post Office* [1974] AC 1 shows that the courts give the word 'floor' a wide meaning. In that case it was held that part of a floor in a lift motor room which was situated on a flat roof, on which certain employees were accustomed to walk, constituted a floor within the meaning of the section.

Staircases must be provided and maintained with handrails or handholds (s. 16(2) and (3)). A staircase with two open sides must have a handrail or handhold on both sides as must a staircase which, owing to the nature of its construction or condition, is specially liable to cause accidents (s. 16(2)). Any open side of a staircase which is required to be provided with a handhold or handrail must be guarded in such a way that persons are prevented from accidentally falling through the space between the handrail or handhold and the steps of the staircase (s. 16(3)).

All openings in floors comprised in premises to which the Act applies must be securely fenced, except insofar as the nature of the work renders such fencing impracticable (s. 16(4)). In *MacKay* v *Drybrough and Co. Ltd* 1986 SLT 624, the pursuer was injured when she fell through a space created by an open hatch in the serving area of a bar where she worked. Lord Weir stated, *obiter*, that such a space was an opening within the meaning of s. 16(4). It was quite irrelevant that the space was not a permanent feature of the floor.

Dangerous machinery

Whereas it is customary to associate dangerous machines with factories, mines etc., it is quite common to encounter such machines in premises to which the OSRPA 1963 applies. Section 17 relates to dangerous machines. The provisions of the section are similar to those contained in the Factories Act 1961, s. 14 (see page 161), and therefore do not merit special attention here. Section 18 makes it unlawful for any person under the age of 18 to clean any machinery if to do so would expose that person to the risk of injury from a moving part of that or any adjacent machinery.

Certain machines in common use can pose a potential danger to the employee if he or she is not adequately trained in the safe use of such machines. No person is permitted to work at any prescribed machine unless that person has been fully instructed as to the dangers arising in connection with it (s. 19). The employee must either receive sufficient training in working at the machine or be under adequate supervision by a person who has thorough knowledge and experience of the machine. The Prescribed Dangerous Machines Order 1964 (SI 1964/971) designates machines, such as guillotines and circular knives, for the purposes of the section.

Communally occupied premises

It often happens that shops, but more commonly offices, are housed in buildings which also accommodate other types of premises to which the provisions of the OSRPA 1963 do not apply. Furthermore, it is common practice for employees working in office or shop premises governed by the provisions of the 1963 Act to use facilities such as toilets, situated outside their place of work. It is therefore important to the welfare of such employees that such facilities are kept in a safe and wholesome state. Section 42 relates to any building in single ownership of which only a part comprises premises to which the Act applies. The owner of the whole building is made responsible for complying with the provisions of the section. Under subsections (2) and (3), the owner of every common part (for example, common passages, stairs, WCs) of a building to which s. 42 applies must keep those parts in a clean condition and suitably lit. Furthermore, s. 42(4) makes the provisions of s. 16 (which relates to the construction and maintenance of floors, stairs etc.) apply to common parts of a building in single ownership. The owner is also responsible for effecting compliance with ss. 9 and 10 of the Act (which relate to the provision of sanitary conveniences and washing facilities respectively) (s. 42(6) and (7)). However, the duty to maintain these facilities in a clean condition etc. falls on the occupier of the premises unless the facilities are shared between the employees who work on the premises and others (e.g., the public) in which case the duty falls on the owner of the premises.

Subsections (11) and (13) of s. 42 allocate responsibility for compliance with certain fire precautions in respect of common parts, with certain exceptions, on the owner of the premises.

Section 43 relates to any building of which different parts are owned by different persons, and which in part consists of premises to which the Act applies. The section allocates responsibility in respect of the maintenance, repair etc. of common parts of such buildings which are used by those employed in premises to which the Act applies. The section gives the expression 'common part' a similar meaning to that contained in s. 42, i.e., a part of the premises that is used for the purposes of, but is not comprised in, a part of the building to which the Act applies.

Exemptions from the Act

In some situations it would be unreasonable to require compliance with the various provisions of the OSRPA 1963. Section 46(1) therefore empowers the appropriate local authority to grant exemptions from the following requirements of the Act: s. 5(2) (which relates to the overcrowding of rooms), s. 6 (which relates to temperature) and s. 9 (which relates to sanitary conveniences). Exemption can be made only if the local authority is satisfied that, in the circumstances, compliance with the Act is not reasonably practicable. The local authority may also grant exemption from the provisions of s. 10 (which relates to the provision of washing facilities) as far as the requirement that the water supplied be running or heated. Exemptions made under the section may be granted for a period not exceeding two years, but the period may be extended for a further period if the local authority is satisfied that compliance is not reasonably practicable and that the person on whom statutory responsibility lies has not failed to do anything which would have rendered compliance reasonably practicable. Any person aggrieved by the refusal of an authority to grant an exemption may appeal to the magistrates' court which has complete powers of review in the matter.

SUBORDINATE HEALTH AND SAFETY LEGISLATION

A veritable plethora of subordinate legislation has been made under the Acts discussed in this chapter. A large portion of such legislation has been prompted by EEC Directives. One can, however, in a general work on environmental health law, make but brief mention of some of the more important statutory instruments which have been made under the Health and Safety at Work etc. Act 1974, the Factories Act 1961 or the Offices, Shops and Railway Premises Act 1963.

Workplace (Health, Safety and Welfare) Regulations 1992 (SI 1992/3004)

These regulations give effect to Directive 89/654/EEC and, with a few exceptions, apply to most places of work. A duty is placed on every employer to ensure that every workplace under his control complies with the provisions of the regulations. The regulations make provision for, *inter alia*, the ventilation, temperature, lighting, cleanliness, room dimensions, sanitary conveniences and washing facilities in workplaces.

Manual Handling Operations Regulations 1992 (SI 1992/2793)

Under these regulations an employer is placed under a duty to avoid so far as is reasonably practicable, the need for employees to undertake any manual handling operations at work which involve a risk of being injured. In any case where this is not reasonably practicable, a suitable and sufficient assessment must be made of manual handling operations which involve a risk of injury (reg. 4).

Health and Safety (Display Screen Equipment) Regulations 1992 (SI 1992/2792)

These regulations place a duty on an employer to carry out an analysis of display screen equipment for the purpose of assessing the health and safety risks to the relevant users (reg. 2). Any display equipment which is first used after 1 January 1993 must also meet the requirements of the schedule to the regulations (reg. 3). Users of display screen equipment are required to be allowed a sufficient number of breaks from the use of such equipment (reg. 4).

Management of Health and Safety at Work Regulations 1992 (SI 1992/2051)

These regulations place a duty on every employer to make a suitable and sufficient assessment of the risks to the health and safety of employees to which they are exposed whilst they are at work and also the risks to the health and safety of other persons arising out of or in connection with the work. A similar obligation is placed on the self-employed (reg. 3). The appropriate arrangements must be commensurate, *inter alia*, with the nature of the activities being undertaken as well as the size of the undertaking (reg. 4). A duty is also placed on an employer to provide employees with information on the risks to health identified by any assessment (reg. 8).

Provision and Use of Work Equipment Regulations 1992 (SI 1992/2932)

These regulations place a duty on every employer to ensure that work equipment is so constructed as to be suitable for the purpose for which it is provided (reg. 5) and to ensure that work equipment is suitably maintained (reg. 6). Every employer is placed under a duty to ensure that all persons who use work equipment have available to them adequate health and safety information and, where appropriate, written instructions relating to the use of the work equipment (reg. 8).

Control of Substances Hazardous to Health Regulations 1988 (SI 1988/1657)

These regulations have been prompted by Directive 80/1107/EEC. They require employers to protect their employees and others from risk to health arising from exposure to harmful substances. An employer may not carry on any work which is liable to expose any employee to any substance hazardous to health unless a sufficient assesment has been made of the risks (reg. 6). Regulation 7 provides that every employer must ensure that the exposure of employees to substances hazardous to health is either prevented or, where this is not reasonably practicable, adequately controlled. Where employees are liable to be exposed to a substance hazardous to health the circumstances of which fall within the scope of the regulations, the employer is under a duty to ensure that the employees in question are under suitable health surveillance.

Control of Asbestos at Work Regulations 1987 (SI 1987/21150) as amended by the Control of Substances Hazardous to Health (Amendment) Regulations 1990 (SI 1990/2026)

These regulations impose various duties on an employer in relation to employees, and (with some exceptions), as far as reasonably practicable, in relation to any other person who may be affected by the work in question. An employer is under a duty to prevent the exposure of employees to asbestos and, where this is not reasonably practicable, to reduce exposure to the lowest level reasonably practicable by measures other than the use of respiratory protective equipment (reg. 8). An employer who provides control measures must ensure, so far as is reasonably practicable, that such measures are properly used (reg. 9). The employer is also under a duty to take steps to monitor the exposure of employees, where such monitoring is appropriate, for the protection of their health of those employees (reg. 15).

Noise at Work Regulations 1989 (SI 1989/1790)

These regulations impose requirements on an employer to reduce the risk of damage to the hearing of employees from exposure to noise to the lowest level reasonably practicable (reg. 6). The employer is also under a general duty, in certain circumstances, to reduce the exposure to noise of employees (reg. 7). In certain circumstances, a duty is imposed to provide the employee, at the latter's request, with suitable and sufficient personal ear protectors.

NINE

Housing

In this chapter attention is turned to the legal controls governing the habitability of houses. The state of the nation's houses is of the utmost importance in environmental health. Although concern about the insanitary condition, as well as general lack of, working-class houses was at the forefront of the Victorian public health reform movement, it was not until after the First World War that legislation was passed to remedy such an unsatisfactory state of affairs by facilitating the erection of houses for the poorer members of society by local authorities. The limited role of State intervention in housing clearly epitomises the doctrine of *laissez-faire* which characterised the nature of government in the 19th century. While to us it may seem quite inexcusable for the government to have allowed such squalid conditions to remain in existence for so long, one should remember that not even the most ardent public health reformer of that period would have considered it incumbent on the State to provide houses for the labouring classes. It should also be remembered that for most of the 19th century a large section of the working class did not have a vote and were thus denied as effective Parliamentary representation as would otherwise have been the case.

The development of the public health control of housing, as far as the law of England and Wales is concerned, was cholera driven and began with the nuisance removal provisions of the Public Health Act 1848 under which local authorities were empowered to deal with houses which constituted a nuisance. The Shaftesbury Act of 1851 (14 and 15 Vict c. 34) which gave local authorities power to acquire land for the building of working-class houses was unpopular for a variety of reasons and remained a dead letter. Of greater import however, were the Cross Act of 1868 (31 and 32 Vict c. 130) and the Torrens Act of 1875 (38 & 39 Vict c. 36). These gave local authorities power to demolish insanitary property and allow speculative builders to erect buildings in their place. While the improvement schemes carried out under these Acts resulted in the eradication of some of the most squalid houses of our great towns, the overall benefit was limited since local authorities were unwilling to spend a sufficient amount of money to allow large areas to be tackled. However, in 1903 the Housing Act of that year enabled central government, in the form of the Local Government Board, to force local authorities to implement the Cross and Torrens Acts. The Housing Act 1909 went further in that it allowed the Board to compel local authorities to build houses for the working classes.

It is not intended to chart the development of housing law during the 20th century. It suffices to point out that the legislation has recognised that houses should be provided with basic minimum facilities, be in a good state of repair, and fit for human habitation. Another feature of housing law is the duty placed on local authorities to give grants for the improvement of dwellings.

The law is now contained in the Housing Act 1985 (HA 1985), which is a consolidating Act. It has been substantially amended by the Local Government and Housing Act 1989.

Before embarking on a discussion of the modern law relating to the public health control of housing it should be pointed out that this chapter deals exclusively with local authority controls over housing conditions. No attempt is made to discuss the law relating to landlord and tenant where both statute and the common law have intervened to imply terms in leases relating to both the state of repairs and the general habitability of leasehold premises.

This chapter divides into:

(a) Houses in disrepair and unfit houses.
(b) Renewal areas.
(c) Slum clearance.
(d) Overcrowding.
(e) Houses in multiple occupation.
(f) Common lodging-houses.
(g) Grants.

HOUSES IN DISREPAIR AND UNFIT HOUSES

Part VI of the Housing Act 1985 deals with repair notices and gives local authorities power to deal with houses which are unfit for human habitation as well as those which are in a state of disrepair though not unfit for human habitation. A local housing authority is placed under a duty to inspect its area from time to time to ascertain what action should be taken in respect of the powers conferred on it by part VI.

Repair notices

Under the Housing Act 1985, s. 189(1) (as amended), if a local housing authority is satisfied that a dwellinghouse or house in multiple occupation is unfit for human habitation then it must serve a repair notice on the person having control (see s. 207) of the house, provided it is satisfied in accordance with s. 604A (see below) that serving such a notice is the most satisfactory course of action. Section 189(1A) makes similar provision in relation to flats.

In the case of a house in multiple occupation a repair notice may be served on the person managing instead of the person having control of the house (s. 189(1B)).

The notice must require the person on whom it is served to execute the works specified in the notice and to begin the works within a reasonable date, being not earlier than the 28th day after the notice is served, and to complete the works within such reasonable time so specified. The notice becomes operative if no appeal is brought on the expiration of 21 days from the date of service of the notice and is final and conclusive as to matters which could have been raised on an appeal (s. 189(4)).

Subject to certain exceptions, no notice may be served under either subsection (1) or subsection (1A) of s. 189 if the authority determines that the premises concerned form part of a building which would be a qualifying building in relation to a group repair scheme (see page 211).

The expression 'dwellinghouse' is defined by s. 207(2) as including any yard, garden or outhouse. There is little authority on the meaning of 'house'. It has been held that a tenement divided into separate dwellings is a house (*Quiltotex Co. Ltd* v *Minister of Housing and Local Government* [1966] 1 QB 704). In *Re Ross and Leicester Corporation* (1932) 96 JP 459 it was held that a common lodging-house ranked as a dwellinghouse for the purposes of the Housing Act 1930. However, in *R* v *Lambeth London Borough Council, ex parte Clayhope Properties Ltd* [1988] QB 563, it was held that the expression 'house' meant a separate building for the purposes of part II of the Housing Act 1957, therefore a flat was not a house. The expression 'flat' is defined for the purposes of the 1985 Act by s. 183(3) as a dwellinghouse which is not a house.

Section 604A provides that in deciding whether the most satisfactory course of action is to proceed under s. 189 (in contradistinction to making a closing order, demolition order or declaring the area in which the house etc. is situated to be a clearance area) the local authority is required to have regard to guidance given by the Secretary of State. See Department of Environment Circular 6/90.

Meaning of unfitness

One of the fundamental flaws of housing legislation in the past has been its insistence on employing the concept of 'unfit for human habitation' as a condition precedent for the local authority taking remedial action in relation to houses. This often had the effect of discouraging local authorities from taking action to close or demolish such houses since it was often difficult to establish a causal connection between the unsatisfactory state a house was in and prejudice to human health. The situation is to some extent improved by the Housing Act 1985. The term 'unfitness' is now defined by the new s. 604 inserted by the Local Government and Housing Act 1989. The section provides:

(1) Subject to subsection (2) below, a dwellinghouse is fit for human habitation for the purposes of this Act unless, in the opinion of the local housing authority, it fails to meet one or more of the requirements in paragraphs (a) to (i) below and, by reason of that failure, is not reasonably suitable for occupation—

(a) it is structurally stable;
(b) it is free from serious disrepair;
(c) it is free from dampness prejudicial to the health of the occupants (if any);
(d) it has adequate provision for lighting, heating and ventilation;
(e) it has an adequate piped supply of wholesome water;
(f) there are satisfactory facilities in the dwellinghouse for the preparation and cooking of food, including a sink with a satisfactory supply of hot and cold water;
(g) it has a suitably located water-closet for the exclusive use of the occupants (if any);
(h) it has, for the exclusive use of the occupants (if any), a suitably located fixed bath or shower and wash-hand basin each of which is provided with a satisfactory supply of hot and cold water; and
(i) it has an effective system for the draining of foul, waste and surface water;

and any reference to a dwellinghouse being unfit for human habitation shall be construed accordingly.

(2) Whether or not a dwellinghouse which is a flat satisfies the requirements in subsection (1), it is unfit for human habitation for the purposes of this Act if, in the opinion of the local authority, the building or part of the building outside the flat fails to meet one or more of the requirements in paragraphs (a) to (e) below and, by reason of that failure, the flat is not reasonably suitable for occupation—

(a) the building or part is structurally stable;
(b) it is free from serious disrepair;

(c) it is free from dampness;
(d) it has adequate provision for ventilation; and
(e) it has an effective system for the draining of foul, waste and surface water.

Section 604(3) provides that s. 604(1) applies in relation to a house in multiple occupation with the substitution of a reference to the house for any reference to a dwellinghouse. The Secretary of State is empowered by order to amend the provisions of s. 604(1) or (2).

It can be seen that the concept of reasonable suitability replaces that of unfitness for human habitation. It is simpler for a local authority to prove that a given state of affairs renders a dwellinghouse not reasonably suitable for occupation than to prove that it is unfit for human habitation. Whether or not a dwellinghouse is not reasonably suitable for occupation would, it is suggested, be a question of fact which would fall to be determined on the circumstances of the case.

Houses in disrepair but not unfit

If a local housing authority is satisfied that a dwellinghouse or house in multiple occupation is in such a state of disrepair that, although not unfit for human habitation, substantial repairs are necessary to bring it up to a reasonable standard, having regard to its age, character and locality, the authority may serve a repair notice on the person having control of the dwellinghouse or house in multiple occupation (s. 190(1)).

If a building which contains a flat is in such a state of disrepair that, although the flat is not unfit for human habitation, substantial repairs are necessary to a part of the building outside the flat to bring it up to a reasonable standard, having regard to its age, character and locality, the local authority may serve a repair notice on the person having control of the part of the building concerned. Similar powers also apply where a building containing a flat is in such a state of disrepair that, although the flat is not unfit for human habitation, the condition of a part of the building outside the flat is such as to interfere materially with the personal comfort of the occupying tenant (s. 190(1A)).

No notice may be served either under subsection (1) or (1A) unless there is an occupying tenant of the dwellinghouse or flat in question, or the dwellinghouse or flat falls within a renewal area within the meaning of the Local Government and Housing Act 1989 (see below). In the case of a house in multiple occupation, a repair notice may be served on the person managing the house instead of the person having control of it.

Appeals

An appeal against a repair notice can be made to the county court. If an appeal against a notice is made this has the effect of suspending the notice becoming operative until a decision on the appeal confirming the notice is given and the period within which an appeal to the Court of Appeal may be brought expires without any such appeal having been brought. If a further appeal to the Court of Appeal is brought the order does not become operative until a decision on that appeal is given concerning the notice (s. 191).

Execution of work by local authority by agreement

Section 191A allows a local housing authority by agreement with the person having control of any premises to carry out works which that person is required to execute in respect of a repair notice served under s. 189 or s. 190.

Default powers

Section 193 empowers a local housing authority to carry out works if a repair notice is not complied with.

RENEWAL AREAS

It is normally much more advantageous for houses which are unsatisfactory from a public health viewpoint to be dealt with collectively rather than on a piecemeal basis. This principle has been recognised in housing law since the 19th century. The modern law is set out in part VII of the Local Government and Housing Act 1989. Section 89(1) of that Act provides:

> Where a local housing authority, upon consideration of such a report as is mentioned in subsection (3) below and of any other matters which the authority consider relevant, are satisfied —
>
> (a) that the living conditions in an area within their district consisting primarily of housing accommodation are unsatisfactory, and
> (b) that those conditions can most effectively be dealt with by declaring the area to be a renewal area,
>
> then, subject to the following provisions of this part, they may cause the area to be defined on a map and by resolution declare it to be a renewal area.

It should be noted that there is no requirement that all or any of the houses are unfit for human habitation before the area can be designated a renewal area.

The report specified in s. 89(3) is one prepared at the request of the local housing authority by normally an environmental health officer and must include, *inter alia*, the living conditions in the area concerned, the ways in which the living conditions may be improved and the powers available to the authority if the area is declared to be a renewal area.

Before exercising its power to declare an area to be a renewal area the local housing authority is required to have regard to guidance given by the Secretary of State (s. 89(4)).

By s. 90(1), an area may not be declared a renewal area unless:

    (a) the area contains not less than a specified minimum number of dwellings;
    (b) of the dwellings in the area, not less than a specified proportion are privately owned;
    (c) such conditions as may be specified with respect to the physical condition of the dwellings in the area and the financial circumstances of those living in the area are fulfilled; and
    (d) such other conditions as may be specified are fulfilled.

The power to specify appropriate requirements by way of directions is given to the Secretary of State.

Publicity etc.

Section 91 of the Housing Act 1985 requires a local housing authority to publicise adequately the fact that an area is to become a renewal area by, *inter alia*, placing adverts in the press.

Powers of local housing authority

After a local housing authority has declared an area to be a renewal area, the authority is empowered to exercise the powers conferred by s. 93. In order to fulfil the objectives specified in s. 93(3), for which the powers may be used, the authority is empowered by s. 93(2) to acquire by agreement, or compulsorily purchase, any land in the area on which there are premises consisting of or including housing accommodation or which forms part of the curtilage of any such premises. The local authority is empowered to provide housing accommodation on any land acquired under the section. The objectives referred to in s. 93(3) are:

    (a) the improvement or repair of the premises, either by the authority or by a person to whom they propose to dispose of the premises;
    (b) the proper and effective management and use of the housing accommodation, either by the authority or by a person to whom they propose to dispose of the premises comprising the accommodation; and

(c) the well-being of the persons for the time being residing in the area.

Power is conferred on the local housing authority to acquire land by agreement, or by way of compulsory purchase, in order to improve the amenities in the area. Power is also given to the authority to carry out and assist in carrying out works on land (s. 93(4) and (5)).

SLUM CLEARANCE

One of the traditional weapons against insanitary houses which has been available to local authorities since the Victorian era is the power to close or demolish houses which fail to conform to certain criteria. The current law is now set out in part IX of the Housing Act 1985 as substituted by the Local Government and Housing Act 1989.

Closing orders

A closing order is an order prohibiting the use of premises to which the order relates for any purpose not approved by the local housing authority (s. 267(2)).

Section 264(1) of the Housing Act 1985 provides that if a local housing authority is satisfied that a dwellinghouse or house in multiple occupation is unfit for human habitation and that, in accordance with s.604A (see page 181) taking action under the subsection is the most satisfactory course of action, it must make a closing order in respect of the premises.

Section 264(2) relates to buildings containing one or more flats, some or all of which are unfit for human habitation. Power is given to the local housing authority to make a closing order with respect to the whole or part of the building. In deciding for the purpose of s. 264(2) whether to make a closing order with respect to the whole or part of a building or in respect of which part of a building to make a closing order, the local housing authority are required to have regard to such guidance given by the Secretary of State under section 604A.

It is an offence for a person, knowing that a closing order has become operative and applies to the premises concerned, to use the premises in contravention of the order or to permit the premises to be so used (s. 277).

The local housing authority is required to determine a closing order on being satisfied that the premises have been rendered fit for human habitation (s. 278). If the authority is satisfied only in relation to part of the premises concerned, it is required to determine the order insofar as it relates to that part. An aggrieved person can appeal to the county court against the refusal of the local housing authority to determine a closing order either in whole or in relation to part of the premises to which it relates.

Subject to certain exceptions, s. 279 allows a local housing authority, after it has made a closing order, to revoke it and make a demolition order. The section provides that the provisions of the Act relating to demolition orders including the right of appeal against such orders, applies to s. 279.

Demolition orders

Section 265(1) of the Housing Act 1985 provides that if a local housing authority is satisfied that a dwellinghouse (which is not a flat or a house in multiple occupation) is unfit for human habitation and that, in accordance with s. 604A (see page 181) taking action under s. 265 would be the most satisfactory course of action, it must make a demolition order with respect to the dwellinghouse. Section 265(2) makes a similar provision in relation to a building containing one or more flats, some or all of which are unfit for human habitation.

When a demolition order is made the premises must be vacated within a specified period of at least 28 days from the date on which the order becomes operative and be demolished within six weeks after the end of the period, or, if not vacated before the end of that period, after the date on which they are vacated, or, in either case, within such longer period as in the circumstances the authority considers it reasonable to specify (s. 267).

Section 270 requires the local housing authority, after a demolition order has become operative, to serve on the occupier of the premises or any part of the premises a notice stating the effect of the order and specifying the date by which the premises must be vacated. When a demolition order has become operative, the owner of the premises is required to demolish the premises to which the order relates within the time limited by the order. If the premises are not demolished within that time the local authority is permitted to enter the premises, demolish the building and sell the materials (s. 271). Expenses may be recovered from the owner of the premises (s. 272).

Service of a demolition order may prompt the owner to effect improvements to the premises concerned. Section 274 therefore provides that where a demolition order has become operative the owner of the premises, or any other person who in the opinion of the local authority is or will be in a position to put the proposals into effect, may submit proposals to the authority for the execution of works designed to secure the reconstruction, enlargement or improvement of the premises. If the owner or any other person who has an interest in the premises submits proposals to the local housing authority for a purpose other than human habitation, the authority may, if it thinks fit, determine the demolition order and make a closing order in its stead.

Section 304 of the Housing Act 1985 prevents a local housing authority making a demolition order in relation to a house which is listed under the

Town and Country Planning Act 1971 s. 54 (now the Planning (Listed Buildings and Conservation Areas) Act 1990, s. 1). Instead a closing order must be made.

Service of notice and right of appeal

Where a local housing authority has made a demolition or closing order it is required under s. 268 to serve a copy of the order on any person who is an owner of the premises and every mortgagee of the premises whose identity it is reasonably practicable to ascertain. An order against which no appeal is brought becomes operative at the end of the period of 21 days from the date of service of the order and is final and conclusive as to matters which could have been raised on appeal. An appeal can be made, within 21 days after the date of the service of the order, to the county court which has complete powers of review.

Obstructive buildings

It sometimes happens that a building, by virtue of its proximity to other buildings, has a deleterious effect on their habitability, for example, by depriving them of light or ventilation. Obstructive buildings are given special attention in the Housing Act 1985. Section 283 defines an obstructive building as a building which, by virtue only of its contact with or proximity to other buildings, is dangerous or injurious to health. Section 284 gives a local housing authority power to serve on every owner of a building which appears to it to be an obstructive building, notice of a time and place at which the question of ordering the building to be demolished will be considered by the authority. The owner is given the right to be heard by the local authority. If the authority decides to demolish the obstructive building the authority is required to make an order requiring that the building be demolished and that the building be vacated for the purpose of the demolition within two months from the date on which the order becomes operative. The order becomes operative if no appeal is brought against it after the expiration of 21 days from the date of service of the notice. Appeal lies to the county court against an order.

If the occupier of the building fails to remove from the building after the appropriate date, the local housing authority is empowered by s. 286 to apply to the county court for an order for vacant possession of the building. The order is then placed under a duty to grant such an order.

The owner of a building which is the subject of an obstructive building order may, under s. 287, offer to sell it to the authority at a price to be assessed as if it were compensation for a compulsory purchase under s. 290. The authority is then placed under an obligation to accept the offer and carry out the necessary demolition. If no such offer is made, however, the responsibility for demolishing the building rests with the owner of the building.

Clearance areas

It has been recognised since the second half of the Victorian era that it is preferable to deal with unsatisfactory housing on an area basis. The Housing Act 1985 allows a local housing authority to establish clearance areas. Section 289(1) defines such an area as an area which is to be cleared of all buildings in accordance with the provisions of part IX.

Section 289(2) (as amended by the Local Government and Housing Act 1989) requires a local housing authority to declare an area to be a clearance area if it is satisfied:

> (a) that the buildings in the area which are dwellinghouses or houses in multiple occupation or contain one or more flats (in this section referred to as 'residential buildings') are unfit for human habitation or are by reason of their bad arrangement, or the narrowness or bad arrangement of the streets, dangerous or injurious to the health of the inhabitants of the area, and
> (b) that the other buildings, if any, in the area are for a like reason dangerous or injurious to the health of the inhabitants of the area,

and in accordance with subsection 604A that the most satisfactory course of action is the demolition of all the buildings in the area.

A residential building containing one or more flats is to be treated for the purposes of s. 289 as unfit for human habitation if some or all of the flats are unfit for human habitation (s. 289(2A)).

Section 289(2B) makes provision for persons who either have an interest in the buildings concerned or are occupiers to be informed of the authority's intention to declare a clearance area. Such individuals are given the opportunity to make representations to the authority. The authority is required to consider such representations. In the light of such representations the authority may decide to declare the area to be a clearance area, or it may decide to declare a clearance area but exclude some buildings or it may decide not to declare the area to be a clearance area (s. 289(2F)).

Section 289(3) requires an authority which has decided to declare an area a clearance area to define the relevant area on a map so as to exclude from the clearance area:

> (i) any residential building which is not unfit for human habitation or dangerous or injurious to health;

(ii) any other building which is not dangerous or injurious to health; and

(iii) any residential buildings which, by virtue of subsection (2F)(b), they have decided to exclude from the area.

Thereafter the authority is required to pass a resolution declaring the area to be a clearance area.

Clearing houses *en bloc* may cause overcrowding in other parts of the local authority's area. This often happened in the 19th century when local authorities were making improvement schemes. It is imperative therefore that those displaced by the clearance area are suitably accommodated. Before establishing a clearance area, a local housing authority must be satisfied that insofar as suitable accommodation does not already exist for the persons who will be displaced by the clearance, the authority can provide or secure the provision of necessary accommodation, in advance of the displacements, as the demolition of the buildings in the area, or in different parts of it, proceeds and that the resources of the authority are sufficient for the purpose of carrying the resolution into effect (s. 289(4)).

After a local housing authority has declared an area to be a clearance area it must secure the clearance of the area by purchasing the land and then itself undertaking or otherwise securing the demolition of the buildings (s. 290). After the land has been purchased the authority is required to cause every building on the land to be vacated. It may then itself demolish every building on the land or dispose of the land subject to a condition that the buildings on the land be demolished forthwith. In the case of the local housing authority deciding to demolish the buildings itself, it has six weeks from the date a building is vacated, or such longer period as the authority considers reasonable, to demolish the building.

OVERCROWDING

It was not only the poor physical state of the houses of the working classes which attracted the attention of the public health reformers of the 19th century, it was also the grossly overcrowded condition of the houses. It was not uncommon for several families to occupy one room of a house. Both national legislation and local authority by-laws have made provision since then to proscribe the overcrowding of houses. The current law is contained in part X of the Housing Act 1985.

Definition of overcrowding

Under s. 324 of the Housing Act 1985 a dwelling is overcrowded for the purposes of part X of the Act when the number of persons sleeping in the dwelling is such as to contravene either the standard specified in s. 325 (the

Housing

room standard) or the standard specified in s. 326 (the space standard). For the purposes of part X 'dwelling' means premises used or suitable for use as a separate dwelling. The definition is therefore wide and includes premises not built as housing accommodation.

Room standard

Under s. 325 the room standard is contravened when the number of persons sleeping in a dwelling and the number of rooms available as sleeping accommodation is such that two persons of opposite sex who are not living together as husband and wife must sleep in the same room. For the purposes of the section, children under the age of 10 must be left out of account. Furthermore, a room is to be regarded as available for sleeping accommodation if it is of a type normally used in the locality either as a bedroom or a living-room.

Space standard

Under s. 326 the space standard is contravened when the number of persons sleeping in a dwelling is in excess of the permitted number, having regard to the number and floor area of the rooms of the dwelling available for sleeping accommodation. For the purposes of the section no account is to be taken of a child under the age of one. A child aged one or over but under 10 falls to be reckoned as a half unit. A room is available as sleeping accommodation if it is of a type normally used in the locality either as a living-room or a bedroom.

By s. 326(3) the permitted number of persons in relation to a dwelling is whichever is the less of:

(a) the number specified in table 9.1 in relation to the number of rooms in the dwelling available as sleeping accommodation, and

(b) the aggregate for all such rooms in the dwelling of the numbers specified in column 2 of table 9.2 in relation to each room of the floor area specified in column 1.

No account is to be taken for the purposes of either table of a room having a floor area of less than 50 square feet.

Table 9.1

Number of rooms	Number of persons
1	2
2	3
3	5
4	7½
5 or more	2 for each room

Table 9.2

Floor area of room	Number of persons
110 sq ft or more	2
90 sq ft or more but less than 110 sq ft	$1\frac{1}{2}$
70 sq ft or more but less than 90 sq ft	1
50 sq ft or more but less than 70 sq ft	$\frac{1}{2}$

Power is given to the Secretary of State to prescribe by regulations how floor area is to be ascertained (see the Housing Act (Overcrowding and Miscellaneous Forms) Regulations 1937 (SR & O 1937/80).

Offence of causing house to be overcrowded

The occupier of a dwelling who causes or permits it to be overcrowded commits a summary offence (Housing Act 1985, s. 327). Liability under the section is strict it is suggested. However, an occupier is not guilty of an offence if the overcrowding falls within the exceptions specified in ss. 328 or 329 or by virtue of anything done under the authority of a licence granted by the local housing authority under s. 330.

If a dwelling, which would not otherwise be overcrowded, becomes overcrowded by reason of a child attaining the age of one or 10 and the occupier applies to the local authority for suitable alternative accommodation, or has so applied before the date when the child attained the age in question, then the occupier does not commit an offence under s. 327 so long as all the persons sleeping in the dwelling were living there when the child attained that age and thereafter continuously live there, or were children born after that date (s. 328). The exception provided by the section ceases to apply if suitable alternative accommodation is offered to the occupier and he or she fails to accept it. The exception ceases to apply if there is a person who lives in the dwelling but is not a member of the occupier's family and it would be reasonably practicable for that person to move out, having regard to all the circumstances (including the availability of suitable alternative accommodation for that person), and the occupier fails to require his or her removal.

Section 329 makes exception to liability under s. 327 if the persons sleeping in an overcrowded dwelling are members of the occupier's family but are living there only temporarily.

The expression 'family' is not defined in the Act. It is suggested, however, that the expression is not a term of art and should therefore be given its ordinary meaning in common parlance.

An occupier may also avoid liability under the Act by obtaining a licence from the local authority authorising him or her to permit more than the permitted number of persons to sleep in the dwelling.

Duty to inform local housing authority of overcrowding

In order that a local housing authority is informed or overcrowding in its area, subject to certain exceptions, a duty is imposed by the Housing Act 1985, s. 333, on the landlord of an overcrowded dwellinghouse and any agent of the landlord, to inform the authority if it comes to the relevant person's notice that the house is overcrowded.

HOUSES IN MULTIPLE OCCUPATION

Houses which are occupied by members of more than one household are more likely to be misused and to present a public health problem for both the residents of the premises and the general public. There is also a tendency for such premises not to be of high amenity as far as facilities are concerned. Furthermore, there is a greater likelihood that those who reside in houses in multiple occupation are prone to exploitation. During the late 1950s and early 1960s the activities of the notorious landlord, Peter Rachman, who exploited those living in houses in multiple occupation focused public as well as government attention to this aspect of housing. The current law governing houses in multiple occupation is contained in part XI of the Housing Act 1985, which has been heavily amended by the Local Government and Housing Act 1989.

Meaning of house in multiple occupation

The term 'house in multiple occupation' means a house which is occupied by persons who do not form a single household (Housing Act 1989, s. 345(1)). 'House' here includes (by s. 345(2)) any part of a building which, apart from the provisions of the subsection, would not be regarded as a house and was originally constructed or subsequently adapted for occupation by a single household.

It was held in *R v Hackney London Borough Council, ex parte Evenbray* (1987) 86 LGR 210 that premises comprising 14 bedrooms and six bathrooms, the rooms charged on a nightly basis, constituted a house.

The expression 'household' is not defined in the Act, and the case law is unhelpful. In *Hackney London Borough Council v Ezedinma* [1981] 3 All ER 438 it was held that what constituted a household was a matter of fact and degree.

Premises cannot be in multiple occupation unless they are occupied. In *R v Hackney London Borough Council, ex parte Thrasyvoulou* (1986) 84 LGR 823 the premises in question offered bed and breakfast accommodation. Several described themselves as hotels. Rooms were let at a daily rate. They were occupied in the main by individuals who were sent there by the local authority in fulfilment of its statutory duty to house the homeless. It was held that the premises were occupied. However, Balcombe LJ stated, *obiter*, that it could not be said that a person who has a regular home of his own and stays overnight in a hotel occupied the hotel.

Registration schemes

A local housing authority may make and submit to the Secretary of State, for confirmation, a scheme for compiling and maintaining a register for its district of houses in multiple occupation (Housing Act 1985, s. 346). The registration scheme need not be for the whole of the housing authority's area and need not extend to all the houses which are in multiple occupation. In other words an authority can simply register the houses which are in need of attention. The scheme comes into force on the date specified in the scheme provided it has been confirmed by the Secretary of State. It is an offence to fail to comply with the scheme.

The scheme may contain control provisions, that is to say, provisions for preventing, *inter alia,* multiple occupation of a house unless the house is registered and the number of households or persons occupying the house does not exceed the number registered for it (s. 347). Of practical importance is the power given by s. 348 to a local housing authority to refuse to register or vary the registration of a house in multiple occupation either on the ground that the house is unsuitable and incapable of being made suitable for such occupation or on the ground that the person having control of the house or the person intended to be the person managing the house is not a fit and proper person. Furthermore, the authority can require as a condition of registration that such works are carried out as will make the house suitable for occupation.

An appeal lies to the county court against the decision of the local housing authority to refuse to register a house in multiple occupation.

Before the scheme is submitted to the Secretary of State and after the latter approves it, the local housing authority must publicise the scheme in one or more newspapers (s. 349). See the Houses in Multiple Occupation (Charges for Registration Schemes) Regulations 1991 (SI 1991/982).

Power to require execution of works

It is obviously important that a local housing authority should be able to compel the owners etc. of houses in multiple occupation to effect appropriate improvements to their premises. Section 352 of the Housing Act 1985, as amended, therefore provides:

(1) Subject to section 365 the local housing authority may serve a notice under this section where in the opinion of the authority, a house in

multiple occupation fails to meet one or more of the requirements in paragraphs (a) to (e) of subsection (1A) and, having regard to the number of individuals or households or both for the time being accommodated on the premises, by reason of that failure the premises are not reasonably suitable for occupation by those individuals or households.

(1A) The requirements in respect of a house in multiple occupation referred to in subsection (1) are the following, that is to say —

(a) there are satisfactory facilities for the storage, preparation and cooking of food including an adequate number of sinks with a satisfactory supply of hot and cold water;

(b) it has an adequate number of suitably located water-closets for the exclusive use of the occupants;

(c) it has, for the exclusive use of the occupants an adequate number of suitably located fixed baths or showers and wash-hand basins each of which is provided with a satisfactory supply of hot and cold water;

(d) subject to section 365, there are adequate means of escape from fire; and

(e) there are adequate other fire precautions.

The notice must specify the works which, in the opinion of the local housing authority, are required to render the house in question reasonably suitable for occupation by the individuals and households for the time being accommodated there, or for a smaller number (specified in the order) of individuals or households. The notice may not specify any works to any premises outside the house (s. 352(2)).

The notice must be served on the person either having control or managing the house in question (s. 352(3)).

An appeal against the notice may be made to the county court on a number of specified grounds (s. 353).

If the work is not carried out the authority may carry it out and recover the expenses (s. 375). It is an offence for a person wilfully to fail to comply with a notice served under s. 352 (s. 376).

Power to limit number of occupants

We have seen how a local housing authority has power under the Housing Act 1985, s. 352, to require the carrying out of remedial works to houses in multiple occupation. In order to supplement such powers, s. 354 gives an authority power, for the purpose of preventing the occurrence of, or remedying, a state of affairs which would call for a notice to be served under s. 352, to serve a notice limiting the highest number of individuals or households or both who should, having regard to the requirements set out in s. 352(1A), occupy the house in its existing condition. An authority can also exercise such powers in relation to a part of a house and also set separate limits where different parts of a house are, or are likely to be, occupied by different persons. It is an offence for the occupier, or other person who is for the time being entitled or authorised to permit individuals to take up residence, knowingly to permit individuals to occupy the house in question in excess of the notified limits (s. 355).

Overcrowding in houses in multiple occupation

Overcrowding in a house in multiple occupation presents a particular problem. The Housing Act 1985, s. 358, therefore empowers a local housing authority to control such a situation. The section allows an authority to serve an overcrowding notice on the occupier of premises if it appears to the authority that an excessive number of persons are being, or are likely to be, accommodated on the premises, having regard to the rooms available. Prior to serving the overcrowding notice the occupier of the premises and any person managing the house in question must be given the right to make representations. Appeal lies (under s. 362) to the county court against such a notice.

It is an offence to contravene an overcrowding notice.

It may happen that the circumstances which prompted the local housing authority to serve the overcrowding notice change, in which case s. 363 empowers the authority on the application of a person having an estate or interest in the premises to revoke the overcrowding notice or vary it so as to allow more people to be accommodated on the premises. An appeal lies to the county court against the refusal of an authority to revoke or vary a notice. The court has full powers of review.

Means of escape in the event of fire

The Housing Act 1985, s. 365(1) as amended, provides that where a local housing authority has the power to serve a notice under s. 352 (see page 194) in respect of a house in multiple occupation and the reason or one of the reasons is the inadequacy of means of escape from fire, the authority has power to accept an undertaking or make a closing order under s. 368 (see below) in relation to the house. By s. 365(2) the authority must exercise such powers in relation to a house which falls within such description or is occupied in such a manner as the Secretary of State specifies by order (see the Housing (Means of Escape from Fire in Houses in Multiple Occupation) Order 1981 (SI 1981/1576)). Under s. 368 if it appears to the authority, subject to s. 365, that the means of escape from fire would in fact be adequate if part of the house were not used for human habitation, it can require that the relevant part is not used. The authority is empowered to accept an undertaking that the relevant part will not be used for human habitation without the permission of the local authority. It is an offence for a person who, knowing that such an undertaking has been accepted, uses the part of the house to which the undertaking relates in contravention of the undertaking or permits the part to be so used.

Standards of management in houses in multiple occupation

The Secretary of State has power to make regulations governing standards of management of houses in multiple occupation (Housing Act 1985, s. 369). The relevant regulations are the Housing (Management of Houses in Multiple Occupation) Regulations 1962 (SI 1962/668) and 1990 (SI 1990/830).

Power to require execution of works

It is important that a housing authority can require remedial work to be carried out to houses in multiple occupation. The Housing Act 1985, s. 372, therefore empowers an authority to serve notice on the person managing a house if it is defective in consequence of neglect to comply with the regulations made under s. 369 (see the preceding paragraph). The person (either the owner, lessee or mortgagee of the house) on whom notice is served, may appeal to the county court under s. 373 on the grounds specified in that section. If a notice is not complied with the authority may carry out the work itself and recover costs (s. 375). Section 376 makes it an offence for a person wilfully to fail to comply with a notice served under s. 372.

Control orders

The most serious measure which a local housing authority can take under the Housing Act 1985 in relation to a house in multiple occupation is to make a control order. Section 379(1) as amended allows an authority to make such an order if:

    (a) a notice has been served in respect of the house under section 352 or 372 (notices requiring the execution of works),
    (b) a direction has been given in respect of the house under section 354 (direction limiting number of occupants) or
    (d) it appears to the authority that the state or condition of the house is such as to call for the taking of action under any of those two sections.

A control order comes into force on being made. Its effect is to give the authority the right to possess the premises and do anything which a person having an estate or interest in the premises would have been able to do. The section confers the right on the authority to create an interest in the premises which has the attributes of a lease. The above powers would in practice only be employed in the face of extreme conditions, probably as a last resort.

Any person having an estate or interest in a house to which a control order relates may appeal on specified grounds to the county court against the making of the order.

When the control order is in force the authority is given wide powers of management by s. 385. Such powers include the carrying out of remedial work on the premises.

After making a control order, a local housing authority must prepare a management scheme in respect of the premises (s. 386). The content of a scheme is governed by part 1 of sch. 13 to the Act.

A control order ceases to have effect after five years commencing from the date on which it came into force (s. 392) or it may be revoked at any time by the local housing authority either on application or on its own initiative. An appeal lies to the county court against the refusal of a county court to revoke a control order (s. 393).

COMMON LODGING-HOUSES

The heyday of the common lodging-house was in the 19th century when it was customary for persons of modest means who were visiting towns to reside in such premises. Unfortunately, it was not unusual for common lodging-houses to be kept in an insanitary condition. From the earliest days of the public health movement it was recognised that the common lodging-house was a potential source of infectious disease. The various Public Health Acts dating from that time invariably contained provisions relating to such premises. Local authorities also made by-laws to control common lodging-houses and similar premises.

The current statute law relating to common lodging-houses is contained in the Housing Act 1985, part XII.

Controls over common lodging-houses

The expression 'common lodging-house' is defined as a house (other than a public assistance institution) provided for the purpose of accommodating by night poor persons, not being members of the same family, who resort to it and are allowed to occupy one common room for the purpose of sleeping or eating, and includes, where part of a house is so used, the part so used (Housing Act 1985, s. 401). For premises to fall within the definition of common lodging-house, there must be one common room for the purposes of either sleeping or eating.

The main instrument of control over common lodging-houses since the 19th century has been a requirement that keepers of such premises must be registered. Section 402 of the 1985 Act provides that no person may keep a common lodging-house or receive a lodger in such premises unless that person is registered as the keeper of the premises.

A housing authority is required to keep a register of common lodging-houses in which the names and addresses of the keepers are entered as well as the locations of the lodging-houses (s. 403). An authority is required to register, or renew the registration of, a common lodging-house if the keeper, his deputy, if any, and the premises are suitable and the lodging-house will not cause inconvenience or annoyance to persons residing in the neighbourhood. The registration of a person as keeper of a lodging-house remains in force for such period, not exceeding 13 months, as may be fixed by the authority (s. 404). An appeal lies to the magistrates' court by an aggrieved person against the refusal of a local housing authority to grant or renew registration (s. 405).

Traditionally local authorities have made by-laws for regulating the sanitary condition of common lodging-houses. Section 406 of the Act empowers a local housing authority to make by-laws for such purposes.

Offences, power to disqualify keepers etc.

Section 408 of the Housing Act 1985 makes it an offence for a person to contravene, or fail to comply with, any of the provisions of the Act relating to common lodging-houses. If the keeper of a common lodging-house is convicted of an offence under part XI of the Act, or a by-law made under it, or an offence under s. 39(2) or 49(2) of the Public Health (Control of Disease) Act 1984 (failure to notify in case of infectious disease or failure to comply with closing order made on account of notifiable disease) then the Housing Act 1985, s. 409, empowers the court by which the keeper is convicted to cancel the registration as a common lodging-house keeper and may order that the person in question be disqualified for such period as the court thinks fit.

Section 411 gives wide powers to an authorised officer of the local housing authority to enter common lodging-houses to ascertain, *inter alia*, if the provisions of the Act are being complied with.

IMPROVEMENT GRANTS

One of the hallmarks of the changing face of housing law in the postwar years has been a recognition that the State should give financial assistance towards the improvement of dwellinghouses. The relevant law is now contained in part VIII of the Local Government and Housing Act 1989 which is now discussed.

Grants for improvement and repair

Under the Local Government and Housing Act 1989, s. 101, grants are payable by local housing authorities towards the cost of works required:

(a) for the improvement or repair of dwellings, houses in multiple occupation or the common parts of buildings containing one or more flats; and

(b) for the provision of dwellings or houses in multiple occupation by the conversion of a house or other building; and

(c) for the provision of facilities for disabled persons in dwellings and in the common parts of buildings containing one or more flats.

No grant is payable under the Act, *inter alia*, to any local authority, new town corporation, urban development corporation or housing action trust (s. 101).

Grant applications and conditions

In order to obtain an improvement grant an application must be made in writing to the local housing authority (s. 102). A local housing authority may not entertain an application for a grant (other than for a common parts grant) unless it is satisfied that the applicant has, or proposes to acquire, an owner's interest in the land on which the works are to be carried out, or, in the case of an application for a renovation grant (other than an application in respect of works required for the provision of one or more dwellings by the conversion of a house or other building), the applicant is a tenant of the dwelling but does not have or propose to acquire an owner's interest in the dwelling (s. 104). For the purposes of part VIII of the Act, the expression 'owner's interest' means an interest which is held by the applicant alone or jointly with others and is either an estate in fee simple absolute in possession (i.e., freehold) or a term of years absolute (i.e., leasehold). However, the Secretary of State may give directions to a local housing authority to the effect that insofar as an applicant for a grant must have an owner's interest that requirement is satisfied if the applicant has simply an interest in part of the land concerned.

Common parts grants

The expression 'common parts' in relation to a building is defined by s. 138 as including the structure and exterior of the building and common facilities provided, whether in the building or elsewhere, for persons who include the occupiers of one or more flats in the building.

A local housing authority may not entertain an application for a common parts grant unless it is satisfied that, at the date of the application, at least the required proportion of the flats in the building concerned are occupied by occupying tenants and the application is either a landlord's common parts application or a tenants' common parts application (s. 105(1)). The required proportion is three-quarters or such other proportion as may be prescribed for the purposes of s. 105 by an order made by the Secretary of State or an order approved by the Secretary of State in relation to a particular case or description of case on application made by the local housing authority concerned.

The expression 'occupying tenant' in relation to a flat in a building includes a tenant who holds one of the following interests: a lease of which not less than five years remains unexpired at the date of the application, an assured tenancy, a protected occupancy or a secured tenancy (s. 105(2)(a)). The expression 'landlord's common parts application' is defined, in relation to works to the common parts of a building, as an application for a common parts grant made by a person who has, alone or jointly with others, either the freehold or the leasehold of the building and has a duty to carry out the works (s. 105(2)(b)). The expression 'tenants' common parts application' is defined, in relation to works to the common parts of a building, as an application for a common parts grant made by at least three-quarters of the occupying tenants of the building who under their tenancies have a duty to carry out or make a contribution to some or all of the works (s. 105(2)(c)).

Certificate of future occupation
Section 106 provides that, subject to ss. 126 and 136, a local housing authority may not entertain an application for a renovation grant or a disabled facilities grant unless it is accompanied by one of four kinds of certificate specified in the section. The certificates are:

(a) An 'owner-occupation certificate'. This certifies that the applicant has, or proposes to acquire, an owner's interest in the dwelling or building and that the applicant, or a member of his or her family, intends to live in the dwelling or, as the case may be, a flat in the building as his or her or that member's only or main residence for a period of not less than 12 months beginning on the certified date.

(b) A 'tenant's certificate'. This certifies that the applicant is a tenant who is required by the terms of his or her tenancy to carry out the relevant works and the tenancy is not of a description excluded by an order made by the Secretary of State or the tenancy is of a description specified by the Secretary of State and the applicant or a member of his or her family intends to live in the dwelling or, as the case may be, a flat in the building as his or her or that member's only or main residence.

(c) A 'certificate of intended letting'. This certifies that the applicant has, or proposes to acquire, an owner's interest in the dwelling or building and has let, or intends to let, the dwelling or, as the case may be, one or more flats in the building as a residence:

    (i)   to someone other than a member of the applicant's family; and
    (ii)   for a period of not less than five years beginning on the certified date; and
    (iii)   except where the application relates to a disabled facilities grant, on a tenancy which is not a long tenancy (as defined in Housing Act 1985, s. 115).

(d) A 'special certificate'. This certifies that the applicant has, or proposes to acquire, an owner's interest in the dwelling or building and is an applicant of a class prescribed for the purposes of the section.

Notwithstanding the fact that the applicant has the requisite certificate, s. 106 provides that in certain circumstances a grant is not payable unless certain requirements are met. Under s. 106(6) a local housing authority may not entertain a tenant's application unless it is also accompanied by a certificate of intended letting made by the person who at the time of the application is the landlord under the tenancy or the authority considers it unreasonable in the circumstances to seek such a certificate. Section 106(7) provides that the authority may not entertain an application for an HMO (house in multiple occupation) grant unless it is accompanied by a certificate that the applicant has or proposes to acquire an owner's interest in the house and intends to license the use of it as a residence to someone other than a member of the applicant's family and for a period of not less than five years beginning from the certified date and, except where the application relates to a disabled facilities grant, on a tenancy which is not a long tenancy, or the applicant intends to let part of the house as a residence for the aforementioned purposes.

An application for a common parts grant must be accompanied by a certificate signed by the applicant, or each of the applicants, which specifies the interest of the applicant, or, as the case may be, each of the applicants, in the building or in the flat in the building and certifies that the required proportion as defined in s. 105(5) of the flats in the building is occupied by occupying tenants. The subsection specifies a proportion of three quarters or such other proportion specified by order of the Secretary of State.

Exclusion of certain dwellings and works from grant aid

In certain situations it would be inappropriate for grant to be given for the carrying out of works of renovation. The Local Government and Housing Act 1989, s. 107, provides that, unless the application is for a mandatory grant (see page 205) and either completion of the works is necessary to comply with a notice served under the Housing Act 1985, s. 189 (repair notice requiring works to render premises fit for human habitation), or it is a landlord's application, no grant may be paid if:

(a) The dwelling or house is not fit for human habitation, and the local housing authority considers that the works will not be sufficient to render it fit for human habitation.

(b) If, or to the extent that, the works have been completed before the date of service of a notice of refusal under s. 116 (see page 208).

(c) If, within three months after service of a notice of refusal, the local housing authority intends to make a closing order under the Housing Act 1985, s. 264 or a demolition order under s. 265 (see pages 187).

(d) If, within 12 months after service of a notice of refusal, the authority intends to declare a clearance area under the Housing Act 1985, s. 289 (see page 189), for an area which includes the dwelling, house or building.

Furthermore, by s. 107(5), unless it is a landlord's application for a mandatory grant, a local housing authority may not approve an application for an HMO grant so far as it relates to works which relate to means of escape from fire or other fire precautions and which are required to be carried out under or by virtue of any enactment, whenever passed.

It is important that the local housing authority approves a proposal before work begins. Section 108 therefore provides that an authority may not approve an application for a grant if the works have been commenced before the application is approved and must in consequence serve a notice of refusal to that effect on the applicant. This does not apply to an application for a mandatory grant if either completion of the works is necessary to comply with a notice under the Housing Act 1985, s. 189, or it is a landlord's application. It also does not apply if the authority is satisfied that there was genuine error or good reason for beginning the work before the application was approved. In such a case the authority may, with the consent of the applicant, treat the application as varied so that the relevant works are limited to those that remain to be completed at the date of the application.

Grants to owner-occupiers and tenants

In certain circumstances the Local Government and Housing Act 1989 makes provision for means testing in relation to grants. Section 109 provides that where an application for a grant is accompanied by an owner-occupation certificate, a tenant's certificate or a special certificate, then if the financial resources of the applicant exceed the applicable amount, the amount of any grant which may be paid must be reduced by the amount calculated in accordance with regulations made by the Secretary of State (see the Housing Renovation etc. Grants (Reduction of Grant) Regulations 1990 (SI 1990/1189) amended by SI 1992/705).

Grants to landlords

In determining the amount of a grant to a landlord, a local housing authority must have regard to the cost of the relevant works as well as, *inter alia*, the amount of rent payable and any increase which might reasonably be expected in that rent to take account of the works when completed (Local Government and Housing Act 1989, s. 110).

Tenants' common parts grant applications

When considering a tenants' common parts grant, the local housing authority is required to decide how much of the cost of the works is attributable to the applicants (Local Government and Housing Act 1989, s. 111(2)). This figure is referred to in s. 111 as the 'attributable cost' and is equal to the proportion referred to in s. 111(3) of the cost of the works, that is:

(a) where it can be ascertained, the proportion that the aggregate of each of the applicant's respective liabilities to carry out or contribute to the carrying out of the relevant works bears to the aggregate of all such liabilities on the part of all persons (including the applicants) so liable; or

(b) where the proportion mentioned in paragraph (a) above cannot be ascertained, the proportion that the number of applicants bears to the number of persons (including the applicants) liable to carry out or contribute to the carrying out of works to the building;

and in any case where the interest by virtue of which the liability referred to in paragraph (b) above arises is held jointly by two or more persons, those persons shall be regarded as a single person in deciding for the purposes of that paragraph the number of persons so liable.

The attributable cost is apportioned under s. 111(4) to each of the applicants:

(a) in a case where the attributable cost is calculated by reference to the proportion mentioned in paragraph (a) of subsection (3) above, according to the proportion that his liabilities to carry out or contribute to the carrying out of the relevant works bears to the aggregate of the applicants' liabilities mentioned that paragraph; or

(b) in a case where the attributable cost is calculated by reference to the proportion mentioned in paragraph (b) of that subsection, equally.

The amount of grant payable is the aggregate of the grants that would be payable to each of the applicants under s. 109 (see page 203) or, in the case of a participating landlord, under s. 110 (see page 202) if each of the applicants was applying in respect of his or her apportionment of the attributable cost.

Duty to approve certain applications (mandatory grants)

Traditionally one of the main purposes of State grants for the improvement of residential accommodation has been to allow premises unfit for human habitation to be rendered fit. Under the Local Government and Housing Act 1989, s. 112(1), a local housing authority must approve an application for a renovation grant (other than an application in respect of works required for the provision of one or more dwellings by the conversion of a house or other building) in respect of an unfit dwelling if it is satisfied that on completion of the works the dwellinghouse would be fit for human habitation. The expression 'fit for human habitation' has the same meaning as it has under the Housing Act 1985, s. 604 (see page 182). No account must be taken, however, of works for which assistance is available under part XVI of the Housing Act 1985. In determining whether the house is fit for human habitation the authority is required to have regard to any guidance given under the Housing Act 1985, s. 604A (see page 181).

The authority need approve an application for aid for more works than are necessary to cause the dwelling to be fit for human habitation. In such a case, the authority is required to treat the application as an application for a mandatory grant other than in respect of the additional works and, in relation to the additional works, as an application for approval under s. 115 (which gives the authority discretion as to whether or not to approve of the application). An authority is not placed under a duty to approve an application under section 112 if it is accompanied by a certificate of intended letting and is not a tenant's application or if the authority expect within a period of twelve months from the date of receipt of the application, to prepare a group repair scheme in respect of the building which includes or comprises the building.

In practice the desire to carry out improvement works to property may be prompted by the appropriate local authority serving a repair notice under the Housing Act 1985. Section 113 of the 1989 Act provides that a local housing authority is required to approve an application for grant falling within the scope of s. 110(1) (that is, a 'landlord's application') if completion of the works is necessary to comply with repair notices served under one or more of the following provisions:

(a) Housing Act 1985, s. 189 (repair notice requiring works to render premises fit for human habitation),

(b) Housing Act 1985, s. 190 (repair notice in respect of premises in state of disrepair but not unfit), or

(c) Housing Act 1985, s. 352 (requiring works to render premises fit for number of occupants).

No account may be taken of works for which assistance is available under part XVI of the Housing Act 1985 (assistance for owners of defective housing). To the extent that a landlord's application is for works not required by any such notice it is not an application for a mandatory grant and is instead dealt with under s. 115 (see page 207).

A local housing authority must approve an application for grant which is accompanied by an owner-occupation certificate if completion of the works is necessary to comply with a notice served under the Housing Act 1985, s. 190 (repair notice in respect of house in state of disrepair but not unfit).

Applications for facilities for the disabled

The Local Government and Housing Act 1989 makes special provision to encourage the provision of facilities for the disabled in houses. Section 114 places a duty on a local housing authority to approve an application for a disabled facilities grant if the works are for one or more of the purposes mentioned in s. 114(3), which include:

(a) facilitating access by the disabled occupant to and from the dwelling or the building,

(b) facilitating access by the disabled occupant to a room used or usable as the principal family room,

(c) facilitating access by the disabled occupant to, or providing for the disabled occupant, a room used or usable for sleeping,

(d) facilitating access by the disabled occupant to, or providing for the disabled occupant, a room in which there is a lavatory, bath, shower or wash-hand basin, or facilitating the use by the disabled occupant of such a facility.

However, a local housing authority may not approve an application for a disabled facilities grant unless it is satisfied that the works are necessary and appropriate to meet the needs of the disabled occupant and that it is reasonable and practicable to carry out the relevant works having regard to the age and condition of the dwelling or building. The relevant welfare authority must be consulted about whether the works are necessary to meet the needs of the disabled occupant (s. 114(1)).

Discretionary grant approval

Many grant applications are for works going beyond what is necessary to render the dwelling fit for human habitation. It is not the intention of

Parliament to deprive those who effect such works of State assistance. The Local Government and Housing Act 1989, s. 115(1), therefore provides that a local housing authority may approve an application for a grant, other than a common parts grant, in any case where:

(a) the works go beyond or are other than those which will cause the dwelling to be fit for human habitation, but
(b) the authority is satisfied that the works are necessary for one or more of the purposes set out in s. 115(3).

A local housing authority may approve an application for a common parts grant under s. 115(2) if the authority is satisfied that the relevant works:

(a) are necessary for one or more of the purposes set out in paras. (a) and (c) to (g) of s. 115(3), or
(b) will cause the building to meet the requirements mentioned in paras. (a) to (e) of the Housing Act 1985, s. 604(2).

The purposes set out in s. 115(3) are:

(a) to put the dwelling or building in reasonable repair;
(b) to provide the dwelling by the conversion of a house or other building;
(c) to provide adequate thermal insulation;
(d) to provide adequate facilities for space heating;
(e) to provide satisfactory internal arrangements;
(f) to ensure that the dwelling or building complies with such requirements with respect to construction or physical condition as may for the time being be specified by the Secretary of State for the purposes of this section; and
(g) to ensure that there is compliance with such requirements with respect to the provision or condition of services and amenities to or within the dwelling or building as may for the time being be so specified.

In the case of an application for an HMO grant, any reference in s. 115(1) and (3) to the dwelling includes a reference to the house in multiple occupation.

A factor which is of considerable moment when a local housing authority is considering whether or not to approve an application for grant is the expected future life of the building. In considering whether to approve an application for a grant in exercise of its discretion under s. 115(1) or (2), a local housing authority must have regard to the expected life of the building including, where appropriate, the effect of carrying out the works

(s. 115(5)). Furthermore, in determining what constitutes 'reasonable repair' in relation to s. 115(3)(a) the housing authority must have regard to the age and character of the dwelling or building and the locality in which it is situated and the authority is also required to disregard the state of internal disrepair of the dwelling or building (s. 115(9)).

A local housing authority may approve a landlord's application if the works are for the purpose of rendering the dwelling or house fit for human habitation or, in the case of an application for an HMO grant, the works are for the purpose of enabling the house to meet one or more of the requirements in the Housing Act 1985, s. 352(1A) (power to require execution of works to render premises fit for number of occupants) and in either case, the authority is satisfied that the relevant works are necessary for the purpose concerned (Local Government and Housing Act 1989, s. 115(6)).

If proposed works are more or less extensive than is necessary to achieve the result referred to in s. 115(2)(b) or any of the purposes set out in s. 115(3) or (6), the local housing authority can, with the consent of the applicant, treat the grant application as varied to include such works as are necessary for that purpose.

Approval and payment of grants

The local housing authority must notify the applicant for grant in writing as soon as reasonably practicable, and in any event not later than six months after the date of the application concerned, whether the application is approved or refused (Local Government and Housing Act 1989, s. 116). If the authority decides to approve an application it is required to determine which of the relevant works are eligible for grant; the amount of expenses which are properly to be incurred; and the amount of costs which have been or are to be properly incurred with respect to preliminary or ancillary services and charges; and the amount of grant it has decided to pay in respect of the eligible works. These sums must be notified to the applicant in question.

Generally speaking, the local housing authority is not empowered to attach any condition to the approval of any grant with the exception that a condition may be imposed under s. 118(1) to the effect that the works in question be carried out in accordance with the specifications laid down by the authority. It will be seen below, however, that the 1989 Act makes provision for the imposition of conditions for certain types of grants.

The Secretary of State is empowered by s. 118(5) to prescribe by order a maximum amount of grant which a local housing authority may pay in respect of an application for grant. See the Housing Renovation etc. Grants (Grant Limit) Order 1993 (SI 1993/553).

A grant may be paid either in whole after the completion of the works or in part by instalment as the works progress and the balance after completion of the works. Payment of grant is conditional on the works being executed to the satisfaction of the authority and the authority being provided with an acceptable invoice, demand or receipt for payment of the works and any preliminary or ancillary services and charges in respect of which the grant or part of the grant is to be paid (s. 117).

Conditions of grants and repayments

Large sums of public money are spent on grants. It is important therefore that local housing authorities have some control over the quality of the works paid for. An authority may, under the Local Government and Housing Act 1989, s. 118, require as a condition of grant that the works are carried out in accordance with such specifications as it determines. It is also a condition of grant that the eligible works are carried out within 12 months from the date of approval of the application concerned. This period may be extended by the local authority.

In addition to the above conditions, the 1989 Act requires conditions to be attached to grants according to their types. The relevant sections are explained in turn.

Conditions as to availability for letting

Section 119(1) applies where an application for a renovation grant or a disabled facilities grant, other than an application for a disabled facilities grant in respect of works to the common parts of buildings containing flats, has been approved by the local housing authority and the application for the grant was accompanied by a certificate of intended letting. It is made a condition of the grant that throughout the initial period (that is, a period of five years from the certified date):

(a) the dwelling will be let or available for letting as a residence and not for a holiday, on a tenancy which is not a long tenancy by the owner for the time being of the dwelling to a person who is not connected with him, or

(b) the dwelling will be occupied or available for occupation by a member of the agricultural population in pursuance of a contract of service and otherwise as a tenant,

disregarding any part of that period in which neither of the above paragraphs applies but the dwelling is occupied by a person who is a protected occupier under the Rent (Agriculture) Act 1976 or is occupier under an assured agricultural occupancy, within the meaning of Part I of the Housing Act 1988.

Condition requiring repayment of grant on certain disposals of property

Section 120 deals with a situation where a renovation grant (other than a tenant's application) has been approved by a local authority and the application for the grant was accompanied by a certificate of intended letting. It is made a condition of the grant that where the owner makes a so-called 'relevant disposal' other than an exempt disposal of the dwelling with vacant possession within the initial period, the owner is required to pay the local housing authority the amount of the grant.

Section 124 defines the expression 'relevant disposal' as a conveyance of the freehold, or an assignment of the lease of the premises, or a grant of a lease (other than a mortgage term) for a term of more than 21 years otherwise than at a rack-rent. The expression 'exempt disposal' covers a variety of situations including the disposal of the premises to certain classes of individuals and also the vesting of the whole of the dwelling in a person taking under a will or intestacy. Where the owner makes such a disposal otherwise than with vacant possession within the initial period, the owner is required to pay the authority on demand the amount of the grant reduced by one fifth for each complete year which has elapsed after the certified date and before the disposal.

An important provision of the section is that as long as a condition remains in force with respect to a dwelling it is binding on any person who is for the time being an owner of the dwelling. In other words the condition 'runs' with the relevant land.

Section 121 makes provision for the situation where an application for a renovation grant has been approved by the local housing authority and the application for grant was accompanied by an owner-occupation certificate. It is made a condition of grant in such a situation that where an owner makes a relevant disposal (other than an exempt disposal) the owner is required to pay the authority on demand the amount of grant, reduced by one third for each complete year which has elapsed after the certified date and before the disposal. The condition remains in force for three years from the certified date and binds any person who is for the time being an owner of the dwelling.

Conditions relating to HMO grant

As far as houses in multiple occupation are concerned, s. 122 makes it a condition of the grant that throughout the initial period the house will be residentially occupied or available for residential occupation under tenancies or licences by persons who are not connected with the owner for the time being of the house.

Landlord's common parts application

As far as a landlord's common parts application is concerned, s. 123 provides that if the applicant makes a relevant disposal other than an exempt

Housing

disposal of the building within the initial period the applicant must pay the local housing authority on demand the amount of the grant.

Renovation grants relating to two or more dwellings

No application for a renovation grant may be made in respect of more than one dwelling (Local Government and Housing Act 1989, s. 126). However, a single application may be made for a renovation grant towards the cost of works required for the provision of two or more dwellings by the conversion of a house or other building.

Group repair schemes

It is not unusual to find that the exterior of a building containing a number of houses falls into a state of disrepair, in which case it is preferable from a practical point of view to deal with the building as a whole. Section 127 of the Local Government and Housing Act 1989 therefore allows a local housing authority to enter into agreements to secure the carrying out of such external works to buildings (i.e., 'qualifying buildings') to which the scheme relates as will ensure that on completion of the works, the exterior of those buildings will be in reasonable repair. Such a scheme is referred to as a group repair scheme. The scheme must be prepared by the local authority and approved by the Secretary of State. Such approval may be given either in respect to a specific scheme or generally to schemes which fulfil such criteria as the Secretary of State may from time to time specify. In order to be eligible to participate in such a scheme the applicant must have an owner's interest as defined in a dwelling subject to certain exclusions and also meet the conditions specified in s. 127(5).

Qualifying buildings and external works for group repair schemes
A building will qualify for grant in respect of a group repair scheme if the whole or some part of its exterior is not in a state of reasonable repair and the lack of repair affects at least 75 per cent of the houses contained in the building (s. 128(1)). Every group repair scheme must relate to at least one qualifying building (referred to as the 'primary building') which was constructed so as to comprise not less than four separate houses. Under s. 128(2) a scheme may relate to one or more qualifying buildings if the following conditions are fulfilled with respect to each of them:

    (a) the building was constructed so as to comprise at least one house and is contiguous or adjacent to the primary building; and

    (b) the exterior of the building is not in reasonable repair and is in need of works similar to those required to the exterior of the primary building; and

(c) carrying out the works to the building and the primary building at the same time is the most effective way of securing the repair of each of them.

The question whether a building was constructed so as to comprise not less than four houses or at least one house is to be determined according to the configuration of the building at the time of construction (s. 128(3)).

Section 128 goes on to provide that a terrace of houses is to be regarded as one building except that if it appears appropriate to a local housing authority to do so, it may treat only part of the terrace as a building. Furthermore, in the case of one building containing two or more purpose-built flats and one or more houses, the part of the building containing the purpose-built flats and the part or parts of the building containing the houses, are to be regarded as separate buildings.

Contributions by participants in the scheme
Each person who participates in a group repair scheme has to contribute a certain percentage of the cost of the work attributable to the house or other premises in which that person has an interest. The percentages are determined in accordance with s. 129. An unassisted participant contributes 100 per cent. An assisted participant with an interest in premises other than a house (a term which, for the purposes of the subsection, includes a house in multiple occupation) or flat contributes 25 per cent if the qualifying building is in a renewal area and 50 per cent in any other case (s. 129(4)). These percentages may be altered by the Secretary of State by order. In the case of any other assisted participant the rate of contribution falls to be determined by the local housing authority between nil and that which would be appropriate if s. 129(4) applied.

Minor works

In addition to making provision for the grants mentioned above, the Local Government and Housing Act 1989 empowers local authorities to give assistance for the various purposes mentioned in s. 131 which include the provision or improvement of thermal insulation in a dwelling; the carrying out of works of repair to a dwelling which, at the time of the application, is included in a clearance area (see page 189), or which the authority intends to include in such an area within 12 months after the date of the application; and the carrying out of works of repair, improvement or adaptation to premises owned or tenanted by an elderly person. The Secretary of State is empowered by regulations to make provision for the determination of sums payable under the section (see the Assistance for Minor Works to Dwellings Regulations 1990 (SI 1990/388) amended by SI 1992/1845.

Housing 213

Other matters

Brief mention can be made here of the Homes Insulation Grants Order 1988 (SI 1988/1239) which makes provision for grants to allow the insulation of houses to be improved, and the Housing Act 1985, part XVI, which makes provision for assistance to the owner of a defective dwelling, that is, a dwelling which is defective by reason of its design or construction. Essentially, in order to qualify for assistance under part XVI, the applicant must have acquired the dwelling from a public-sector authority before the appropriate cut-off date and the value of the dwelling which governed its price did not take account of the defect.

CARAVAN SITES

Any discussion of the public health control of housing would be incomplete if it failed to accord some attention to the control of caravans and caravan sites since a numerically significant, albeit small, minority of the population reside in caravans either on a temporary or permanent basis. The current legal framework is contained in the Caravan Sites and Control of Development Act 1960 and the Town and Country Planning Act 1990. Only the former will be discussed here. The 1960 Act is, in the main, a planning statute. Its main purport is therefore to prevent the presence of caravans interfering with the amenity of the environment. However, the statute does contain provisions which are directed to securing the health of the occupants of caravans. It is these provisions which are discussed now.

Licensing of caravan sites

The main form of control over caravan sites takes the form of requiring caravan sites to be licensed by local authorities. Section 1(1) of the Caravan Sites and Control of Development Act 1960 provides that an occupier of land must obtain a site licence prior to allowing any part of the land to be used as a caravan site. The expression 'occupier' includes a person who has let land amounting to no more than 400 square yards in area (about 334 square metres) under a tenancy entered into with a view to the use of the land as a caravan site and is entitled to possession of the land but for the rights of the person under the tenancy. The section imposes a penalty for contravening s. 1(1).

The expression 'caravan site' is defined in s. 1(4) as 'land on which a caravan is stationed for the purposes of human habitation and land which is used in conjunction with land on which a caravan is so stationed'. Section 29(1) defines 'caravan' as:

> any structure designed or adapted for human habitation which is capable of being moved from one place to another (whether by being towed, or by

being transported on a motor vehicle or trailer) and any motor vehicle so designed or adapted, but does not include —

(a) any railway rolling stock which is for the time being on rails forming part of a railway system, or
(b) any tent.

In *Wyre Forest District Council* v *Secretary of State for Environment* [1990] 2 AC 357 it was held that a chalet was a caravan for the purposes of the 1960 Act. In *Tyler* v *Woodspring District Council* [1991] JPL 727 it was stated, *obiter*, that a structure which rested on stanchions and not on permanent foundations but was capable of being dismantled in sections and transported was not a caravan.

In certain circumstances it is unnecessary to obtain a site licence. Section 2 provides that no site licence is required for the use of land as a caravan site if such use falls within sch. 1 to the Act. The schedule makes provision for a variety of circumstances in which a licence is not required including the use of land as a caravan site if the use is incidental to the enjoyment as such of a dwellinghouse within the curtilage of which the land is situated. No site licence is needed in relation to land used periodically to accommodate caravans in certain circumstances. Caravan sites run under the aegis of certain organisations are also exempt from the requirement to have a site licence.

An application for a site licence must be made by the occupier of the land (s. 3). The local authority may issue a site licence only if planning permission has been granted under the Town and Country Planning Act 1990 for the use of the land as a caravan site. Indeed the local authority must issue a site licence if planning permission has been granted (s. 3). The site licence lasts as long as the planning permission unless the planning permission was granted by way of a development order (s. 4).

Conditions which may be attached to site licence

Of fundamental importance as far as environmental control of caravan sites is concerned is the power possessed by the local authority to attach conditions to the site licence under the Caravan Sites and Control of Development Act 1960, s. 5(1). A local authority has wide power as to the conditions it can attach to a site licence in the interests of the persons living in the caravan or of any other class of person or of the public at large. Conditions may be imposed for the following purposes:

(a) restricting the occasions on which caravans are stationed on the land,
(b) controlling the types of caravan which are stationed on the land,
(c) regulating the positions in which caravans are stationed,

(d) securing the taking of any steps for preserving or enhancing the amenity of the land,
(e) preventing and combating fire,
(f) securing that adequate sanitary facilities are provided.

In *Babbage* v *North Norfolk District Council* (1988) 57 P & CR 237 it was held that as far as the imposition of a condition to preserve or enhance the amenity of the land was concerned, the local authority could lawfully take into account the appearance of the caravan site from outside the site.

No condition may be attached to a site licence controlling the types of caravans which are stationed on the land by reference to the materials used in the construction of the caravans (s. 5(2)).

The minister is allowed to make model standards in order to assist local authorities as to the conditions which they attach to site licences (see Ministry of Housing and Local Government Circular No. 42/60).

While, as mentioned, the above powers to attach conditions to a site licence are wide, the conditions must be reasonable and relate to the physical user of the land concerned (*Mixnam's Properties Ltd* v *Chertsey Urban District Council* [1964] 1 QB 214; *Pyx Granite Co. Ltd* v *Ministry of Housing and Local Government* [1958] 1 QB 554). Furthermore, the conditions of a site licence are subject to and circumscribed by any conditions imposed on the grant of planning permission (*R* v *Kent Justices, ex parte Crittenden* [1964] 1 QB 144).

Under s. 7 any person aggrieved by any condition (other than a condition relating to the display of a site licence) attached to a site licence may appeal to the magistrates' court. The court, if satisfied that the condition is unduly burdensome, may vary or cancel the condition. In deciding whether any condition is burdensome the court is required to have regard, *inter alia*, to the model standards prepared by the minister. In *Babbage* v *North Norfolk District Council* (1988) 57 P & CR 237 McCullough J was of the opinion that it was not possible to formulate any criteria by which one can clearly and certainly distinguish between conditions which can and cannot be impugned before the courts.

With the passage of time a change in the circumstances affecting the site may necessitate the current conditions attached to the licence being changed. Section 8 allows a local authority to alter conditions attached to a site licence. Prior to doing this the holder of the licence must be given an opportunity to make representations. The holder of a site licence may appeal to the magistrates' court against the decision of the authority to alter the conditions of the licence.

Section 9 makes it an offence for the occupier of land to fail to comply with any condition of a site licence. Where a person convicted under s. 9 has been convicted on two or more previous occasions, the court may, on the application of the local authority, revoke the licence.

TEN
Building control and buildings

BUILDING CONTROL

It is essential that all new buildings are constructed in such a way as to secure the health and well-being of those occupying the building as well as the general public. Building control is mainly concerned with the regulation of the structure, layout, services and facilities provided to buildings, as opposed to the environmental impact of the buildings themselves, which is the preserve of planning law. Since Victorian times at least, the large bulk of the substantive law governing building and buildings has taken the form of local authority by-laws which have governed the safety of buildings and also given local authorities powers of enforcement. This situation obtained until 1965 when the Building Regulations, made under the Public Health Acts 1936 and 1961, came into force. The principal statute which now deals with building control in England and Wales is the Building Act 1984 (BA) which largely repeals and re-enacts the provisions of the 1936 and 1961 Acts. The main provisions of the 1984 Act will now be discussed.

Building regulations

Wide power is given by s. 1 of the Building Act 1984 to the Secretary of State to make regulations for the purpose of securing the health, safety, welfare and convenience of persons in or about buildings and of others who may be affected by buildings or matters connected with buildings. Of interest from a broad environmental viewpoint, is the additional power to make regulations to further the conservation of fuel and power and prevent waste, undue consumption, misuse or contamination of water.

The regulations currently in force are the Building Regulations 1991 (SI 1991/2768). Section 3 of the Building Act 1984 provides that building regulations may exempt a prescribed class of building services, fittings or equipment from all or any of their provisions. In order to provide practical guidance with respect to the requirements of any provision of building regulations, s. 6 empowers the Secretary of State or a body designated for the purpose, to approve and issue any document or, alternately, approve any document issued by some other body. This form of legislation by reference (which has parallels in environmental health law in, for example, the Health and Safety at Work etc. Act 1974 and the Environmental Protection Act 1990) introduces flexibility and also allows new developments in building technology to be taken account of earlier than would normally be the case if changes in the law were to be effected by regulations. It also prevents the building regulations becoming unduly cumbersome. Formerly, the building Regulations were, on the whole, difficult to interpret. Approved documents are written in simple language and employ terms of art more readily understood by those in the building industry. Frequent reference is made in approved documents to British Standards and Codes of Practice.

As far as the legal significance of approved documents is concerned, s. 7 provides that failure to comply with an approved document does not of itself render any person liable to any civil or criminal proceedings. However, failure to comply with an approved document may be relied on as tending to establish liability, whereas proof of compliance with the document in question may be relied on as tending to negative liability.

Relaxation of the building regulations

In certain cases it would be unduly onerous for the provisions of the building regulations to be made to apply. This situation is obviously more likely to occur when building works are being carried out to buildings which were built before the regulations came into force. Section 8 of the Act allows the Secretary of State to grant relaxations of the regulations and this power may be delegated to local authorities as it has been by reg. 10 of the Building Regulations 1991. A body which is considering granting a relaxation is required to advertise the location of the premises in question, indicating that representations may be made on public health or safety grounds, unless it appears that the effect the direction may have on public health is limited to premises adjoining the site, in which case notice must be given to the owner and occupier of the premises. An appeal can be made to the Secretary of State against the refusal of a local authority to dispense with or relax the regulations (s. 39) and then to the High Court on a point of law (s. 42). Section 11 allows the Secretary of State to grant relaxation in relation to particular types of building matter. The relaxation may be given unconditionally or conditionally. If the Secretary of State has 'first-instance' powers of dealing with applications for relaxation, an appeal may be made against the relevant decision to the High Court (s. 42).

Type approval in building

In order to avoid uncertainty as to whether a particular material or mode of construction complies with the building regulations, s. 12 of the Building Act 1984 allows the Secretary of State to approve a particular type of building matter (in effect, building materials or mode of construction of a building) as complying with the building regulations either generally or in a class of case.

Section 13 allows the power to make type approvals to be delegated to any body or person e.g., the Agreement Board.

Neither s. 12 or s. 13 are in force at the time of writing (May 1994).

Passing and rejecting plans

As far as England and Wales is concerned, there is in effect a dual system of building control, split between local authorities and approved inspectors who are individuals vested with powers to pass building plans and inspectorial powers in relation to building works. This will be discussed below.

The cornerstone of the Building Act 1984 is s. 16(1) which relates to the passing or rejection of plans. The section provides that where plans of any proposed work are in accordance with building regulations, the local authority is under a duty to pass the plans subject to any other section of the Act expressly authorising it to reject the plans, unless the plans are defective or they show that the proposed work would contravene any of the building regulations. In certain situations the Act provides that plans must be rejected, for example, if there is insufficient access for the removal of refuse (s. 23), or it is proposed to build on ground filled with offensive materials (s. 29). It should be noted that the local authority is under a mandatory duty to pass the appropriate plans if they are not defective. Therefore, the power possessed by the local authority differs from a system of licensing, where the licensing body has often wide discretion as to whether or not to grant a licence. The Building (Prescribed Fees etc.) Regulations 1985 (SI 1985/1576) deal with fees that local authorities can charge in relation to the passing of plans and inspecting building work.

If plans are defective or indicate that the proposed work would contravene any of the building regulations, the local authority may reject the plans or pass them subject to modifications being made and/or that further plans be deposited with the authority (s. 16(2)). This latter condition would be apposite if the original plans failed to show sufficient detail of the proposals in question. A local authority can only pass plans conditionally if a request to that effect has been made to it by the person by whom or on whose behalf the plans were deposited, or the person concerned has consented to the authority passing the plans conditionally.

However, where plans are accompanied by a certificate given by an approved person (that is to say a person approved by the Secretary of State or by a body designated by the Secretary of State under s. 17) to the effect that the proposed work, if carried out in accordance with the deposited plans, will comply with such provisions of the regulations, prescribed by the building regulations for the purposes of s. 16, as are specified in the certificate, the local authority may not, except in prescribed circumstances, reject the plans on the grounds that they are defective with respect to the building regulations which are specified in the certificate, or on the grounds that the plans show that the proposed work would contravene any of those provisions (s. 16(9)).

In the event of a dispute between the local authority and a person who proposes to carry out work about whether the plans are in conformity with the building regulations or whether the local authority is prohibited from rejecting the plans by s. 16(9), the matter can be referred to the Secretary of State for determination. An appeal may be made to the High Court against the Secretary of State's decision (s. 42).

Section 17(1) provides that the building regulations may make provision for the approval of persons for the purposes of s. 17(9) by either the Secretary of State or by a body corporate which is designated by the Secretary of State for the purpose. Thus far only the National Housebuilding Council (NHBC) has been designated. Any such approval may limit the description of work or the provisions of the regulations in relation to which the person concerned is approved. Furthermore, building regulations may prescribe the insurance cover that is to be provided in relation to any certificate given under s. 16(9).

Building over sewers and drains

Unless special precautions are taken, it is undesirable to erect a building over a sewer since it is possible that the weight of the building will exert pressure causing the sewer to fracture. A local authority must reject plans which show that a building is to be erected over a sewer or drain unless satisfied that in the circumstances of the case it can give consent (Building Act 1984, s. 18).

Provision of drainage

In order to provide accommodation which is satisfactory from a public health viewpoint, a building must be provided with certain essential facilities. Building plans must be rejected unless they show that satisfactory provision will be made for the drainage of the building or the authority is satisfied that in the particular case provision for drainage may be dispensed with (Building Act 1984, s. 21(1)). In *Chesterton Rural District Council* v *Ralph Thompson Ltd* [1947] KB 300, it was held that the phrase 'satisfactory provision for drainage' referred to the drains of the particular building as opposed to the system which the house drains discharged into. Therefore the local authority was not entitled to take into account drains outside the particular building. Section 21(4) provides that in order to meet the requirements of the section, the drain must connect with a sewer, or discharge into a cesspool or some other place (for example, a septic tank). However, no drain may be required to be connected with a sewer unless the sewer is within 100 feet (30.48 metres) of the site of the building or extension, and is also at a level that makes it reasonably practicable to construct a drain or communicate with it. If the sewer is not a public sewer it must be one that the person constructing the drain is entitled to use, and the intervening land must be land through which the person is entitled to construct a drain. The local authority can, however, require a drain to be provided to a sewer that is not within 100 feet of the building but is a sewer which the person constructing the drain is entitled to use, if the authority undertakes to bear the additional cost.

Section 22 provides that in a situation where a local authority might under s. 21 require each of two or more buildings to be drained separately into an existing sewer but it appears to the authority that those buildings may be drained more economically or advantageously in combination, the authority may, when the drains of the buildings are first laid, require that the buildings be drained in combination into the existing sewer by means of a private sewer to be constructed either by the owners of the buildings in such manner as the authority may direct, or, if the authority so elects, by the authority on behalf of the owners.

Provision of other facilities etc.

It is essential from a public health viewpoint that refuse collection services can have access to buildings. Building plans must be rejected unless satisfactory means of access are provided from the building to a street for the purpose of removal of refuse (Building Act 1984, s. 23). There must also be satisfactory means for storing refuse for removal.

It is also necessary, in order to secure the safety of those occupying or visiting the building, that there is provided safe means of access and escape from the building. Section 24 requires the building to be provided with such means of ingress and egress as the authority after consultation with the fire authority deems satisfactory.

The significance of the 1984 Act as a public health statute is emphasised by s. 25 which provides that building plans must be rejected unless a proposal is put before the local authority which satisfactorily provides the occupants of the house with a supply of wholesome water sufficient for domestic purposes by connecting the house to a supply of water in pipes provided by a statutory water undertaker, or, if this is not reasonable, to require the house to be connected to a piped water supply. If, however, no form of piped supply can reasonably be provided to the house itself, the section provides that it is sufficient to provide a supply of water within a reasonable distance of the house.

As far as the meaning of 'wholesome' is concerned it is suggested that the expression simply means that the water is free from contamination and pleasant to drink (see *McColl* v *Strathclyde Regional Council* 1983 SLT 616).

As far as the meaning of 'domestic purposes' is concerned, the courts have palpably failed to enunciate a general working test by means of which one can determine if water put to a given use ranks as domestic use in the eye of the law. The test expounded by Eve J in *Frederick* v *Bognor Water Co.* [1909] 1 Ch 149 is of limited value. There, his lordship, in finding that a supply of water for the use of the inmates of a boarding-school was for domestic purposes, stated that the important point was not the character of the house in which the water was used but the character of the purpose for which the water was used (at p. 157). Probably a more effective working test was put forward by Lord Atkinson in *Metropolitan Water Board* v *Avery* [1914] AC 118 where he stated that water supplied to satisfy or help satisfy the needs, or perform or help in performing the services, which, according to the ordinary habits of civilised life, are commonly satisfied and performed in people's homes, as distinguished from those needs and services which are satisfied or performed outside those homes and are not connected with, nor incident to, the occupation of them, fell to be categorised as water for domestic purposes (at p. 126). In the *Avery* case it was held that water used for cooking and washing plates in a public house was use for domestic purposes. Again in *South Suburban Gas Co.* v *Metropolitan Water Board* [1909] 2 Ch 666, it was held that water supplied to the sanitary conveniences provided for workers in a gasworks was water for domestic purposes. Similarly, in *Metropolitan Water Board* v *Colley's Patents Ltd* [1911] 2 KB 38 water which was supplied to a factory and used for drinking, washing and for the cleaning of urinals ranked as domestic use. In *Pidgeon* v *Great Yarmouth Waterworks Co.* [1902] 1 KB 310, it was held that water supplied to a dwellinghouse where boarders resided ranked as water for domestic purposes. However, in *Barnard Castle Urban District Council* v *Wilson* [1902] 2 Ch 746 it was held that water used for a swimming-pool in a school was not employed for domestic purposes. Finally it has been held that water used for water-closets for staff and customers at a railway station is not for domestic purposes (*Metropolitan Water Board* v *London Brighton and South Coast Railway Co.* [1910] 2 KB 890).

Tests for conformity with building regulations

Wide power is given to a local authority by the Building Act 1984, s. 33, to require a person, on whose behalf work was, is being or is proposed to be, done, to carry out reasonable tests of or in connection with the work, and to take any samples necessary to enable them to carry out such tests. The section goes on to provide that without prejudice to the generality of such a power the authority may have tests carried out on the soil or subsoil of the site of the building or test any material, component or combination of components used in the construction of the building. Such a power would allow tests to be employed, for example, to determine the fire or heat resistance of materials used in the construction. Tests may also be employed in relation to any service, fitting or equipment. Attention should also be drawn to regs. 16 and 17 of the Building Regulations 1991 which allow a local authority to test drains or private sewers and sample materials used in the carrying out of building work respectively.

Lapse of deposit of plans

It would be impracticable to allow approval of plans to remain effective without limit of time. If work is not commenced within three years of the deposit of plans then the local authority may give notice that the deposit is of no effect (Building Act 1984, s. 32). Notice must be given to the person by whom or on whose behalf the plans were deposited before building work has commenced.

Breach of the building regulations

Section 35 of the Building Act 1984 makes it an offence for anyone to contravene any provision of building regulations other than a provision designated as one which does not apply. In *Torridge District Council* v *Turner* (1991) 90 LGR 173 it was held that the offence of building contrary to building regulations was not a continuing offence. Rather the offence was complete when the person responsible for constructing the building did so in a way which did not comply with the building regulations. Moreover, in *Antino* v *Epping Forest District Council* (1991) 155 JP 663 it was held that an offence under s. 35 was complete when the offending works were purported to have been completed by the builder in question, the builder having had no intention of completing the works in conformity with the regulations. Lack of the requisite intention could be inferred from abandonment of the work. It was possible, furthermore, for a part of a building to be regarded as completed for the purposes of the section, if the builder was proved to have no intention of remedying the defects in that part.

Building control and buildings

Removal of unauthorised work etc.

It is important that a local authority has power to deal with building work which contravenes the regulations especially if the building in question is unsafe or unstable. The Building Act 1984, s. 36, provides that if any work, to which building regulations are applicable, contravene the regulations, the local authority may, without prejudice to its right to take proceedings for a fine in respect of the contravention, issue a notice requiring the owner to pull down or remove the work. The owner, however, is also given the option of making the building comply with the building regulations. If provisions of the Act other than s. 16 expressly require plans to be rejected, the local authority may require the work to be removed or make the owner comply with the requirements it might have imposed as a condition precedent to the passing the plans. If the owner fails to comply with an s. 16 notice, the local authority may pull down or remove the work or carry out remedial works.

An appeal against an s. 36 notice lies to the magistrates' court (s. 40) and then to the Crown Court (s. 41). In *Rickards v Kerrier District Council* (1987) 151 JP 625 it was held that while the burden of proof was on the local authority, the evidential burden shifted to the appellant if the authority showed that the works did not comply with the approved plans. It was then up to the accused to show that, nonetheless, the requirements of the regulations were complied with.

Supervision of work by approved inspectors

In order to introduce more flexibility into the system of building control, reduce public expenditure, and afford builder and client a greater degree of choice, the Building Act 1984 introduces an entirely new concept of building control, in which an independent approved inspector, as opposed to the local authority, can, under certain conditions, supervise building works.

Section 47 makes provision whereby an approved inspector can assume the powers of inspection which would otherwise be exercised by the local authority. In order that an approved inspector can assume inspectorial powers under the Building Act 1984 an 'initial notice' must be given to the local authority jointly by the person intending to carry out the building work and the approved inspector. The initial notice must be accompanied by such plans of the work as may be prescribed, and must be accompanied by appropriate evidence that an approved scheme applies (see below) or the prescribed insurance cover has been, or will be, provided in relation to the work. When the initial notice is accepted by the local authority, then, so long as it continues in force, the approved inspector by whom the notice is given, essentially assumes the statutory inspectorial powers that would otherwise be performed by the local authority under the Act.

If an initial notice is served on a local authority, it may not reject the notice except on prescribed grounds. The notice may be accepted conditionally or unconditionally (s. 47(2)).

The Secretary of State is empowered to approve, for the purposes of the section, any scheme that appears to secure the provision of adequate insurance in relation to work that is specified in the initial notice and is work to which the scheme applies (s. 47(6)). Building regulations may prescribe, for the purposes of s. 47, the insurance cover that is to be provided in relation to any work that is specified in an initial notice and is not work to which an approved scheme applies. The regulations may prescribe the form and content of policies of insurance applicable to such work (s. 47(7)).

Effect of initial notice

The practical effect of the initial notice is that as long as the notice continues in force, the building control powers which would otherwise be exercisable by the local authority in respect of the works in question, cease to be exercisable (Building Act 1984, s. 48). The local authority may not, therefore, serve a notice under s. 36(1) (see page 223) nor may the local authority institute proceedings under s. 35 for contravention of the regulations.

Section 48(2) provides that for the purposes of the enactments specified in s. 48(3), the giving of an initial notice accompanied by the relevant plans is to be treated as the deposit of the plans. The acceptance or rejection of an initial notice ranks as the passing or rejection of the plans. The cancellation of an initial notice under s. 52(5) (see page 225) is to be treated as a declaration under s. 32 that the deposit of plans is of no effect.

Approved inspectors and their powers

Section 49 of the Building Act 1984 gives both the Secretary of State and any body designated by the Secretary of State power to approve inspectors for the purposes of the Act (see the Building (Approved Inspectors etc.) Regulations 1985 (SI 1985/1066) amended by SI 1992/740). An approving body has the right to limit the description of work in relation to which a person is an approved inspector. For example, an inspector could be confined to inspecting dwellinghouses. Under reg. 7 of the 1985 regulations, the Secretary of State must maintain a list of bodies which are for the time being designated to confer approval on inspectors. So far only the NHBC has been designated.

An approved inspector may make charges for work.

An approved inspector may delegate powers to another person. However, a delegate may not give a plans certificate or a final certificate under ss. 50 or 51 (see below). Nor does the act of delegation affect the civil or criminal liability of the approved inspector. If the approved inspector does delegate powers, the inspector concerned still continues capable of exercising the powers in law (*Huth* v *Clarke* (1890) 25 QBD 391).

If an approved inspector is of the opinion that plans of the work specified in an initial notice are in conformity with the building regulations and has complied with prescribed requirements as to consultation or otherwise then the inspector, if requested by the person intending to carry out the relevant work, must give what is known as a 'plans certificate' to the local authority and to the person making the request (s. 50(1)). Any dispute between the approved inspector and a person who proposes to carry out any work about whether or not the plans are in conformity with the building regulations may be referred to the Secretary of State for determination (s. 50(2)). A plans certificate, which may relate either to the whole or only to part of the work specified in the initial notice, does not have effect unless it is accepted by the local authority to whom it is given (s. 50(5)). The local authority to whom a plans certificate is given may not reject the certificate except on prescribed grounds and must reject the certificate if any of the prescribed grounds exist (s. 50(6)).

Where an approved inspector is satisfied that the work specified in the initial notice has been completed, the inspector is required to give to the local authority by whom the initial notice was accepted and to the person by whom the work was carried out, a certificate known as a 'final certificate'. Once a final certificate has been accepted by the local authority, the initial notice ceases to apply to the work. However, the supervisory powers of the local authority remain suspended in relation to the work (s. 51).

Section 52 makes provision for the cancellation of an initial notice. In practical terms the most common ground for cancelling an initial notice is that there is a contravention of the building regulations and that the approved inspector has, in accordance with the building regulations, given notice of the contravention to the person carrying out the work and that person has failed to carry out the appropriate remedy within the prescribed period. Power is also given to a local authority to cancel an initial notice if it appears to the authority which accepted it that the work has not commenced within three years from the date on which the initial notice was accepted.

Section 53 makes provision for the initial notice ceasing to be in force by virtue, *inter alia*, of it being cancelled by way of a notice under s. 52 or because of the expiry of the appropriate period of time. In the event of a final certificate being given in relation to part of the work specified in the initial notice, the fact that the initial notice has ceased to be in force does not affect the continuing operation of s. 48(1) so that the local authority's enforcement powers continue not to be exercisable in relation to the work (s. 53(3)).

Work carried out by public bodies

The Building Act 1984, s. 54, allows a public body which is approved by the Secretary of State to exercise supervisory powers (which the relevant local authority would otherwise possess) in relation to its own building works. Before the public body can assume such powers notice must be given to the relevant local authority and the latter must accept the notice before it becomes effective. The notice may not be rejected except on prescribed grounds but it must be rejected if the prescribed grounds exist. The local authority is empowered to impose similar requirements as a condition of accepting the notice to those it can impose under the Act as a condition of passing plans.

Appeals

A person aggrieved by a local authority's rejection of, *inter alia*, an initial notice, plans certificate or a final certificate may appeal to a magistrates' court, and from there to the Crown Court (Building Act 1984, s. 55).

The meaning of 'person aggrieved' in the context of the section under discussion has not been determined in any reported case. However, it is suggested that the phrase would encompass owners, builders etc. whose rights are being directly affected by the local authority's decision. Others, for example, persons occupying land neighbouring that on which the building works are or could take place, would not be 'persons aggrieved' (see, e.g., *Buxton* v *Minister of Housing and Local Government* [1961] 1 QB 278).

Offences concerning notices and certificates

It is an offence subject to a penalty for any person to give a notice or certificate (e.g., an initial or final notice or a plans certificate) which contains a statement which the person knows to be false or misleading in a material particular or for any person to recklessly give a notice or certificate that purports to comply with the requirements governing such notices and certificates and which contains a statement which is false or misleading in a material particular (Building Act 1984, s. 57). In *NHBC Building Control Services Ltd* v *Sandwell Borough Council* (1990) 50 BLR 101 it was held that the appellant, which was an approved inspector, and which employed a system of random sampling in carrying out its building control functions, did not act recklessly in terms of s. 57 by failing to ascertain that a building failed to meet the requirements of the building regulations and subsequently certifying that the building was satisfactory.

BUILDINGS

Building services and facilities

The Building Act 1984 is a comprehensive statute which deals with existing as well as new buildings. Part III makes provision in relation to services and facilities provided to buildings.

Drainage and water supply to buildings

Section 59 of the Building Act 1984 deals with drainage to premises. Section 59(1)(a) provides that a local authority is empowered to serve notice on the owner of a building to make satisfactory provision for drainage to the building where satisfactory provision has not been made. Notice may also be served under s. 59(1)(c) to compel the owner or occupier of the building to renew, repair, cleanse any cesspool, drain, sewer, pipe, sink provided for the building which is prejudicial to health or a nuisance. In *Swansea City Council v Jenkins* (1994) *The Times*, 1 April 1994 which concerned a nuisance emanating from a blockage to a private sewer, it was held that the local authority were entitled to serve notice only on owners of buildings above the defect and not on all those served by the drainage system.

Provision of sanitary conveniences

It is imperative that buildings are adequately provided with sanitary conveniences.

Section 64 provides:

(1) If it appears to a local authority—
  (a) that a building is without sufficient closet accommodation,
  (b) that a part of a building being a part that is occupied as a separate dwelling is without sufficient closet accommodation, or
  (c) that any closets provided for or in connection with a building are in such a state as to be prejudicial to health or a nuisance and cannot without reconstruction be put in a satisfactory condition,
the authority shall by notice to the owner of the building, require him to provide the building with such closets or such substituted closets being in each case either water-closets or earth closets as may be necessary.

Section 64(2) provides that the authority may not require the provision of a water-closet except in substitution for an existing water closet.

An appeal against a notice served under s. 64 may be made under s. 102. Section 64(6) excludes from the provision of the section a factory, a building used as a workplace and premises to which the Offices, Shops and Railway Premises Act 1963 applies.

Provision of sanitary conveniences in workplaces

Section 65 requires that sufficient and satisfactory sanitary conveniences are provided to a building used as a workplace. If both sexes are employed separate accommodation must be provided.

Food storage

The Building Act 1984, s. 70, makes provision for food storage accommodation in houses. Power is given to a local authority, if it appears to it that a house or part of a building occupied as a separate dwelling, is without sufficient and suitable accommodation for the storage of food, by notice, to require the owner of the house or building to provide it with suitable accommodation for that purpose. An appeal may be made to the magistrates' court against the notice. One of the grounds for appeal is that it is not reasonably practicable to comply with the notice.

Entrances, exits to buildings

It is of prime importance that suitable means of access and egress are provided to buildings. The Building Act 1984, s. 71, therefore empowers a local authority, if it appears to it that a building to which the section applies is not provided with such means of ingress and egress and passages or gangways as the authority after consultation with the fire authority deem satisfactory, to issue a notice requiring the provision of the requisite means of entrance etc. The section applies to certain types of buildings to which the public have access, such as theatres, halls, restaurants, churches, warehouses and shops. An appeal lies to the magistrates' court against a notice served under the section. Power is also given to the local authority to apply to the magistrates' court for a temporary order to have the premises closed or access thereto restricted, in relation to a building in respect of which a notice has been served under the section, if the authority considers that such immediate action is necessary. A duty is placed on the person having the control of any building to which the section applies to take steps to secure that the means of access and egress to the building are kept free and unobstructed except insofar as the local authority after consultation with the fire authority otherwise approves.

Cellars, rooms below subsoil water level

Rooms which are situated below ground level have a tendency to become damp and uninhabitable unless special precautions are taken. The Building Act 1984, s. 74, prohibits the construction of a cellar or room in, or as part of, a house, shop, inn, hotel or office if the floor level of the cellar or room is lower than the ordinary level of the subsoil water on, under or adjacent to the site of the house. The section does not apply to the construction of certain cellars or rooms, for example, certain cellars or rooms contained in licensed premises, shops, hotels or offices. It is an offence to construct a cellar or room in contravention of the section.

Defective, dangerous premises

Defective premises

Premises, whether domestic, commercial or recreational, may fall into such a state of disrepair that they begin to pose a danger to the occupants of the premises as well as to the general public. It is important that local authorities have statutory power to deal with such premises speedily. The Building Act 1984, s. 76(1), provides that if it appears to a local authority that any premises are in such a state as to be prejudicial to health or a nuisance, and unreasonable delay in remedying the defective state would be occasioned by using the procedure contained in the Environmental Protection Act 1990, s. 80, the local authority may serve on the person on whom it would have been appropriate to serve an abatement notice under s. 93 of the 1936 Act (now s. 79(1) of the 1990 Act) a notice stating that the local authority intends to remedy the defective state and specifying the defects it intends to remedy. After the expiration of nine days after service of the notice the local authority is empowered to execute such works as may be necessary to remedy the defective state and recover the expenses reasonably incurred in so doing from the person on whom the notice was served. If, however, the person on whom notice is served serves a counter-notice that the person intends to remedy the defects in question, the local authority may not take any action unless the person who served the counter-notice fails within a reasonable time to begin to carry out the necessary remedial works or, having begun to execute the works, fails to make such progress towards their completion as the local authority considers reasonable.

A local authority may not serve a notice under the Building Act 1984, s. 76, if the execution of the work would be in contravention of a building preservation order under the Town and Country Planning Act 1947, s. 29.

Dangerous buildings

The Building Act 1984 makes special provision for buildings which are dangerous. Section 77 provides that if it appears to a local authority that a building or structure is in such a condition or is used to carry such loads as to be dangerous, the authority may apply to a magistrates' court. The court may, where the danger arises from the condition of the building or structure, make an order requiring the owner to execute such work as may be necessary to obviate the danger or, if that person so elects, to demolish the building or structure or any dangerous part of it. If the danger arises from the overloading of the building or structure, the court may make an order restricting the use of the building until a magistrates' court, satisfied that the necessary works have been executed, withdraws or modifies the restriction. The section gives the local authority power to execute works and recover costs in the face of default on the part of the owner concerned. The owner in such a case is liable on summary conviction to a fine. A building may be in such a state that immediate danger is posed to personal safety. Section 78 therefore provides that if it appears to a local authority that immediate action should be taken to remove the danger, it can take the necessary action. Notice of its intention to do so must be given to both the owner and occupier of the building or of the premises on which the structure is situated. Under general principles of administrative law it would seem that there would be no need to give the owner or occupier a hearing before the action was taken (see, e.g., *Earl of Lonsdale* v *Nelson* (1823) 2 B & C 302). The local authority may recover from the owner expenses which have reasonably been incurred by it in taking action under the section.

Ruinous buildings

Ruinous buildings present an indubitable blight on the environment. Such buildings are dealt with under the Building Act 1984, s. 79, which provides that if it appears to a local authority that a building or structure is, by reason of its ruinous or dilapidated condition, seriously detrimental to the amenities of the neighbourhood, the local authority may by notice require the owner to execute the necessary repair, restoration or demolition. Appeal against the notice lies to the magistrates' court.

Local authority's powers in relation to demolition operations

It is important that certain precautions are taken during the course of demolition works in order to protect the occupants of adjoining buildings, the adjoining buildings themselves as well as the general public. Sections 80 to 82 of the Building Act 1984 in essence give a local authority power by notice to require that a person carrying out demolition work on a building effects, for example, shoring and weatherproofing to adjacent buildings, the repair and making good of any damage to adjacent buildings, and the disconnection and sealing of any drain in or under the building.

Powers of entry to premises

Wide power is given to authorised officers by the Building Act 1984, s. 95, to enter any premises, *inter alia*, for the purpose of ascertaining whether there is or has been a contravention of the Act or the building regulations in relation to the premises, or generally for the purpose of performance by the local authority of its functions under the Act or the building regulations. However, admission to premises other than a factory or workplace may not be demanded as of right unless 24 hours' notice of the intended entry has been given to the occupier.

FIRE PRECAUTIONS

It is of fundamental importance that precautions are taken to ensure that the risk of injury from fire to persons using buildings is minimised. The most important statute concerning fire precautions in buildings is the Fire Precautions Act 1971 (as amended, mainly by the Fire Safety and Safety of Places of Sport Act 1987) the main provisions of which are briefly discussed.

Under s. 1 of the 1971 Act a certificate from a fire authority is required in respect of any premises designated under the section. The Secretary of State is empowered to designate by order premises which require a fire certificate. However, no order may be made in relation to premises unless the use falls within at least one of the following classes:

(a) use as, or for any purpose involving the provision of, sleeping accommodation;
(b) use as, or as part of, an institution providing treatment or care;
(c) use for purposes of entertainment, recreation or instruction or for purposes of any club, society or association;
(d) use for purposes of teaching, training or research;
(e) use for any purpose involving access to the premises by members of the public, whether on payment or otherwise;
(f) use as a place of work.

An order may provide that a fire certificate is not required for any premises of any description specified in the order, notwithstanding the premises are put to a designated use. The order may also designate descriptions of premises which qualify for exemption by a fire authority under s. 5A.

To date, orders under s. 1 have been made in respect of hotels and boarding-houses (SI 1972/238) and factories, offices and shops (SI 1989/76).

Section 2 exempts certain types of premises (such as places used for public worship) from the requirement to have a fire certificate.

An application for a fire certificate must be made to the relevant fire authority. The authority must issue the certificate if it is satisfied that the premises are provided with suitable fire escapes, with the means of securing that the fire escape can be used at all material times as well as the means of fighting fire, and suitable fire alarms (s. 5). The fire authority is also empowered to grant exemption from the need to have a fire certificate in respect of particular premises.

A fire certificate must specify the particular use or uses of the premises which the certificate covers, the means of escape in case of fire and the means with which the relevant building is provided for securing that the means of escape provided can be safely and effectively used (s. 6).

A person who is aggrieved by the refusal of a fire authority to issue a fire certificate can appeal to the magistrates' court. If any premises to which the Act applies are used without a fire certificate then the occupier of the premises is guilty of an offence (s. 7(1)).

Section 12 gives the Secretary of State power to make regulations as to the fire precautions which must be employed in premises which the Secretary of State has power to designate under s. 1 of the Act (see the Fire Precautions (Sub-surface Railway Stations) Regulations 1989 (SI 1989/1401)).

Section 19 gives inspectors appointed under the Act power to enter premises to which the Act applies, *inter alia*, to inspect the premises and require the production of and inspect any fire certificate in force.

ELEVEN
Control of communicable disease

Traditionally one of the most important functions which has been carried out by local authority public health departments has been the suppression of communicable disease. It has already been mentioned that the fear of cholera in the 1830s sparked off a revolution in the attitudes of central and local government as well as the general public to environmental matters. The first public general statutes dealing with the suppression of infectious disease, for example, the Nuisance Removal Acts of 1848 and 1856, placed great emphasis on nuisance removal since it was believed, before the germ theory became established, that disease, especially enteric diseases, emanated from organic matter. However, once the cause of infectious disease became known it became imperative for Parliament to introduce legislative measures to compel the notification of disease, to prevent, where appropriate, sufferers coming into contact with the general public and also to allow the local authority to deal with infected articles. Such controls have constituted the mainstay of infectious disease legislation mainly in the form of the Public Health Acts the most recent of which were those of 1936 and 1961. The main statute which now deals with infectious disease is the Public Health (Control of Disease) Act 1984 (the '1984 Act') which largely repeals and re-enacts the relevant provisions of the Public Health Act 1936. The main provisions of the 1984 Act are now discussed.

Notification of infectious diseases

It is of prime importance that the authorities responsible for controlling infectious disease are made aware of the identity of those suffering from the disease. However, there was much debate in the 19th century about the prudence of compelling medical practitioners to notify the relevant local authority that their patients were suffering from infectious disease. Resistance to compulsory notification came mainly from doctors who believed that compulsory notification tended to flout the fiduciary relationship which existed between doctor and patient. The Infectious Disease (Notification) Act 1889 made notification of infectious disease compulsory by doctors in London and elsewhere where the Act was adopted. Section 11 of the 1984 Act now provides that if a registered general practitioner becomes aware or suspects that a patient whom he or she is attending is suffering from a notifiable disease or from food poisoning then that disease must be notified to the proper officer of the authority for the district giving, *inter alia*, the name, age and sex of the patient, and stating particulars of the disease. Under s. 10 the expression 'notifiable disease' means the following:

(a) cholera;
(b) plague;
(c) relapsing fever;
(d) smallpox; and
(e) typhus.

This list has been extended considerably by the Public Health (Infectious Diseases) Regulations 1988 (SI 1988/1546) to include meningitis, diphtheria, mumps and measles. Aids is not included.

Of further significance is the power given to local authorities by s. 16 to add to this list of notifiable diseases by order. Any such addition must be approved by the Secretary of State before it has legal effect.

It is particularly important that environmental health authorities are able to take appropriate measures on the occurrence of an infectious disease. Section 18 empowers a local authority to require the occupier of any premises in which there is or has been any person suffering from a notifiable disease or food poisoning to furnish such information within that person's knowledge as that officer may reasonably require for enabling the appropriate measures to be taken to prevent the spread of disease or to trace the source of the food poisoning. It is an offence to fail to furnish the requisite information or to furnish information which is known to be false. While the section applies to a wide variety of premises, the section could be of particular value in relation to hostels, lodging-houses etc. which tend to accommodate itinerants.

Exposure of persons and things

Some communicable diseases can be spread by droplet infection. Fewer can be spread by touch. It is important that the host, that is, the person afflicted with a communicable disease, is isolated from the general public. The compulsory isolation of such individuals has featured in public health law since the 19th century. Some other communicable diseases are spread by fomites, that is to say, by inanimate objects such as bedlinen with which the host of the disease has come in contact. As far as the modern law is concerned, s. 17(1) of the 1984 Act provides:

A person who —

    (a) knowing that he is suffering from a notifiable disease, exposes other persons to the risk of infection by his presence or conduct in any street, public place, place of entertainment or assembly, club, hotel, inn or shop,
    (b) having the care of a person whom he knows to be suffering from a notifiable disease, causes or permits that person to expose other persons to the risk of infection by his presence or conduct in any such place as aforesaid, or
    (c) gives, lends, sells, transmits or exposes, without previous disinfection, any clothing, bedding or rags which he knows to have been exposed to infection from any such disease, or any other article which he knows to have been so exposed and which is liable to carry such infection,

shall be liable on summary conviction to a fine.

No person incurs liability under the section by transmitting with proper precautions any article for the purpose of having it disinfected (s. 17(2)).

As far as para. (a) is concerned it would be sufficient that the accused simply shut his or her eyes to the state of his or her health, for liability to lie (*James and Son Ltd* v *Smee* [1955] 1 QB 78; see also *Knox* v *Boyd* 1941 JC 82). Furthermore there is authority to the effect that where the accused deliberately refrains from making enquiries which would bring the facts to his or her knowledge, this constitutes knowledge of the facts in the eye of the law (*Knox* v *Boyd* 1941 JC 82).

Stopping work

Infectious diseases are often transmitted in the workplace to employees. Certain diseases, especially food poisoning, can also be transmitted to the general public by workers who handle food. It is therefore particularly important that such employees refrain from working. Section 20 of the 1984 Act (as amended by the Food Safety Act 1990) therefore empowers the proper officer of a local authority to request any person to discontinue his or her work in order to prevent the spread of a notifiable disease or:

(a) enteric fever (including typhoid and paratyphoid fevers);
(b) dysentery;
(c) diphtheria;
(d) scarlet fever;
(e) acute inflammation of the throat;
(f) gastro-enteritis; or
(g) undulant fever.

The local authority must compensate any person who has suffered any loss in complying with such a request.

Children

Children are more susceptible to infectious disease than adults. Furthermore, children often tend not to take the necessary precautions to prevent the spread of disease. The 1984 Act therefore makes special provision for children. Under s. 21 a duty is placed on a person having care of a child who is or has been suffering from a notifiable disease or has been exposed to infection of a notifiable disease not to send that child to school or permit the child to attend school until the person in charge has obtained from the proper officer a certificate that in his or her opinion the child may attend school without undue risk of communicating the disease to others.

In order to allow local authority environmental health departments to be informed of the identity of pupils suffering from a notifiable disease, s. 22 requires the principal of the school in question, if requested by the proper officer of the local authority, to furnish that officer within a reasonable time, of the names and addresses of such pupils, not being boarders, in or attending the school. It is an offence for the principal (that is, the person in charge of the school) to fail to comply with the provisions of the section.

Section 23 gives local authorities wide power to exclude persons aged 16 and under from public places such as theatres, public halls, swimming-baths and theatres. It is an offence for any person responsible for the management of premises who is served with a notice published under the section to the effect that children are excluded from the premises in question, to admit any person under the prescribed age. This would normally place managers in an invidious position. Section 23(6) therefore provides that in any proceedings for an offence under the section it is a defence to prove that there were reasonable grounds for believing that the person admitted had attained the prescribed age.

Infected articles

It is particularly important that fomites, that is, inanimate objects capable of transmitting infectious disease, are controlled. The Public Health (Control of Disease) Act 1984 therefore makes special provision for infected articles.

Clothes etc.
It is an offence to send or take to any laundry or public wash-house any article which is known to have been exposed to infection from a notifiable disease unless that article has been disinfected by or to the satisfaction of the proper officer (usually the environmental health officer) or a registered medical practitioner, or the article in question is sent with proper precautions to a laundry for the purpose of disinfection with notice that it has been exposed to infection (s. 24). The occupier of any building in which a person is suffering from a notifiable disease must, if required by the local authority, provide it with the address of any laundry, wash-house or other place to which the articles from the house have been or will be sent during the continuance of the disease for the purpose of being washed or cleaned. It is an offence to contravene the section.

Library books
It is an offence for any person who knows that he or she is suffering from a notifiable disease to take, cause to be taken or use any book taken from any public or circulating library (s. 25).

Infected waste
In order to protect, in the main, refuse collectors, s. 26 makes it an offence for anyone to cause or permit to be placed, in a dustbin or ash-pit, any matter which that person knows to have been exposed to infection from a notifiable disease and which has not been disinfected.

Infected premises

Since the cholera-inspired infectious disease provisions of the Public Health Act 1848 and Nuisance Removal Act of that year, legislation has made special provision for preventing disease spreading from premises which are infected. The Public Health (Control of Disease) Act 1984 makes special provision for premises.

For centuries it has been the custom in certain trades for work to be done at home. Articles made in a house etc. where infectious disease exists could therefore pose a threat to human health. Section 28 allows a local authority to make an order prohibiting the giving out of any work to which the section applies. The section applies to the making, cleaning, washing, altering etc. of clothing.

Certain communicable diseases are capable of spreading by means of dust which can adhere to the walls, floors and furnishings of premises. It is an offence for a person who is either concerned in the letting of a house, or part of a house, or has recently ceased to occupy the house or part of the house, if questioned by any person negotiating for the hire of the house or any part of it as to whether there has been in any part a person suffering from an infectious disease, to make a false answer to the question (s. 29).

It is an offence for a person who ceases to occupy a house or part of a house, in which, to his or her knowledge, a person has within six weeks previously been suffering from a notifiable disease, to fail to have the house and all relevant contents disinfected, or to fail to give the owner of the house or part of the house notice of the previous existence of the disease, or to make a false answer on being questioned by the owner as to whether within the preceding six weeks there has been in it any person suffering from any notifiable disease (s. 30).

Section 31 gives a local authority, on a certificate of the proper officer, power to cleanse and disinfect any premises as well as destroy any articles therein.

Section 32 allows the authority power to remove the residents of premises in which someone is suffering from an infectious disease.

Public conveyances

The capacity of infectious disease to spread by droplet infection is enhanced in crowded and unventilated places such as buses and trains. Section 33 of the Public Health (Control of Disease) Act 1984 makes it an offence for any person who knows that he or she is suffering from a notifiable disease to enter any public conveyance used for the conveyance of persons as separate fares or to enter any other public conveyance without previously notifying the owner or driver that he or she is so suffering. The owner, driver or conductor of public conveyance used for the transport of passengers at separate fares must not convey in it a person whom he knows to be suffering from a notifiable disease (s. 34).

Medical examination

In the vast majority of cases those having the misfortune to fall ill with or to become carriers of infectious disease are willing to enlist medical assistance. However, it may sometimes happen that such persons are unwilling to allow themselves to be examined in which case the Public Health (Control of Disease) Act 1984, s. 35, provides that if a justice of peace is satisfied, on a written certificate issued by a registered medical practitioner nominated by the local authority for the district, that there is or has been someone either suffering from a notifiable disease or someone who is a carrier of such a disease, the justice may order that person to be medically examined if such examination is in the interest of that person or that person's family or the public. No examination may be ordered, however, if the justice is satisfied that the patient is under the treatment of a registered medical practitioner unless the latter consents to the examination. References to persons being examined include references to the being submitted to bacteriological and radiological tests (e.g., X-ray examinations). The section could therefore be employed to compel carriers of food poisoning micro-organisms to submit faecal specimens for investigation.

Section 36 allows a justice of the peace to order the entire members of a group to be examined if there is reason to believe that a member of that group is a carrier of the disease. The section could be put to good use particularly in respect of employees of a food factory where one or more such employees is suspected of being a carrier of food-poisoning bacteria. There is no statutory guidance or judicial authority on the meaning of the expression 'group'. It is possible that it could embrace a numerically large number of persons.

Removal to hospital

The majority of those suffering from infectious disease will be willing to avail themselves of hospital treatment. Occasionally a person in need of such treatment is unwilling to be hospitalised. On the application of a local authority, a justice may order the removal of a person to hospital if satisfied that inadequate precautions are being taken to prevent the spread of infectious disease and that serious risk of infection is thereby caused to others (Public Health (Control of Disease) Act 1984, s. 37). In practice this section has been used mainly in respect of itinerants. Similar powers are conferred by s. 38 to detain persons suffering from an infectious disease in hospital if such persons would not on leaving hospital have suitable accommodation in which proper precautions could be taken to prevent the spread of the disease.

Regulation 5 of the Public Health (Infectious Diseases) Regulations 1988 allows a justice of the peace, on the application of a local authority, to make an order for the detention in hospital of an inmate of that hospital suffering from Aids, if the justice is satisfied that on the patient leaving hospital, proper precautions to prevent the spread of that disease would not be taken in his or her lodging or accommodation or in other places to which he or she may be expected to go if not detained in hospital.

Common lodging-houses

Common lodging-houses have traditionally posed problems as far as infectious disease control is concerned. This is first because the persons who normally resort to such premises tend to do so only for short periods and can therefore spread infectious disease. Secondly, the habits of the inmates often tend to conduce to the spread of infectious disease. Thirdly, the facilities provided in such premises are often of a rudimentary character. Since the Victorian era, which was the heyday of the common lodging-house, there have been legislative controls over them. Under s. 39 of the Public Health (Control of Disease) Act 1984, a duty is imposed on the keeper of a common lodging-house to give notice of the presence of anyone suffering from infectious disease on the premises. It is an offence to fail to comply with this provision.

The expression 'common lodging-house' is defined in s. 74 as a house (other than a public assistance institution) provided for the purpose of accommodating by night poor persons, not being members of the same family, who resort to it and are allowed to occupy one common room for the purpose of sleeping or eating, and, where part only of a house is so used, includes the part so used.

Sections 40 and 41 make provision for the medical examination of the inmates of a common lodging-house as well as the removal to hospital of such persons, in the event of the occurrence of infectious disease. Section 42 allows a magistrates' court to order the closure of a common lodging-house where there is or has been a recent case of infectious disease on the grounds that such closure is necessary in the interests of the public health.

Persons dying of infectious diseases etc.

Sections 43 to 48 of the Public Health (Control of Disease) Act 1984 make detailed and extensive provision for the disposal etc. of the bodies of those dying from infectious disease. The gist of the provisions is to ensure that the risk of infection from the corpses of the deceased is minimised.

Canal boats, tents and vans

Special provision is made in the Public Health (Control of Disease) Act 1984 for canal boats, tents and vans on account of the restricted space normally found in such places. A duty is placed on the Secretary of State to make regulations governing, *inter alia*, the number of persons who can lawfully reside in canal boats as well as cleanliness in boats (see the Canal Boats Regulations 1878 (SR & O Rev 1948, vol. 3, p. 429)).

Provisions of the Act relating to, *inter alia*, the control of disease are made to apply to tents, vans and sheds by s. 56. A local authority is also given power by the section to make by-laws for preventing the spread of infectious disease as far as tents, vans and sheds etc. used for human habitation.

Powers of entry etc.

Section 61 of the Public Health (Control of Disease) Act 1984 gives wide power to an authorised officer, normally the environmental health officer, of a local authority to enter premises at all reasonable hours for the purpose, *inter alia*, of ascertaining whether there is or has been any contravention of provisions of the Act. Admission to any premises other than a factory or workplace may not be demanded as of right unless 24 hours' notice has been given to the occupier.

Default powers

In the event of any local authority etc. failing satisfactorily to discharge its duties under the Public Health (Control of Disease) Act 1984, s. 71 gives the Secretary of State power to declare by order any body exercising powers under the Act in default and direct it to discharge its functions in such a manner and within such a time as is specified in the order. In the event of the body failing to comply with the order, the Secretary of State is empowered to take over the functions.

Crown premises

An interesting provision of the Public Health (Control of Disease) Act 1984 is contained in s. 73 which allows the Crown and a local authority to make agreements about which government property the provisions of the Act should apply to.

Verminous persons etc.

It is possible that infectious and other diseases can be spread by insects and parasites. Measures are needed, therefore, to control the spread of disease from premises and articles which are infested.

Section 83 of the Public Health Act 1936 empowers a local authority, upon consideration of a report from any of its officers (normally an environmental health officer), or other information in its possession, to the effect that any premises are in such a filthy or unwholesome condition as to be prejudicial to health or are verminous, to give notice to the owner or occupier of the premises requiring them to be cleaned. In the face of default, the local authority is empowered to carry out the necessary works and recover expenses from the person on whom notice was served.

As far as verminous articles are concerned, under s. 84, where it appears to a local authority, upon a certificate of its proper officer, that any article in any premises:

    (a)   is in so filthy a condition as to render its cleansing, purification or destruction necessary in order to prevent injury, or danger of injury, to the health of any person in the premises; or

(b) is verminous, or by reason of its having been used by, or having been in contact with, any verminous person is likely to be verminous,

the local authority shall cause that article to be cleansed, purified, disinfected or destroyed, as the case may require, at their expense and, if necessary for that purpose, to be removed from the premises.

It happens from time to time that persons, commonly itinerants, become infested by virtue of their way of life. Section 85 of the 1936 Act allows a county council or local authority to take the necessary measures to free verminous persons and their clothing from vermin. If a verminous person refuses to allow himself or herself to be cleansed, the county council or local authority may apply to a magistrates' court, which can make an order for the removal of the appropriate person to a cleansing station. Section 86 gives a county council or local authority power to provide cleansing stations.

Control of aircraft and ships

It is of prime importance that infectious diseases should not be brought into the country by those who have been in foreign countries. Conversely, there must be control over persons suffering from infectious diseases who intend to visit other countries. Section 13 of the Public Health (Control of Disease) Act 1984 allows regulations to be made for the control of infectious disease from aircraft and ships. The Public Health (Aircraft) Regulations 1979 (SI 1979/1434) makes detailed provision for the examination of persons leaving or embarking on an aircraft and the notification of infectious disease on board aircraft. The Public Health (Ships) Regulations 1979 (SI 1979/1435) make similar provision in respect of ships.

Tuberculosis

Tuberculosis was at its height in the 19th century. An important source of the disease was the milk supply since milk cows were often kept in grossly insanitary conditions and were underfed. It is important therefore that milk supplies are prevented from contamination. The Public Health (Prevention of Tuberculosis) Regulations 1925 (SR & O 1925/757) provide for the prevention of contamination of milk by persons suffering tuberculosis of the respiratory tract and prohibit such persons working in connection with a dairy where this would involve milking cows, treating milk or handling milk vessels. Power is also given to a local authority to prohibit such persons working in a dairy.

Anthrax

Anthrax is a communicable disease with a high death rate. The micro-organism responsible for the disease is spore forming and has the capacity to survive in the ground or in fomites for years. Special precautions are therefore necessary to prevent the spread of the disease. The Anthrax Prevention Order 1971 (SI 1971/1234) made under the Anthrax Prevention Act 1919 prohibits the import of goat hair and certain types of animal hair unless certain precautions are observed.

The Anthrax Order 1991 (SI 1991/2814) made under the Animal Health Act 1991 makes provision for the prevention of the spread of anthrax from farm animals.

Burial and cremation

Since at least medieval times local authorities have had legal power to dispose of the dead in the interest of the health of the public. The so called 'paupers' graves' in many municipal graveyards indeed provide sombre evidence of this fact. As far as the current law is concerned, the Public Health (Control of Disease) Act 1984, s. 46, places a duty on a local authority to either bury or cremate the body of any person who has died or been found to be dead in its area where it appears to the authority that no suitable arrangements for the disposal of the body have been or are being made otherwise than by the authority. The section also allows a local authority which is a local authority for the purposes of the Local Authority Social Services Act 1970 to bury or cremate the body of any deceased person who immediately before his or her death was being provided with accommodation under part III of the National Assistance Act 1948 by, or by arrangement with, the council or was living in a hostel provided by the council under s. 29 of the 1970 Act. The authority may not, however, cremate any body if it has reason to believe that this would be against the wishes of the deceased.

TWELVE

Pests

Vermin present a particular risk to human health. Epidemic diseases such as the dreaded plague were caused by parasites of rats. Less dramatic, but unfortunately endemic diseases such as salmonellosis also are on occasion attributable to rats and mice. Parasitic diseases such as trichinosis can also be caused by rats. Weil's disease, which is spread by rat's urine, can sometimes be fatal. Rats and mice also present an economic risk in that they can do great damage to farming produce. It is therefore of prime importance that legislation should specifically deal with them. The main statute dealing with such pests in England and Wales is the Prevention of Damage by Pests Act 1949, the main sections of which are now discussed.

Enforcement

The responsibility for enforcing the provisions of part I of the Act rest with the Common Council of the City of London, the councils of London boroughs and district councils.

Duties of local authorities

Section 2 of the Act places a duty on every local authority to take such steps as may be necessary to secure so far as practicable that its district is kept free from rats and mice. The local authority is required to carry out inspections, to destroy rats and mice on land which it occupies and to keep such land so far as practicable free from rats and mice, and to enforce the duties of owners and occupiers of land under part I of the Act.

Duties to notify local authority

A duty is placed on the occupier of land by s. 3 to give immediate notice in writing to the local authority on learning that rats or mice are living on or resorting to the land in substantial numbers. However, there is no duty to give notice as far as infestations of agricultural land are concerned. Furthermore, there is no duty to inform the local authority if the occupier has a duty to give notice to the Minister of Agriculture, Fisheries and Food under part II of the Act (which relates to the infestation of food). If a duty to inform the local authority does exist, failure to so notify is an offence.

Powers of local authority to require destruction of rats

Section 4 of the Act allows a local authority to serve notice on the owner or occupier of land if it appears to the local authority that steps should be taken either for the destruction of rats or mice on the land or otherwise for keeping the land free from rats or mice. The notice may require the owner or occupier to take reasonable steps for the destruction of the rats or mice within a reasonable period. The notice may require the employment of any form of treatment specified in the notice as well as the carrying out of any structural repairs to the premises. In *Perry* v *Garner* [1953] 1 QB 335, it was held that the notice must specify what the owner or occupier must do to destroy the rats. An appeal may be made to the magistrates' court against a notice requiring the carrying out of structural works. In the face of default by the person on whom notice is served, the local authority is empowered by s. 5 to carry out the works and recover costs.

Treatment of a group of premises

It is often preferable from an operational viewpoint, when dealing with an infestation of rats and mice on land in different occupation, to treat the land as one unit for the purpose of destroying the rats or mice. Section 6 therefore allows a local authority to deal with land comprising premises in different occupation which is frequented by rats or mice in substantial numbers. The local authority is empowered to enter the land without serving notice under s. 4 and destroy the rats and mice. At least seven days' notice of the local authority's intention to enter the premises must be given to the occupier of the land. A local authority is not authorised to carry out structural works in the exercise of its powers under s. 6.

Any expenses reasonably incurred by a local authority in carrying out the powers conferred by s. 6 may be recovered by the authority from the occupiers of the premises comprised in the land in such proportion as may be just having regard to the cost of the work done on the several premises.

Hayricks

Hayricks provide an environment favourable to rats and mice. The Act makes special provision for this under s. 8 which allows the minister to make regulations to prevent rats or mice escaping from ricks in the course of dismantling.

Default powers

If the minister is satisfied that a local authority is not performing satisfactorily the powers and duties conferred on it by part I of the Act then the minister may, by order, empower any person named in the order to exercise the relevant functions on behalf of the local authority. Before such an order is made the local authority must be allowed to make representations.

Infestation of food

The presence of rodents or insects in food can cause considerable damage. Part II of the Act is devoted to the infestation of food. Section 13(1) requires every person carrying on a business which consists of or includes the manufacture, storage, transport or sale of food, to give notice to the minister forthwith if it comes to that person's knowledge that any infestation is present:

 (a) in any premises or vehicle, or any equipment belonging to any premises or vehicle, used or likely to be used in the course of that business for the manufacture, storage, transport or sale of food;

 (b) in any food manufactured, stored, transported or sold in the course of that business, or in any other goods for the time being in his possession which are in contact or likely to come into contact with food so manufactured, stored, transported or sold.

A similar obligation to inform the Minister is placed by s. 13(2) on a person who manufactures, sells, repairs or cleans containers on learning that any infestation is present in any container for the time being in that person's possession.

 The minister is empowered to make regulations, *inter alia*, for relaxing or excluding the requirements of s. 13 or for prohibiting or restricting the delivery in the course of business of any food or other goods in respect of which notice is or is required to be given to the minister under the section. The Prevention of Damage by Pests (Infestation of Food) Regulations 1950 (SI 1950/416) have been made under this section.

Section 14 allows the minister to give directions to certain persons, such as manufacturers and warehousemen, as to the steps necessary to prevent or mitigate damage to food by virtue of an infestation. Where the direction requires the carrying out of any structural work or the destruction of any food or container, an appeal may be made under s. 15 to the magistrates' court. In the case of default on the part of the relevant person on whom notice is served under s. 14, the minister is given power under s. 16 to exercise default powers to secure compliance.

Powers of entry

Section 22 confers on persons authorised in writing by either a local authority or the minister wide powers to enter land at any reasonable time, *inter alia*, for the purpose of carrying out an inspection under the Act and to ascertain whether there has been a failure to comply with any requirement under part I of the Act.

Fumigation safety measures

Several regulations govern the safety precautions which must be taken when premises or ships are being fumigated with hydrogen cyanide. Such fumigation is normally carried out to eradicate pests. The regulations governing buildings are the Hydrogen Cyanide (Fumigation of Buildings) Regulations 1951 (SI 1951/1759) and those for ships are the Hydrogen Cyanide (Fumigation of Ships) Regulations 1951 (SI 1951/1760).

Index

Abatement notices
  defective premises 229
  litter 90–1
  noise nuisance 22
  statutory nuisance 17
Adulteration of food 5
Aerodrome noise 29–30
Air pollution
  19th century 33–4
  alkali industry 33–4
  authorisations 48–51
    appeals 54–5
    fees and charges 51
    revocation 53, 55
    transfer 51
    variations 51–3, 54
  best available technique condition 49–50
  best practicable environmental option (BPEO) 50–1
  burning
    cable insulation 42
    straw and stubble 58
  charges 51
  chimneys
    height 38–9
    new buildings 39
  Clean Air Act 1993
    default powers 46
    domestic provisions 39–43
    industrial provisions 34–9
    offences 45–6
    powers of entry 46
    special cases 43–5
    see also individual aspects e.g., smoke
  colliery spoilbanks 44

Air pollution — *continued*
  Crown premises 45
  dark smoke 14, 15, 34, 35
  emission limits 48
  enforcement of EPA 53–4
  enforcement notice 53, 54, 55
  Environmental Protection Act 1990 44, 46–58
    appeals 54–5
    authorisations 48–53
    enforcement 53–4
    offences 57–8
    publicity 56–7
    see also individual aspects
  fees 51
  fumes and gases 45
  grit arrestment plant 36–7
  grit and dust 36–8
  information 42–3
  inspectors
    appointment 55
    powers 55–6
  integrate pollution control 46–57
  investigations and research 43
  local authority pollution control 46–7
  London smog 1952 6, 33
  motor fuel 42
  'polluter pays' principle 51
  prescribed processes 46–7
  prohibition notice 53, 54, 55
  publicity 56–7
  railway engines and vessels 44
  research 43, 45
  smog 6, 33
  smoke 33, 34–5

Index

Air pollution — *continued*
    dark smoke   14, 15, 34, 35
    from furnaces   35–6
    Ringlemann Chart   34
    smoke control areas   39–42
        adaptations   41–2
        exempted fireplaces   41
        grants   42
        igniting apparatus   42
        remedial works   41
        smokeless fuel   40, 41
    straw and stubble burning   58
Aircraft noise
    aerodrome noise   29–30
    flight noise   29
    low-flying aircraft   29, 30–1
    military aircraft   30–1
Alkali industry   33–4
anthrax   242–3

Batho Committee   22
Beaver Committee   6, 33
Best available technique condition   49–50
Best practicable environmental option (BPEO)   50–1
'Best practical means' defence   17–18
Building regulations   216–17
    access and egress   220
    appeals   226
    breaches   222
    building over sewers or drains   219
    constructions sites   23–4
    disputes   219
    drains   219–20
    final certificate   225, 226
    fire escape   220
    initial notice   224, 226
    inspectors
        delegation of powers   224
        supervision by   223–4
        work of   224–5
    lapse of deposit of plans   222
    noise insulation   32
    offences   226
    passing and rejecting plans   218–19
    plans certificate   225, 226
    refuse collection access   220
    relaxation   217
    removal of unauthorised work   223
    supervision by approved inspectors   223–4
    tests for conformity   222
    type approval   218
    water supply   221
    work by public bodies   225–6
    see also Buildings
Building societies   5

Buildings
    abatement notices   229
    below subsoil water level rooms   228
    cellars   228
    dangerous buildings   229–30
    defective premises   229
    demolition powers   230
    drainage   227
    entrances   228
    entry powers   230
    exits   228
    facilities   226
    fire precautions   230–2
        certificate   231
        exits   228, 232
    food storage   228
    powers of demolition   230
    powers of entry   230
    ruinous buildings   230
    sanitary conveniences   227
        workplace provision   227
    services   226
    water supply   227
    see also Building regulations; Housing
Burial of dead   243
Burning
    cable insulation   12
    straw and stubble   58
By-laws, noise   27–8

Caravan sites
    conditions attached to licence   214–15
    definition of caravan   213–14
    definition of site   213
    licensing   213–14
    model standards   215
    planning permission   215
    revocation of licence   215
    when licence not required   214
Carson, Rachel   6
Cesspools   77
Chadwick, Edwin   4
Chimneys
    height   38–9
    new buildings   39
Cholera   2, 3, 4, 95–6, 179
Clean Air Act *see* Air pollution
Cleanliness, at work   164, 170
Collection of controlled waste
    cesspools   77
    commercial waste   78–9
    conveyance of waste   77
    disposal of waste *see* Disposal of waste
    duties of WCAs   76–7
    Garchey system   77
    household waste   77–8
    industrial waste   76–7

Collection of controlled waste
— *continued*
  receptacles for 78–9
  interference with sites 85
  privies 77
  receptacles
    for commercial waste 78–9
    for household waste 77–8
    for industrial waste 78–9
    interference with 85
  recycling
    payments 84
    plans 80
    powers 85
    transport of waste for 79–80
  Secretary of State powers 89
  septic tanks 77
  waste disposal plans 81–3
  waste management licences 89
  waste recycling plans 80–1
Colliery spoilbanks 44
Common lodging-houses
  controls over 199
  definition 198
  diseases in 239–40
  disqualification of keepers 199
  offences 199
  register 199
Common parts grant *see* Improvement grants
Communicable diseases *see* Diseases
Construction site noise
  building regulations 23–4
  local authority consent 23–4
  notice 23
  site traffic 22
Contagion theory 3–4
Conveyance of controlled waste 62
Cremation 243
Crown premises
  air pollution control 45
  disease control 241

Dark smoke 14, 15, 34, 35
Demolition
  local authority powers 230
  orders *see* Housing
Director General of Water Services 96, 97
Disabled facilities grant 206
Diseases
  19th century 95–6, 233
  aircraft 242
  anthrax 242–3
  burial and cremation 243
  buses 238
  canal boats 240
  children 236

Diseases — *continued*
  common lodging-houses 239–40
  contagion theory 3–4
  cremation 243
  Crown premises 241
  default powers 241
  disposal of bodies 240
  exposure of persons or things 234–5
  food handling 235–6
  germ theory 233
  industrial revolution 2–3
  infected articles 236–7
    clothes 237
    library books 237
    waste 237
  infected premises 237–8
  information requirement 234
  isolation of persons or things 234–5
  medical examination requirement 238–9
  miasmatic theory 3–4
  notifiable diseases 234
  notification of infectious diseases 233–4
  personal hygiene 2
  powers of entry 240–1
  public conveyances 238
  removal to hospital 239
  ships 242
  stopping work 235–6
  tents 240
  trains 238
  tuberculosis 242
  vans 240
  verminous persons 241–2
  see also Pests
Disposal of waste 79–80
  controlled waste 83–4
  functions of WDAs 83–4
  household waste 83, 220
  payments 84
  plans 81–3
  recycling
    payments 84
    plans 80–1
    powers 85
    transport of waste for 79–80
  refuse collection access 220
  Secretary of State powers 89
  waste disposal plans 81–3
Ditches, nuisance from 14, 16
Drainage
  building over drains 219
  building regulations 219–20
  buildings 227
  drainage districts 5
  industrial revolution 2, 5
  investigation of defective drain 109, 113

Index

Drainage — *continued*
  power to alter systems 109
  sanitary areas 5
  see also Sewerage; Trade effluent
Dumping of waste, control 61–76
  authorised persons 66–7
  authorised transport purposes 66–7
  'causing' 61
  civil liability 63–4
  closed landfills 75–6
  codes of practice 67
  conveyance of controlled waste 62
  defences 63
  documents required 67
  domestic waste 62
  'due diligence' 63
  duty of care 65–7
  exempt activities 61
  Health and Safety Executive 69
  information access 74–5
  'knowingly causing' 61
  'knowingly permitting' 61
  NRA 69, 72, 76
  offences 67
  'permitting' 61, 62
  powers of entry 76
  public registers 74–5
  'reasonable precautions' 63
  refuse dumping 87–8
  removal of unlawful deposits 64–5
  site licence 68, 69
  waste management licences *see* Waste management licences
Dust pollution *see* Air pollution; Grit and dust pollution

Employment, health and safety *see* Health and safety at work
Epidemics 2
  see also Diseases
Exempted fireplaces 41

Factories Act *see* Health and safety at work
Fire certificates 232
Fire exits
  building regulations 220
  buildings 228
  houses in multiple occupation 196–7
Fire precautions 230–2
Fireplaces, exempted 41
'Five percent philanthropy' movement 5
Fluoridation 104
Food
  adulteration 5
  consumer protection 127–30
    advertisements 129–30
    false description 129–30

Food — *continued*
  'nature' 127–8
  presentation likely to mislead 130
  'quality' 127, 128–9
  'substance' 127, 128
contamination in milk 142
defences
  due diligence 133–5
  fault of another person 132–3
  reasonable precautions 133–5
definition 114–15
disease in handler 138, 235–6
emergency controls 126–7, 137
  prohibition notices and orders 125–7
European Community obligations 131–2
Food Safety Act 1990 114–36
  consumer protection *see* consumer protection
  defences 132–5
  enforcement 115–16
  food authorities 115–16
  human consumption intention 115
  materials covered in 115
  see also injurious food; substandard food *and individual notices or orders e.g.,* improvement notices
human consumption intention 115
hygiene 3
  general requirements 137–8
  handlers 138, 235–6
  markets and stalls 140
  premises 138–9
  reform proposals 141
  regulations 137–41
  temperature control 139–40
  training 135
  washing facilities 139
improvement notices 123
infestation 246–7
injurious food 116–17
licensing of premises 132
milk and dairies
  buildings 141–2
  contamination 142
  hygiene 141–2
    handling 142
  impure milk 142
  inspection of cattle 141
  registration of premises 141
  types of milk 142
  water supply 141–2
premises
  exemptions 140
  hygiene regulations 138–9
  registration and licensing 132
prohibition orders 123–6
promotion of safety 135–7

Food — *continued*
  registration of premises 132
  safety
    emergency controls 137
    hygiene training 135
    sampling and analysis 136–7
    shellfish cleansing facilities 135–6
  sampling and analysis 136–7
  shellfish cleansing facilities 135–6
  storage accommodation in houses 228
  subordinate legislation 130–2
  substandard food 117–23
    bulk quantities or batches 120–1
    commercial dealing 117
    contamination 119–20
    'has in his possession' 117–18
    inspection and seizure 121–3
    procedure for dealing with 121–3
    unfit for human consumption 118–19
  temperature control 139–40
Furnaces
  domestic 36, 37
  grit and dust 36–8
  smoke from 35–6

Garchey system 77
General Board of Health 4
Germ theory 233
Grit arrestment plant 36–7
Grit and dust pollution 36–8
  see also Air pollution
Group repair schemes
  contributions by participants 212
  primary building 211
  qualifying building 211

Health and safety at work
  19th century 147
  access, safe 168–9
  asbestos control 177–8
  cleanliness 164, 170
  codes of practice 157–8
  common law controls 143–7
  competent staff 147
  Control of Asbestos at Work Regulations 1987 177
  Control of Substances Hazardous to Health Regulations 1992 177
  controllers of premises, duties 154–6
  criminal offences
    codes of practice 158
    HASAWA 161
  display screen equipment 176
  duties of controllers of premises to non-employees 154–6
  duties of employees 156–7
  duties of employers 149–52

Health and safety at work — *continued*
  nature of duty to employee 150
  'reasonably practicable' 149
  to non-employees 153–4
  types of risks 150
  duties of manufacturers of equipment 156
  employees' duties 156–7
  employers *see* duties of employers
  enforcement of legislation 158
  equipment instructions 177
  equipment manufacturers 156
  exposure to harmful substances 177
  Factories Act 1961 161–9
    definitions 162–3
    fencing of machinery 164–7
    general provisions 163–4
  'factory' meaning 162
  family premises 170
  floors 167–8, 173–4
  general public 153–4
  Health and Safety at Work etc. Act 1974 148–61
    criminal offences 161
  Health and Safety Commission 157
  Health and Safety (Display Screen Equipment) Regulations 1992 176
  Health and Safety Executive 157, 158
  hearing damage 178
  improvement notices 160, 161
  independent contractors 148, 151, 153
  inspectors
    appointment 159
    powers 159–60
  lifting heavy weights 169
  lighting 164, 171
  machinery
    defined 165
    fencing 164–7
    'in motion' 166–7
    offices, shops and railway premises 174
  Management of Health and Safety at Work Regulations 1992 176–7
  Manual Handling Operations Regulations 1992 176
  'manual labour' meaning 162–3
  manufacturers of equipment, duties 156
  Noise at Work Regulations 1989 178
  obstructions to floors and passageways 167–8
  'office premises' meaning 169–70
  offices, shops and railway premises
    accommodation for clothing 172
    cleanliness 170
    communally occupied premises 174–5
    dangerous machinery 174
    eating facilities 173

Index

Health and safety at work — *continued*
  floors, passages and stairs 173–4
  overcrowding 171
  sanitary conveniences 171–2
  seating 172–3
  temperature 171
  ventilation and lighting 171
  washing facilities 171–2
  Offices, Shops and Railway Premises Act 1963 169–75
    exemptions 175
  overcrowding 164, 171
  passageways 167–8, 173–4
  practical jokers 147
  prohibition notices 160–1
  prophylactic measures 146
  Provisions and Use of Work Equipment Regulations 1992 177
  'railway premises' meaning 170
  regulations 148–9
  safe means of access 168–9
  safe place of employment 168–9
  safe place of work 144–5
  safe plant and machinery 144
  safe system of work 145–7
  sanitary conveniences 171–2
  self-employed persons 148, 153
  'shop premises' meaning 170
  staircases 173–4
  statutory control 147–75
  subcontractors 151
  subordinate legislation 175–8
  'system of work' meaning 145–6
  temperature 164, 171
  ventilation 164, 171
  warnings of dangers 146
  washing facilities 171–2
  Workplace (Health, Safety and Welfare) Regulations 1992 176
  written safety policy 152–3
Health and Safety Commission 157
Health and Safety Executive 69, 157, 158
Highways
  abandonment of vehicles on 88
  litter 89
Household appliance noise 31–2
Housing
  19th century 5
  caravan sites
    conditions attached to licence 214–15
    definition of caravan 213–14
    definition of site 213
    licensing 213–14
    model standards 215
    planning permission 215
    revocation of licence 215
    when licence not required 214

Housing — *continued*
  closing order 181
  common lodging-houses
    controls over 199
    definition 198
    diseases in 239–40
    disqualification of keepers 199
    offences 199
    register 199
  demolition orders 181, 187–8
    listed property 187–8
    service of notice and right of appeal 188
    service of order 187
  development of law 179–80
  in disrepair *see* unfit houses
  group repair schemes *see* Improvement grants
  improvement grants *see* Improvement grants
  multiple occupation
    control orders 197–8
    fire escape 196–7
    management standards 197
    meaning 193–4
    overcrowding 196
    power to limit number of occupants 195–6
    power to require execution of works 194–5, 197
    registration schemes 194
  overcrowding
    definition 190–1
    duty to inform local authority 193
    multiple occupation 196
    offence of causing house to be overcrowded 192
    room standard 191
    space standard 191–2
  public health control of 179–80
  renewal areas 184–6
    powers of local housing authority 185–6
    publicity 185
  repair notices 180, 181, 183–4
  slum clearance
    clearance areas 189–90
    closing orders 186–7
    demolition orders 187–8
    obstructive buildings 188–9
    service of notice and right of appeal 188
  unfit houses 180–4
    closing order 181
    default powers 184
    demolition order 181
    in disrepair but not unfit 183

Housing — *continued*
    execution of work by local authority 184
        meaning of unfitness 181–3
        repair notices 180, 181, 183–4
    see also Buildings
Hygiene
    food *see* Food, hygiene
    personal 2
Hypersensitive plaintiff 11

Ice cream van noise 24–5
Improvement grants 199–213
    applications 200
    approval 208
    certificate of future occupation 201–2
    certificate of intended letting 201–2
    common parts grants 200–1, 210–11
        tenant's application 204–5
    conditions 200
        HMO grant 210
        letting availability 210
        multiple occupation 210
        repayment on disposals 210
    disabled facilities grant 206
    discretionary grant approval 206–8
    exclusion of certain dwellings and works 202–3
    expected future life of building 207–8
    group repair schemes
        contributions by participants 212
        primary building 211
        qualifying buildings 211
    improvement and repair grants 200
    insulation 212, 213
    local authority approval 203, 206
    mandatory grants 205–6
    minor works 212
    owner-occupation certificate 201
    payment 209
    renovation of two or more buildings 211
    repayment 210–11
    special certificate 202
    tenant's certificate 201
    thermal insulation 212, 213
    to landlord 204, 210–11
    to owner-occupiers 203–4
    to tenants 203–4
        common parts grant 204–5
Improvement notices, health and safety at work 160, 161
Independent contractors 148, 151, 153
Industrial plant design, noise and 27
Industrial revolution 1–3
    drainage 2
    public health reform 3–5
    temperance reformers 2

Industrial revolution — *continued*
    urbanisation 1–2
    water supply and drainage 2
Infectious diseases *see* Diseases
Insulation of buildings, noise 30, 32
Integrated pollution control 46–57
    see also Air pollution

Landfill sites *see* Dumping of waste, control
Lead, in motor fuel 42
Lighting
    food premises 139
    health and safety at work 164
    offices, shops and railway premises 171
Litter
    abatement notices 90–1
    control areas 89–90
    fixed penalties 89
    grants to encourage public 92
    highways 89
    maintenance of bins 92
    places controls apply over 88
    public registers 92
    street litter control notices 91
    strict liability 89
    summary proceedings by private individuals 90
Local authorities
    air pollution control 46–7
    improvement grant approval 203, 206
    noise
        construction site consent 23–4
        noise abatement zones powers 25
        noise level register 25–6
    overcrowding notification 193
    sewerage functions 105
    unfit housing works 184
    vermin and 245, 246
    water supply functions 103–4
Locality principle 9–10
London smog 1952 6, 33

Metropolitan district councils 6–7
Miasmatic theory 3–4
Mice *see* Pests
Milk and dairies
    buildings 141–2
    contamination 142
    hygiene 141–2
        handling 142
    impure milk 142
    inspection of cattle 141
    registration of premises 141
    types of milk 142
    water supply 141–2
Motor fuels, lead and sulphur content 42
Motor vehicles, abandoned 87–8

Index

Multiple occupation of houses *see* Housing, multiple occupation

National parks 31
National Rivers Authority
  dumping of waste 69, 72, 76
  waste disposal plans 82
Nature Conservancy Council for England 69
Neighbourhood noise 21
Noise
  abatement notice 22
  aerodrome noise 29–30
  aircraft noise
    aerodrome noise 29–30
    flight noise 29
    low-flying aircraft 29, 30–1
    military aircraft 30–1
    noise certification 29
  boats in national parks 31
  building regulations 32
  by-laws 27–8
  construction sites
    building regulations 23–4
    local authority consent 23–4
    notice 23
    traffic 22
  employment 178
  Environmental Protection Act 1990 28
  Health and Safety at Work etc. Act 1974 28
  household appliances 31–2
  ice cream vans 25
  industrial plant design 27
  insulation of buildings 30, 32
  Land Compensation Act 1973 32
  licensed premises 28–9
  Licensing Act 1964 28–9
  loudspeakers in street 24–5, 28
  neighbourhood noise 21
  noise abatement zones 25–7
    local authority powers 25
    new building construction 26–7
  noise level register 25–6
  nuisance examples 20–1
  permeation of buildings 28
  planning law and 27
  road traffic 31
  statutory control 21–9
  statutory noise nuisance
    action by local authorities 21–2
    action by private individuals 22
  street noise 24–5, 28
  Town and Country Planning Act 1990 27
  vibrations 21, 28
Non-metropolitan county councils 7
Nuisance
  abatement notice 17

Nuisance — *continued*
  default proceedings 18–19
  noise nuisance 22
  accumulation 14, 15–16
  animal keeping 14, 16
  avoidance of 11–12
  coming to nuisance defence 9, 12–13
  common law 8–13
    defences 12–13
    remedies 13
  damage remedy 13
  dark smoke 14, 15
  declaration remedy 13
  default proceedings 18–19
  duration 10
  fault requirement 12
  indigenous state of affairs 9–10
  injunction remedy 13
  intensity 10
  interference with reception 11
  liable persons
    author 12
    occupier 12
  locality principle 9–10
  motive of defendant 9
  noise *see* Noise
  originating outside local authority's area 18
  prejudicial to health 14, 15
  prescription defence 13
  proceedings by private individuals 19
  sensitivity of plaintiff 11
  several authors 18
  smoke 14, 15
  social utility of conduct 9
  state of affairs 9–10, 11
  state of premises 14–19
  statutory authority 13
  statutory nuisances 14–19
    abatement procedure 17
    best practical means defence 17–18
  time of day 11
  watercourses, ditches etc 14, 16

Offices *see* Health and safety at work, offices, shops and railway premises
Overcrowding
  health and safety at work 164
  houses
    definition of overcrowded 190–1
    duty to inform local authority 193
    multiple occupation 196
    offence of causing house to be overcrowded 192
    room standard 191
    space standard 191–2
  offices, shops and railway premises 171

Pests
  default powers 246
  duties of local authorities 245, 246
  enforcement 244
  fumigation safety measures 247
  group of premises 245
  hayricks 246
  infestation of food 246–7
  local authority
    duties 245
    notification 246
    powers to require destruction of rats 245
  notification of local authority 246
  powers of entry 247
  ships 247
  treatment of group of premises 245
  see also Disease
Planning law, noise and 27
'Polluter pays' principle 61
Private individuals
  litter proceedings 90
  statutory noise nuisances action 22
Privies 77
Prohibition notices, health and safety at work 160–1
Public health
  19th century reform 3–5
  food control see Food
  see also Diseases
Public sewers see Sewerage

Rachman, Peter 193
Radioactive waste 93–4
Railway engines and vessels, air pollution control 44
Railway premises see Health and safety at work, offices, shops and railway premises
Rats see Pests
Recycling of waste
  payments 84
  plans 80–1
  powers 85
  transport of waste to plant 79–80
Renewal areas 184–6
  powers of local housing authority 185–6
  publicity 185
Repair notices, houses 180, 181, 183–4
Ringlemann Chart 34
Road traffic noise 31
Robens Committee 148

Sanitary areas 5
Sanitary Condition of the Labouring Population of Great Britain (Chadwick) 4
Sanitary conveniences
  buildings 227
  offices, shops and railway premises 171–2

Self-employed persons 148, 153
Septic tanks, emptying 77
Sewerage
  adoption of sewers and disposal works 106–7
  building over sewers 219
  connection to public sewers 107–8
  disposal works, adoption 106–7
  duty to provide system 104–5
  general sewerage schemes 109
  investigation of defective sewer 109, 113
  local authorities and 105
  maps of sewers 113
  power to alter drainage system 109
  public sewers
    adoption of sewers 106–7
    duty of care 106
    industrial revolution 2
    provision 106
    right to communicate with 107–8
    trade effluent discharge into 110
  restrictions of use of sewers 108–9
  sewer maps 113
  'sewer' meaning 105
  see also Drainage; Trade effluent
Ships
  disease control 242
  fumigation of pests 247
Shops see Health and safety at work, offices, shops and railway premises
Silent Spring (Carson) 6
Slum clearance
  clearance areas 189–90
  closing orders 186–7
  demolition orders 187–8
  obstructive buildings 188–9
  service of notice and right of appeal 188
Smog 6, 33
Smoke 33
  dark smoke 14, 15, 34, 35
  from furnaces 35–6
  nuisance 14, 15
  Ringlemann Chart 34
Smoke control areas 39–42
  adaptations 41–2
  exempted fireplaces 41
  grants 42
  igniting apparatus 42
  remedial works 41
  smokeless fuel 40, 41
Straw burning 58
Street litter control notices 91
Stubble burning 58
Sulphur, in motor fuel 42

Temperature at work 164, 171

Index

Trade effluent
  agreements for disposal 112–13
  consents
    appeals 111–12
    conditions of 111
    special category effluent 110–11
    variation 112
  discharge into public sewer 110
  see also consents
Transport of controlled waste 62, 92–3
Tuberculosis 242

Unfit for human habitation see Housing, unfit houses
Urbanisation 1–2

Ventilation
  food premises 139
  health and safety at work 164
  offices, shops and railway premises 171
Vermin see Pests
Verminous persons 241–2
Vibrations 21, 28

Washing facilities
  food premises 139
  offices, shops and railway premises 171–2
Waste
  abandonment of vehicles 87–8
  authorities 59–61
  collection of controlled waste see Collection of controlled waste
  controlled
    collection see Collection of controlled waste
    transport 62, 92–3
  default powers of Secretary of State 87
  disposal see Disposal of waste
  dumping see Dumping of waste, control
  infected waste 237
  inspectors
    appointment 86
    powers 86–7
  litter see Litter
  neighbourhood amenity destruction 88
  non-controlled waste 85–6
  radioactive 93–4
  recycling
    payments 84
    plans 80–1
    powers 85
    transport of waste for 79–80
  Secretary of State powers 85, 87
  special waste 85–6
  waste collecting authorities 60–1, 64–6
    public access to information 74–5
  see also Collection of controlled waste

Waste — *continued*
  waste disposal authorities 60, 77, 79
    functions 83–4
  waste management licences see Waste management licences
  waste regulation authorities 59–60
    inspector appointment 86
    public access to information 74–5
    waste disposal plans 81–3
  see also Trade effluent
Waste management licences 67–74
  appeals 73–4
  application 68–9
  fees 71
  fit and proper person 68, 69
  hearings 73–4
  revocation 68, 69–71, 72
  site licence 68
  supervision of licensed activities 71–2
  surrender 68, 76
  suspension 69–71, 72
  terms and conditions 67–8
  transfer 71
  variation 69–71
Water supply
  19th century 95
  building regulations 221
  buildings 227
  cistern requirement 101
  connection expenses 98
  contamination 101–3
  Director General of Water Services 96, 97
  disconnections 99–100
  diseases see Cholera; Diseases
  domestic connections 98
  domestic supplies 98–9
  'droplet' method 2, 95
  duty to supply 96
  fluoridation 104
  hosepipe bans 103
  industrial revolution 2
  local authority functions 103–4
  major suppliers 96–7
  means 100
  non-domestic supplies 99
  persons entitled to require water main 97–8
  pressure of supply 100–1
  privatisation of public water supply 97
  quality of water 101–2
  requests to supply 97–8
  service pipe 100
  wastage 102–3
  wholesomeness 101–2
Watercourses, nuisance from 14, 16
Work health and safety see Health and safety at work